THE TAO OF THE UNBREAKABLE MAN

by
Manny Wolfe

Let's Tell Your Story Publishing
London

COPYRIGHT

Title: The Tao of the Unbreakable Man

First published: 2016

Publisher: Let's Tell Your Story Publishing

Address: 3 Century Court, Tolpits Lane, Watford, WD18 9RS UK

ISBN: 978-1-910600-05-4

Cover concept: Mercy Kay

Edited by: Colette Mason

For publicity enquiries, please email manny@mannywolfe.com in the first instance.

*This book is dedicated to Jilly, Kamila, Colette
and Mercy. I am quite certain that had it not been for
each of your efforts, at one point or another,
this book would never have come to life.*

Thank you.

FREE READER OFFER

Download my FREE Five Pillars of Charisma audio file. For more details visit www.mannywolfe.com.

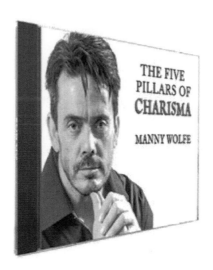

Publishers note

Some names mentioned in this book have been changed to protect people's identities.

This book includes strong language that may not be suitable for minors.

CONTENTS

ACKNOWLEDGEMENTS

Thanks to everyone who has helped me write the book – although it is based on my memories, I could not have done it alone.

Thank you to Michael and Dan for reading the pre-release copy and kindly writing a foreword.

Also thanks to my eagle-eyed beta-readers, Vicki Irvin, Jill Blanco, Jane Akshar, Mercy Kay and Sean O'Connor who gave me feedback and helped move it forward.

Kamila, I don't even know where to begin to thank you. You have been with me since the very start.

Colette, you have been the saving grace at the eleventh hour. You made a job that I can't even comprehend look effortless.

Finally, thanks to my supporters in my 'TOTUM launch' Facebook group for helping to spread the word when my book was complete.

FOREWORD

Michael Allen Williamson, author of 'The Immense Center.'

*"This Manny guy seems like a pompous jerk." I said to my wife
as she entered my studio.*

I had Manny's web site up in my browser listening to an episode of his podcast. He had Jordan Harbinger from 'The Art of Charm' as a guest. I had listened to numerous episodes of Jordan's podcast on my own. I hold the same unfounded prejudices with him, too.

*"Who's Manny?" My wife sidled up to me to look over my
shoulder.*

*"Oh, that Emmanuel Wolfe guy that I'm scheduled to be a guest
on his podcast."*

"Manny?"

My wife's mocking tone sliced through as she asked. She leaned down to look at his headshot on his website.

"Well, at least he's cute."

"Yeah, exactly."

Manny seemed precisely like the kind of person I don't like being around. You know, charm, charisma, luck, blessed, fortunate... and completely clueless as to how difficult life can be for the rest of us. These guys either squander their blessings and make a complete mess out of their life, or they leverage their luck to become successful 'Kings of Mountains'. All the while, they act like it's easy and the rest of us are lazy for being less lucky. I avoid these guys with disdain.

But, I had a book to promote and I'm a self-serving prick, so I proceeded to be a guest on 'The Steep Side of the Mountain with Emmanuel Wolfe'. I hate self-promotion but I must do this. So, fuck him. He may have a theme, or agenda for his show but I'm going to make damn sure I talk about my book as much as possible. He has lots of success coming his way, 'I'm going to leverage him like he leverages others.'

Then we became friends.

How that happened and why are a bit complicated and it makes sense only to a rare minority of people. If you're reading this book, there's a good chance you are one of them.

I'm pretty sure this is very common for middle-aged men and probably for women, too. We reach a point in our lives where we ask, 'What the fuck am I doing? This is not the life I had in mind when I was younger.' We commonly call this the 'mid-life crisis.'

Well, I got started early. When I was 28, I had a CD-player alarm clock with Pink Floyd's 'Dark Side of the Moon' in it. I thought I was clever by putting 'Time' as my wake-up track because the song begins with this cacophony of clock chimes and bells ringing. It's like having a clockmaker's shop as your wake-up call. Every morning for months, this track woke me. One morning, I had the luxury of not needing to be up early, so I let the CD play as I lazily lay in bed.

> *"And then one day you find, ten years have got behind you.*
> *No one told when to run, you missed the starting gun.*
> *So you run and you run to catch up with the sun but it's sinking*
> *Racing around to come up behind you again.*
> *The sun is the same in a relative way but you're older,*
> *Shorter of breath and one day closer to death.*
> *Every year is getting shorter never seem to find the time.*
> *Plans that either come to naught or half a page of scribbled lines"*
>
> *Time, Pink Floyd*

'Ten years? I graduated high school ten years ago. What am I doing?' I vowed then and there to make things better.

I'm in my 40s now and I'm still working on it.

I've written three books. I've started my own company. I have my name as inventor on patents. I've composed most of a symphony, written songs, graduated college, raised two amazing boys, somehow managed to stay married to a beautiful wife, drawn some amazing pictures, built some amazing software, live in a state I love, by mountains I love, I have friends and family and a modicum of health.

I still haven't done anything with my life.

I'm lucky. I'm blessed. I'm fortunate and I have no fucking clue how good I've got it. All I can do is destroy myself over how much I haven't done. There is this insane cultural pressure to achieve, to succeed, to 'do more.'

It's destroying us and we are destroying each other.

You read the news and you see that Americans are working more hours than ever and US suicide rates are skyrocketing. Truly gifted and amazing people are taking their lives and they all share the same lament.

I still haven't done anything with my life.

We move throughout our days wearing masquerade costumes pretending to be people we are not. These empty adult husks and shells that resemble nothing that our pure, raw, youthful passion envisioned for us when we were young. We are fake, self-hating, pretentious, pompous, and destructive. We take advantage of each other and push each other down and grasp at anything that feels like success to us. We put on fake smiles and go to church with people just like us that we'll never get to know because nobody is honest about who they really are... even to themselves.

And, most of us turn to drugs. Not just narcotics, but sex, and junk food, and dysfunctional relationships serve us like narcotics to make us feel better about our shitty existence. Some of us end up in A.A., N.A. or S.A.

Some of us end up fat on a couch watching pointless television. Some of us turn into workaholics, drowning in success-oriented escapism. We are feeding the engine that is spinning our world out of control. We are killing ourselves.

And a few of us – a very small number of us – manage to see a different way. A way that zips past the rest of us in a blur as we spin in circles. You can learn about this way in the A.A. / N.A. / S.A. twelve steps if you don't let it become your religion. You can learn this way in therapy if your therapist is good and if you pay very close attention. You can learn about this way in a very small number of spiritual institutions scattered here and there. There's a small number of voices out there talking about this one secret.

"Sometimes I get tired of pins and needles,
Facades are a fire on the skin.
And I'm growing fond of broken people,
As I see that I am one of them.
I'm one of them."

Paul Meany, MUTEMATH

I am broken.

Being authentic and real – being genuine and humble is not what you think it is. There are a lot of people that are really good at looking humble but it's inauthentic. Real authenticity, real humility is very hard. You have to wake up every day and admit to yourself, 'I am broken. I don't have anything figured out. I have no room to judge others. I'm going to make the most of today.' You must admit to yourself, and to others that you have seriously fucked up – that you've made a mess – that you are an addict (of something) and you need help.

Authentic people are great friends to have. Authentic people have great shoulders to cry on. Authentic people make great business partners. Authentic people make great spouses, and parents, and neighbors.

Emmanuel Wolfe, my friend, is genuine, authentic, and real. Sure, he's been lucky and doesn't realize it – but, so have we all. At least Manny isn't too proud to say he's made a mess of things. Manny is the kind of guy that doesn't judge – but just gives willingly of himself.

You can read this book and think, 'Wow, this guy is a braggadocious hoodlum,' especially when you read about all the shenanigans he and his friends pull. You can read this book and think, 'Wow, this guy is a typical womanizer,' when you look at how he slept around with girls and has the audacity to call girls that sleep around as 'trashy.' You could read this book and think, 'This guy is so lucky, and just screws it up.' You could read this book and think, 'This guy is a dead beat dad trying to convince me he's a good guy.'

You could. But, you'd be dead wrong.

It's hard to recognize genuine, authentic, real vulnerability. It's hard to relate to somebody saying, 'Man, I really fucked this up,' but still marches forward. 'Nobody is this honest... nobody is this real.' We say this to ourselves because we are inwardly terrified of being this honest and vulnerable to the world and even to ourselves.

When you read this book, just keep in mind, 'What would my life be like if I was this honest about my mistakes?' Let go of judgement. Stop playing the game. Stop thinking about comparing yourself to Manny, or the Jones's next door. Exercise a little empathy and recognize how incredibly difficult it is to write, and publish, this kind of memoir – this confession – in book form.

Could you be this honest?

If you can be this honest, let's talk, because I love having friends like you.

Dan G Rice, owner, Leading From Anywhere

Nature or nurture? Which is more responsible for shaping Manny Wolfe?

In the short time I've known Manny personally, I'll admit I've wanted to know. I'll also admit that all I'd known prior to picking up 'The Tao' was that he was the product of a cult, a long series of addictions and a life of fighting for one thing or another.

I knew barely anything else about the real Manny Wolfe...

How does someone come through these things to become the man we know today? The charismatic coach, speaker and consultant who is clearly a leader in his field?

Whilst my middle class upbringing in Hampshire (England) is a long stretch from the roughest areas of America where Manny grew up. I strongly believe there are similarities in the way we've had to break ourselves down, examine our very weakest elements and fight like a son of a bitch when we didn't like what we saw.

And boy did he have a fight on his hands!

As a result of my own challenges, I've emerged as a man that admires great leaders. I am now even making a career of studying people that take it upon themselves to learn how to better themselves and the world around them driven by a higher purpose.

People like Manny.

I still do not know whether it was nature or nurture that shaped the Manny Wolfe we know. The man who made the decision to make a change and never look back...

What I do know is that within the story you are about to read he pulls no punches. He understands the cold hard reality of pain and you will begin to understand how Manny has been shaped by his harrowing past.

"Only through the gauntlet of adversity is true character formed."

Manny Wolfe

PROLOGUE

Dear Reader,

You hold my life in your hands. Well, actually my life story but hopefully much more than that as well. It is my hope and my intention just as I have learned many valuable lessons from the intense struggles of my early life you too can learn from all I have gone through. I am going to share with you the story of an innocent little boy who experienced difficult and even dangerous circumstances, many of them unthinkable to most people.

We will trace the trajectory of a life marked by things such as brainwashing, neglect, violence, addiction, abuse, incarceration and destitution. But also, a life defined by a refusal to give up, a hunger for something better an unrelenting belief in the self and our ability to transcend.

Before publishing this book, many of my friends graciously agreed to be 'beta readers', and many of them said to me in their feedback, they found the story of my life to be very intense and they wished that the book were written with more happy moments.

To that concern, I admit I tried to tell this story with the highest level of emotional truth I could achieve. I had no interest in representing things in any way other than how I experienced them. It would be inaccurate to say much of my young life was happy. Indeed, contrary to some of the popular mythology surrounding addiction, I firmly believe happy children don't find themselves with massive alcohol and chemical addictions by the time they reach high school. The writing of this story represents the first time my life has ever had a cohesive, emotional narrative. It is the first time it all 'made sense.'

Painting the truth of my upbringing in sunny hues would be doing a disservice to the truth of my childhood. I also don't want you to feel sorry for me. I am a firm believer true character is forged in the gauntlet of adversity. Today, I am happy, content, satisfied, fulfilled and at peace. I was able to take something extremely valuable from each challenge, obstacle and setback I experienced.

A Life Defined by Service

Today, I live a life defined by service, contribution, growth, love, success, and legacy. I have done more than simply survive the bizarre, almost fantastical childhood and young adult life I had. Through desire, determination, and drive, I have extracted potent lessons and insights from all of my struggles and found a way to forge what many might consider suffering into a strength that I now use to teach and empower others.

Where I was once cripplingly insecure, I have become confident. Where I was alarmingly thin and skinny, I have become fit and muscular. Where once there was frailty, I am now tempered and resilient. I say these things not to brag or to boast but to serve as proof and a reminder there is nothing we can't overcome and indeed take strength and wisdom from, if we want it badly enough.

Indeed, if you were to read this book and feel sorry for me in anyway, then I have failed to do what I set out to do. If only one reader amongst you finds something positive here and it influences them to pursue the best that is within them – then to me – this book is a success.

Lessons Learned

A big part of the struggle in my younger life was my chronic inability to hold down a job. I attribute this inability mainly to the brainwashing aspect of my life that I mentioned earlier.

From my birth to age 14, I was taught money was evil. The world outside the doors of the cult I was born into was not a place I would ever have any desire to live in or interact with, and outside of the confines of the cult, I essentially did not have any value whatsoever.

At 14, I was suddenly required to find a way to get a job and make financial contributions. I was never able to reconcile that conflict of 'money being evil' yet being sent out to 'earn it' at the same time. The unintended upside was that I was born with a fierce entrepreneurial streak. I was never supposed to be a 'nine-to-five' type of guy.

In my twenties and well into my late thirties, I secured and subsequently sabotaged approximately one hundred jobs. I'd walk in off the street, charm my way into being hired and never bothered to show up for the first day.

Whether I worked one day or one year, I found a way to sabotage and undermine every job I ever had. I had many entry-level jobs. Before management even had my name memorized, I came up with ways I thought could improve their systems. None of my ideas were ever implemented of course, unless by implemented we were to mean something along the lines of 'termination of employment.' In which case, there was a great deal of implementation.

I think it's fair to say, because of my rebelliousness, I have always been unemployable. However – and this may apply to you as well as to me – being unemployable doesn't necessarily mean a person is without certain aptitudes. It simply means they are required, in a purer sense of the meaning, to make their own way. We must fashion our own ships, set off boldly for the horizon, powering forward under our own steam.

Today, I teach entrepreneurs and high performers the art and science of charismatic communication. With the ability to communicate with others at a high-level being both lost in our day-and-age and one of the highest value skill sets people can attain. I've had the privilege of helping people all around the world.

I teach everything from the mechanics of charismatic communication, including powerful vocal delivery, persuasion, storytelling, body language, authenticity and charisma, to mindset coaching to overcome emotional setbacks and limiting beliefs.

I teach people how to have alignment between their thoughts, beliefs, emotions and communication, so they can be the absolute, most powerful and effective version of themselves possible.

Where once, I could not hold down a part time job as a dishwasher, I now coach rising stars, public personalities, and high-figure earners on how to improve themselves in their personal and professional lives.

People often ask me how I came from my background to teaching these particular skills. How does a little kid with an abusive childhood, raised in the ghetto, forced to fight daily, sent off into the world with no guidance weighed down with rampant alcohol and drug addictions become someone who coaches other people on things like charisma, communication, and mindset?

I've given a lot of thought to answering this question and I think the truth sounds something like this. Ever since I could remember, I have had a passion for words and speaking. In addition to my natural tendency towards that area, I think another one of the unexpected upshots of the bizarre childhood that I had was I was exposed to many different 'micro language environments.'

For instance, the cult where I was raised from infancy had its own very stylized, very particular use of language. One of the common threads was as a group we subverted the language of the outside world, deliberately using words in opposite contexts and giving other meanings to words and phrases that were used in the outside world.

I was exposed to one very particular, very idiosyncratic style of communication. As a young boy, I was made to go to public school. When I opened up my mouth to talk to other kids, it became glaringly obvious I did not speak as they did. I got into many fights because of it.

Over time, I have begun to learn this new 'micro-language environment,' that existed among the children in school. Then when I was eight-years-old, the entire cult, as a group, moved from where I was born in the California Bay Area, to the center of the most violent ghetto area in one of the top-most dangerous cities in the United States. All of the children in the commune were terrorized during those years. But even during that period of constant 'fight or flight' and never feeling safe, I still couldn't help but be fascinated by the latest language spoken by the other kids in that ghetto.

At age twelve, my biological family moved away from the ghetto and into a relatively safer neighborhood in the same city. I was exposed to multiple new ways of communication in this culturally and racially mixed neighborhood.

Soon, I was fascinated with language and communication, which was to become a lifelong passion. I was intrigued by all the different styles and examples I was exposed to during my childhood. I had communication mastered... but what about charisma and mindset?

The things I am fascinated by, and now teach, were life and death survival strategies for me growing up. Many people make the incorrect assumption the charisma is something we are born with. Charisma is a learned set of skills. There is a deliberate, systematic and predictable way to teach anyone how to have charisma.

In my case, I learned to be funny and witty at a young age because a well-placed joke or quip could temporarily alleviate the stress and tension of my home life and offer a brief spark of authenticity. I would use same 'quick with the joke' trait when having to talk myself out of dangerous situations. People meet me and often assume I'm just funny, witty or otherwise smart and engaging. While these things may be true now, they are skills I learned.

I found myself at certain points in my life with my back up against the proverbial wall. I realized every time I found myself trapped it forced me to engage in a more creative level of problem solving. In other words, when the pinch was on and the chips were down – and they regularly were – I relied on my unfailing ability to create new solutions to my problems on demand. I was able to shift my mindset rapidly.

Reinventing Myself

I was fascinated by reinventing myself. I became obsessed with trying to understand mindset and self-improvement. I reasoned the potential for a high-level, dynamic problem-solving mindset must come from within me. The onset of tremendous stress allowed me access these hard to reach levels of awareness and ability.

For me, the question became, 'how could I tap into these deeper, more powerful mental resources before the problems arise?' This line of inquiry led me to some great thinkers such as Tony Robbins, Jim Rohn, Zig Ziglar, Napoleon Hill, Gandhi, Dr. Stephen Covey, Freud, Jung and anyone else I could get my hands on. From there, I took my literary quest back in time to study the great teachers of antiquity, Jesus, Buddha, Lau Tzu, Sun Tzu. I sought out virtually anyone who I thought might have potent insight into human behavior and mindset. I didn't know it at the time but I was following something akin to the Tony Robbins 'self-education model.'

Over 20 years, I read and listened to anything and everything I could find that would offer insights. I was cocooning myself. Through a mix of curiosity, desperation, desire and necessity, I was engaging in a self-directed metamorphosis. You will learn later, I nearly died. This transformation I put myself through was of a life or death magnitude for me.

There is absolutely no doubt in my mind, had I not veered sharply off the initial course life seem to have planned for me, I would be dead by now. For sure. I feel as though I have been given a second chance.

If you are reading this book feeling the cards are stacked very much against you, you will find some comfort, confidence and hope from my life story. Just as I stepped off the nightmare merry-go-round, you can too. Join me and let's travel along my former hellish path together, as we learn how I spotted my escape lane and swerved off to that 'better life.' If you are in the midst of your own dark and difficult struggle, perhaps, you can't see the way out of your situation, let me assure you there is one. A complete global change in your life is utterly within your power. I am not talking percentages here, so please do not think otherwise. I am promising that you have within you the power and the ability to reinvent yourself. My years of work with my clients, giving them the confidence and skills to haul themselves out of the depths of despair, for me, is further proof – success is within your grasp.

I urge you – please understand who I once was and where I came from. I was a hopeless, homeless deadbeat, addicted to drink and drugs on a downward spiral. I was a loser who smashed down to rock bottom. The guy writing this book now is most definitely not who I was. My younger self would be staggered I would end up on stage, connecting with an audience by sharing a powerful, transformational message. It is the farthest thing I can possibly imagine from how I was raised and what I believed.

Don't make the mistake of falling back on your old stories like 'it's O.K. for you Manny, but I could never do that. I don't have 'what it takes.'' None of us start out with 'what it takes' when we decide it's time for radical change in our lives. Trust me. Committing 'to become more' and striving for that 'better you' is what will develop the inner strength and resources you need.

I think it would help to share a couple of success stories my clients have had. They really illustrate the power of being willing to step outside of your comfort zone and becoming a 'better you.'

James's story

The following story starts from our first contact. In three short weeks after our first meeting, James spoke at his first public speaking gig at a premier industry event in his field and totally nailed it!

James worked in SEO and marketing. He was a fascinating guy because he was only twenty-three and he was really crushing it. He was getting huge results for his clients with some proprietary something-or-other that he'd developed. However, since he spent his workdays alone, in front of a computer screen, when he was invited to be a keynote speaker at one of the biggest events in his industry, he felt daunted.

We met because we were both members of an online group. One day I noticed an unfamiliar name had given a 'like' to something I'd written. Curious to see who this new person was, I reached out and said 'hello' with a quick private message.

> *"Hi there, thanks for giving me the 'like' are you interested in public speaking?"*

I got a response.

> *"Hey mate. I've been following some of the things you've been sharing on Facebook and I really like what you've got to say, so I'm wondering if I can ask you a question..?"*

> *"Sure." I responded. "What can I do for you, James?"*

I sipped my coffee and waited for the little message alert to indicate he'd replied. 'Bing' – there it was.

> *"I was wondering if I could hear a sample of your work? I've been asked to speak at an industry conference in three weeks and I've never been on a stage in front of people before."*

> *"I'd be happy to" I replied. "Here's a link to one of my podcast episodes. Give it a listen and tell me what you think?"*

I sent him a link to an episode of 'The Steep Side of the Mountain' where I interview people who have faced and overcome extraordinary challenges in pursuit of amazing lives.

He replied a while later.

> *"LOL. I went from one episode straight to another. I couldn't stop listening!"*

I smiled.

> *"O.K. then James. Why don't you tell me a little about what you've got going on?"*

As the conference was less than two weeks away, we were only able to squeeze in four sessions together between all the other prep and normal demands of his company. I remember even staying up until midnight one night so that we could grab a call together at seven am his time.

I was thrilled when he gave me the lowdown after the event.

> *"I felt so strong up there. I was totally confident. Remembering the things you told me, I brought the house down! They loved me!"*

He would wind up bringing in over $60,000 dollars that day from people who were blown away by his presentation.

From my first podcast episode I launched, people had begun to come to me and ask

> *"How do you sound like that?"*

Truthfully, I'd never given it much thought. I mean, it's my voice, right? For me, it's always just 'been there.' Other people, however, were really moved by it. They were impacted by the way I spoke and the way I deliver my messages. I began to get requests to teach people how to have presence and charisma with their own voices, almost immediately upon releasing the show to the public.

In all honesty, it came as a real surprise when I began to get that sort of reaction to my podcast. It rekindled one of my long-dormant dreams – the dream of being a public speaker.

I'd been in love with that idea for many years but had relegated it to the infamous 'back burner' – the place where dreams go to die.

I was trained as an actor, a singer and a speaker, so I'd always had an awareness of the power of my voice but for years, I never really took the time to harness that power. I had the ever-present pressure of needing to earn money NOW. After all, rent doesn't care what your dreams are. I had an incredibly unsupportive family who I listened to far too much (more on that later) and of course, I had a host of insecurities and self-doubts that kept me in check.

I'd begun working with a coach a few months prior to this and I remember her telling me, before the launch of my podcast, 'When we get your podcast out there, within a few months, you won't even recognize your life.' At the time, I didn't remotely understand what she could've meant by that. I did have the somewhat starry-eyed dreams many people have when the first create and launch a new podcast but I didn't expect what was to follow.

I stumbled onto podcasts and they forever changed my life. Some gems I found early on were 'The Art of Charm', 'Smart Passive Income', and 'Entrepreneur on Fire' along with 'The Tim Ferriss Show', 'Mixergy' and others. They were proving the viability of this 'new podcasting thing,' a way to put yourself out there and be heard, potentially, by millions of people. That idea really fired me up.

Podcasts showed me this entire new world of connection-based, entrepreneurs. I created my own podcast, which then lead into the world of Facebook and networking. My circle of friends spread around the world, a top-rated podcast, a new career where my old, dusty dream of being a public speaker reshaped into a flourishing coaching practice.

My coach was right. My life was totally transformed. When I woke to that random inquiry from James, a stranger, asking about what I do and if I could help him, I definitely had to smile.

James was an incredible example of the sheer power you can harness when you're not afraid to step out of your comfort zone, to really push in an effort to become 'more then you were.' He might have needed to spend the money he earned on his building his business. He may never meet his audience members again in the flesh. However, he'll always have the pride of what he achieved that day by becoming a better, more powerful version of himself. And, he'll have those inner resources to use next time. From that day forward, he will always have getting up to speak in front of a crowd and smashing it! Hitting it out of the park! No matter what else happens, he will always have that. As a result, he now has to set his sights on larger goals, thus forcing him to continue growing. Do you see how taking that first tentative step really works?

AJ's story

When I met AJ, he was already very successful. He runs an online coaching agency for entrepreneurs and high performers. A cornerstone of his business and marketing strategy is doing tons of short YouTube videos.

When I found out about the videos during our first call, I asked him if he could send me a couple. After watching the videos, I saw that he was speaking almost exclusively in a very high register. His neck and shoulders were tense.

Whilst correctable, these two issues can take a bit of time for some people to truly master – I guessed in AJ's case we'd need maybe 8 weeks. Thanks to AJ's absolute willingness – no, hunger – to learn new things and improve, with some guidance from me, he fixed things very quickly indeed.

> *"So," I said, "why do you think you keep your shoulders so tight?"*
>
> *"I don't know but they really get sore when I talk for long periods of time."*
>
> *"I see. What about your neck, how does that feel?"*
>
> *"It gets really tight too! How did you know that?"*
>
> *"Well, I can see you straining in the videos. Even though you're smiling, your neck is totally tight."*

I explained to him about the need to keep plenty of air in our lungs while speaking. When we try to talk for too long with too little air to support our words, the muscles in our torso, shoulders and neck will all, automatically, try to come to the aid of our voice. This was the cause of the tension.

During our chat, I had an inkling about something else, so I asked him.

> *"Tell me about growing up. Did you have lots of siblings? How were things like with your mom?"*

"Why do you want to know about that?" he asked.

"Well, often times, when we have certain difficulties with our voices we can trace the cause back to something emotional. For instance, when someone speaks very quickly, with a high-pitched timbre to their voice, it might have to do with literally not feeling heard as a kid."

He paused. His face looked thoughtful.

"That's really weird. Now I think about it, I was raised with lots of brothers and sisters and I always struggled to be heard. I never felt heard in the mix, you know?"

He reclined in his chair and smiled at this realization.

"Do you know how the way we live shows up on our bodies as we get older?" I asked him.

"What do you mean?"

"For instance, if you put ten random, middle-aged people in a line it would be easy to spot the life-long smoker, right? You could tell just by looking at them?"

"Yeah, right." He said.

"Well, the same thing happens to our voices and communication over time. If you know what to look for, you can read a person's emotional life by their voice and how they talk."

AJ raised his eyebrows at this.

"Really?"

"Absolutely. It's fascinating once you know what to listen and look for – it's like this whole world of insight just opens up for you."

"Wow," said AJ, sitting forward in his chair again and smiling, "That's amazing."

AJ and I only had three sessions together but in that short time, he was able to absorb and incorporate some key ideas that changed his presentation skills

---

dramatically. As it was with James, AJ too had a live presentation to give very shortly after we were to start working together. I have had the privilege of watching videos from that presentation, as well as seeing many of the videos he has posted since our working together.

He has absolutely transformed into a powerful, charismatic and passionate speaker. Now that his body language, his vocal tonality and his message are all aligned, he virtually shines in front of the camera.

If you are interested in seeing someone who speaks with a passion, conviction and integrity, I highly recommend that you search AJ Mirhzad on YouTube and see him for yourself.

With both of these client stories, the common thread is they were both willing and eager to push past their comfort zones. The results in both cases meant they were able to incorporate deep lessons that would forever change their skill sets and their abilities. Thanks to their commitment and courage, change was rapid. Some people need longer to get what they want in life and that's fine too. What matters most is choosing to make that change.

Most of us live our day-to-day lives fearing the unknown, being so accustomed to not questioning what else might be out there, what else might be possible and what our true potential might be. Staying firmly within your comfort zone, whilst seeming 'comfortable' at first glance, quickly becomes an invisible, yet very real cage – even a prison. Without even realizing they are doing it, many people create the boundaries and the limitations to their own lives, simply by choosing not to step outside that false friend of a concept, the 'comfort zone.'

I want you to notice something about my story and the experiences I shared about James and AJ. The three of us could not have come from backgrounds and circumstances that are more different. What we all have in common is that at some point in each of our lives, the desire to fulfill our potential, tipped the scales and began to outweigh our fears of the unknown lurking out there, outside our comfort zones.

I encourage you to seek out your tipping point. In a very real way, achieving this tipping point between curiosity and fear, between desire and restraint, is the gateway to all the things that your life can potentially be.

I have been told by those closest to me on more than one occasion, it's as if I am two people, the highly developed man and the little boy, with very little else in between. I happily agree with this sentiment. I feel that one of the unexpected gifts I have been given for coming through all of the challenges that have been put in my path is that I am uniquely in touch with the childlike innocence inside me.

As I finish writing this prologue, the child within me is bursting at the seams, nearly crying with happiness, at the possibility for what your life can become. Right next to him is the grown man that I am today, who deeply hopes that our paths might cross one day or that I might somehow be able to serve you, release you from that invisible cage and help in your quest to become more than you now are.

Manny Wolfe
California
2016

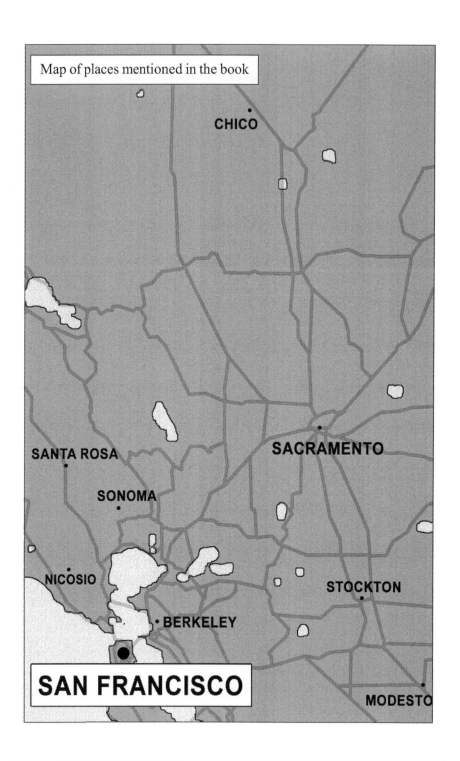

Map of places mentioned in the book

CHICO

SANTA ROSA

SONOMA

SACRAMENTO

NICOSIO

STOCKTON

BERKELEY

SAN FRANCISCO

MODESTO

CHAPTER 1

DENIAL AND CATHARSIS

"We are oft to blame in this – 'tis too much proved – that with devotion's visage and pious action we do sugar o'er the devil himself."

William Shakespeare

I

In the beginning years of the twenty-first century, everyone was grappling with a global financial crisis of truly cataclysmic proportions. We had just lost President George W. Bush who, many felt, had driven not just the U.S. but also most of the developed nations on earth to the brink of collapse. There had been economic policies put in place that enabled unscrupulous lenders to approve huge unaffordable homeowner loans for people. These people had little chance of keeping up with the repayments that proved to be – well – insane. I doubt that anyone reading this will be unfamiliar with the details or the fallout.

It was about three years into President Obama's first term in office before things finally began to show signs of stabilizing. Trillions of dollars needed to be dumped into the economic rescue efforts. It took a long time for the economy to finally show signs of improvement.

By the time the winds began to change, millions of people had lost their homes, which in turn decimated the industries of real estate and construction.

In California alone, construction lost an estimated seven hundred and fifty thousand skilled laborers – a full 25 percent of its labor force. They jumped ship, en masse, in search of something – anything – to sustain them and keep them alive. Many returned to school, changed careers or even left the country in search of some way to put food on their tables.

I was one of those 'construction laborers.'

I remember when things began to dry up. My friends in construction were all starting to complain about how slow a summer we were having, while I was operating at full speed with more work than I could handle. I thought they were either crazy or lazy. I didn't see what all the fuss was about. I was still making money hand-over-fist and had just purchased a new German sports car. I was doing just fine, thank you.

Until my phone, too, simply stopped ringing.

I went eight months without a single work call. During this time, my girlfriend, Lila and I drifted from a state of optimistic denial, through all the successive states, through to utter desperation. We also drifted through our meager savings and her inheritance. We downsized from our nice, spacious home to a smaller one and, ultimately, we downsized out of each other's lives, thinking it better to 'lone wolf' it.

I clawed and scraped my way through the next couple of years, work coming sometimes but not often. I reached out in every direction I could to bring in money, from returning to school for the loans and aid, to trying any shady sales job that Craigslist had to offer. Secretly, I even became a cannabis courier, driving pounds of pot at a time, from growers I knew, to dealers and private customers. Being a drug runner was clearly not a sensible choice with eighteen years of treasured sobriety under my belt but it was money and I had mouths to feed. When I said I reached out in 'every direction,' I meant it,

Then, one day, the phone started to ring again. By this time me, my son, Tobin, my friend Chris and I were all living in a tiny little seven hundred square foot condo, scraping by on macaroni and cheese and frozen veggies and rice – often eating only once a day. I was three months behind on all my bills. I'd been paying rent a couple hundred dollars at a time, if at all. My life had become a constant grind of unanswered calls and feeble excuses, punctuated by the occasional payment when the work slowly began to trickle back into my life.

It's funny what stands out in our minds when we go through something as arduous as the so-called 'Great Recession.' Of all the difficulties I faced during those times, what I remember the most vividly, what made me feel the most helpless and heartbroken is the way my son began to act towards the end. Back then, we had no way of knowing work was finally about to come my way again. Despite his youth, inevitably, it became clear to him we were floundering in a leaky boat, far from shore and there was no help coming. We were going to sink.

Like any child, he liked new stuff and he enjoyed fantasizing about this or that new toy he might want. When gloomy realization hit him – we really had no money at all – he went into this bizarre kind of denial.

He began to compulsively keep mental lists of all the toys and new stuff he wanted Every time we went to the supermarket or department store, he would add it to his list. As our situation grew more desperate, his wants became bigger. His inability to control himself rattling off his wish list items became more prominent. He would go through them with this weird kind of forced, manic happiness in his voice, as if he was trying to use sheer force of will to offset the reality of our situation. Maybe if he believed it hard enough – it might just happen.

He would say things like

> *"Daddy, we should get a new T.V. ours is kinda small, y'know?."*

I'd try to stay even as I said

> *"Well, we can't really afford things like that right now, kiddo, we've gotta watch our money."*

All the while, I was just dying inside. He would say

> *"I know, daddy."*

Then a second later, as if our earlier conversation had never happened

> *"Daddy, we should get a new car, ours is kinda funny looking, y'know?"*

He would carry on like this all day long, listing thing after thing we should buy. If you didn't know him, it would, of course, be easy to dismiss this behavior as being merely the capricious flights of a child's fancy – except he was never like this before. Even, before the crash, when we didn't have money from time to time, all that was required from me was a simple explanation and he would be fine. He was a remarkably reasonable and mature kid. That's what made this utterly out of character. I was watching him develop a stress reaction to our situation and there was nothing I could do.

II

Although the work was slowly beginning to show up again, we were still very deep into the woods and we knew it. It would take time – and money – to get us out of the tight spot we found ourselves in. I did begin to feel a sense of cautious optimism as the small job offers returned, so one evening, I decided to take us out to dinner as a much needed treat. None of us had seen the inside of a restaurant for weeks, maybe even months and the morale boost was very welcome. It seemed like forever since I'd had any 'spare money' in my pocket.

We were all happy, bellies gloriously full, as we returned home. Chatting idly among ourselves, we made our way to the condo only to find an eviction notice taped to the front door. As it happened, I'd just made a partial rent payment two days earlier and thought I'd bought us a little time. Apparently, the property owners didn't feel the same way. They felt the leniency they had been extending me was at an end – and they could no longer afford to extend it. Immediately, I phoned my property manager. I tried and tried but could not wring any more time or compassion out of them. That was that – we were out.

We sat on the couch talking and thinking what we should do next. I put on a pot of coffee as we commiserated. The smell of it was just filling the air and the liquid splashing into my cup when there was a knock at the door. Hoping it might be the property manager coming by with some miracle to pull us back from the edge of the cliff, I answered.

When I opened the door, it was not my property manager but a young man wearing a dirty, grease-covered grey and blue mechanics shirt. I noticed the name on the oval patch on his chest said, rather ironically, 'Lucky.' He was holding a clipboard and sporting ridiculous facial hair, like a goatee but nearly a foot long and five inches wide.

"Are you Emmanuel Wolfe?" he asked.

"That's me. What can I do for you?"

"I need to repossess your vehicle. You do drive the Mitsubishi Montero, right?"

He jerked a thumb towards where my parking space lay.

"Jeezus...really? Yeah, that's mine, how did this happen?"

I tried to sound surprised.

"He looked at his clipboard and looked back at me. It says here that you're three months behind on your payments?"

I sighed.

"Yeah, probably am. Can I pay any of it now and keep the vehicle?"

"Sorry man, by the time I get here, it's pretty much too late."

"All right, let's get it over with then." I said in defeat.

"I noticed you have a lot of stuff inside, I'm not supposed to do this but if you want, you can unload it first."

"O.K. thanks that will help. I appreciate it, man."

"No problem. I'll give you a hand, buddy."

"Really? Thanks man, that's awesome. Thank you."

Together we unloaded all of my work tools and he took that old Mitsubishi away on the back of his tow truck, never to be seen again – by me at least. Slumped and dejected, I headed back toward the apartment I'd soon need to vacate. I walked through the door into a heavy silence. Even my son seemed to appreciate there was really nothing to say. After a time, we began talking again, about nothing much, trying to lighten the mood as best we could.

I began brainstorming ways I could complete the customer jobs that had begun trickling in – which was a little more tricky now, since, I had no way of getting to them! Chris assured me he would drive us so that was no longer a problem. All we needed to figure out was how to transport big, unwieldy things like ladders and other specialist equipment – owing to one inconvenient truth – Chris drove a very small car.

The conversation drifted on to what we might be able to do about a place to live. I ran down all the possibilities I could think of. Chris did the same. We were slap bang in the middle of this discussion when the power suddenly went out.

"Oh now what?" I said to no one in particular.

"Are you kidding me, really?"

Oddly, my outburst didn't cause the power to spontaneously turn on again.

"I'll check the breaker panel," said Chris helpfully.

Click after click from the panel yielded nothing. As I suspected, our power was most definitely 'off.' Of course it was.

In the remaining daylight, I found the stack of mail from the mailbox that day. I began rifling through it for something from the power company that might 'shed some light' on the situation. (No pun intended.) I found the letter that put me in the picture of what had just happened. Just like the car company and the property owner, the power company was out of patience with me too.

There was more. I was about to discard the power company edict in disgust, when my gaze fell on the next letter in the pile. It was from the D.M.V. [The U.S. Department of Motor Vehicles] informing me my driver's license was suspended for lack of insurance. There it was. A four-punch combo, three to the gut, then one to the head. I was wobbling at the sheer improbability of all these things hitting me all at once. I mean 'really?'

The final addition of the D.M.V. kicking a man when he was down sent Chris into a tirade of angry disbelief. He began to threaten the D.M.V. and power company with lawsuits and vandalism, raging impotently and arbitrarily against their totalitarian might. He never was very good beyond a certain level of stress, becoming erratic and irrational rather than focusing and planning. I knew from experience Chris would need to calm down before he could be reasoned with. In the face of such adversity, I knew I would need a different approach, sinking deeper into strategizing mode. Whilst it seemed so sudden and unfair to Chris, I knew we were simply suffering the inevitable outcome of living for so long on borrowed time. The devil always takes his due.

Mom once joked with me that I was like a 'lightning rod', attracting more than my fair share of challenges. That's exactly how I felt. However, one of the good things about being a lightning rod is that you get comfortable, or at least familiar with, having your back against the wall. The situation I was in was one of the worst I'd ever been in but it wasn't totally unfamiliar. I'd been in many scrapes before and the truth was that, somehow, I'd always pulled through. Once I saw in my mind's eye the reality of the situation I was in, the question became one of cost and degree, not of succeed or fail.

One of the things contributing to our tight spot in the first place was that over the last few years, my confidence and clarity of purpose had been shaken as my money problems grew deeper and more severe. During my sobriety years, I'd done a lot of deep, personal improvement work and had become a very focused, effective person in many ways. Lately, though, it was as if there was a foggy disconnect between me and the inner resources, the tools I had developed over time. I could recognize them, I definitely knew I had them but I couldn't seem to latch onto them the way I used to.

This inability to harness what I knew I had inside me was a source of great stress for me. I'd spend hours sometimes in self-examination, feeling like I was on the other side of a curtain from the answer to my problem. However, try as I might, I could not draw the curtain wide to expose it. When I was finally able to pull the curtain back, the answer would hit me like a ton of bricks.

As we sat there in the little condo, pondering what our next move should be, I decided to call my sister for a friendly ear. After a few rings, she answered.

"Hello?"

"Hey sis, it's Manny. What are you doing?"

"Not much, just sitting here with the kids, doing crafts. What are you up to?"

"I just had an incredibly fucked up afternoon..."

"What happened?"

"Well, I don't know where to start, so I'll just lay it all out there. In the last few hours, I've been evicted from my apartment, had my car repossessed, my power shut off, and my license suspended, all today, all this afternoon."

I felt her change gears. There was a momentary silence on the other end of the phone and then she spoke.

"Oh my God."

"I know, right? I can't believe it. I can't wrap my head around it at all."

"Oh my God! I don't know what to say, I'm so sorry."

"I'm sure I'll figure something out, but damn! All that at once? C'mon!"

"Have you talked to mom yet?"

"No, the last of it just happened a little while ago. You're the first person I've called."

"How is Tobin doing?"

"I don't know. He's O.K. I guess. We're just absorbing it all right now... y'know?"

"Yeah, that's a lot to take in... I am so sorry."

"I think maybe he'll need to go stay with his mom for a little bit while I sort this all out. He's not going to like that... I'm not going to like that."

"Poor guy." my sister said sympathetically. *"Paulo and I have actually been talking recently about what we could do if something like this happened to you. We've been worried about you for a while."*

When she said this, a small warning tingle dripped down the back of my scalp and into my spine, like a spider walking across my neck.

III

My sister and I'd had been at our closest as children. I was four years older and was out of the house by the time she was twelve. Over the years, we had developed very archetypal identities for each other. She was the musical prodigy little sister to be protected by me, the menacing, protective older brother, who intimidated all prospective boyfriends. Because of circumstances, we were never able to allow our relationship to flesh out past these one-dimensional roles that we played with each other.

By the time my sister went away to college, I'd been 'out there', in the big wide world, living my own life on my own terms for quite some time. We saw a lot less of each other. I reckon we spent a total of maybe two or three months together between her thirteenth and twenty-third birthdays. I was becoming more and more who I was and she becoming more and more who she was, yet we only had those out-of-date childhood assumptions to guide our thoughts.

It was in college that she met her husband, Paulo. He was, like her, a musical prodigy, or at the very least, highly gifted. Also, he was possibly the single most arrogant person I have ever met. I can't say for sure what opinion he held of me because if I didn't struggle to make conversation or find common ground, we never spoke. For the first years of their relationship, we only saw each other at family functions and holidays. It was only through my efforts that there was any hole whatsoever carved out of his smug, aloof demeanor.

So, when my sister said 'Paulo and I' it set off alarm bells for me but nevertheless I listened.

> *"What, really? Worried? What do you mean?"*

> *"Well we wondered if you wind up in some sort of jam, I mean...
> Y'know... things have been pretty rough for you lately."*

> *"Well that's true with the downturn and stuff but I'm not calling
> to ask for help."*

> *"We want to help. You're my brother and I love you. I want to
> help, I really do."*

I was reluctant to accept. There had always been tension between us about money and I was too raw to deal with old family stuff right now.

"I don't know, sis..."

Then, all at once, she blurted out

*"I'm calling a family meeting! We need to come together and figure
out how we can help you right now!"*

Now, as a rule, my family doesn't do 'family meetings', in fact, I don't ever
remember having one. That really should have been a tip off for me. But the
truth was I was not fully in control of my faculties that evening. I was drained
and overwhelmed. The idea of someone, anyone, coming to my aid did
sound rather good. It gave me the feeling I was calling her to get in the first
place – a sense of belonging – like I mattered.

I agreed to the family meeting, though not without reservations. Something
just didn't feel right about it but I couldn't put my finger on what it might
have been. Pushing my apprehensions aside, we set a date.

IV

The day came and we all met at mom's house. Tobin, my son, was at my
sister's house with their babysitter. We all gathered in the living room as
mom opened the shades she normally kept drawn, letting some warm
afternoon light into the room.

And so it began.

We all got comfortable in our respective seats, pre-arranged in a semi-circle
– myself, my sister Annabel, my brother-in-law, Paulo, mom and my
youngest brother, James.

My sister started.

"So we're all here to see how we can help you right now." she said,
*looking at me "but before we start, there's just something I need to
get off my chest. I want to help you – but I don't trust you."*

I felt like I'd been sharply slapped in the face. It just came out of nowhere.

"What?" I said incredulously. "What are you talking about?"

*"I'm just worried if we give you money now, you'll just be back in
the same situation in a few months or even less."*

Have you noticed; sometimes people can just knock you off your feet with
the briefest of things they say. This was one of those times. There were so
many things wrong in that one small, opening sentence, that I didn't even
know where to start or what to say. I was stunned. I don't know what
bothered me more, the implication I was here to get money from them, the
fact that they wouldn't give any to assistance to a desperate family member
or the more insidious implication that it would just be 'enabling me' in some
way if they did give me money.

I felt heat shoot up inside of me – fast. I went from zero to angry before I
could catch it. What the hell was this? How was this supposed to be helpful?
Had they all discussed this beforehand – behind my back?

"You think I'm here for money?" was all I could manage.

Mom spoke next and without any preamble.

*"What Annabel is saying is you can't seem to get a handle on your
finances and it worries us."*

Now it really did seem like they all discussed this meeting together
beforehand. Suddenly the whole thing felt like an ambush. But why the hell
would you ambush someone you love when they are already down so far?
We were less than a minute into this and already I had a bizarre sensation of
watching the familial safety net I'd always imagined should be there to
support me slowly begin to unravel. Simultaneously, I began to get a sense
of clarity and purpose again, as if I was making a stone of my heart. It was
a very strange sensation.

The meeting continued.

They took turns, one after another, indiscriminately vomiting out every
resentment and concern they had been holding on to about me, with wanton
disregard for me or my feelings. As I sat there, I was at once furious,
horrified, disgusted and fascinated by the morbid spectacle unfolding before
me.

What was supposed to be the gathering of a supportive family, with the aim of finding ways to help someone in a time of crisis, became a freak show from the moment it started. Every single financial decision they found objection with was trotted out and used to crucify me. At one point, I was even accused of spending too much money on haircuts, even though I'd been extremely thrifty using clippers to shave my own head for the last nine months!

I sat there fuming at the injustice of this 'spontaneous' character assassination. I said to myself, 'I didn't ask for any of this hostility. I had expressly told them I did not want any money from them – not a dime.'

My brother-in-law interrupted my sister in mid-rant, blurting out loudly

> "Look, none of us are lending you any money, ever! Do you understand? Not ever!"

Everything stopped at that. The room fell silent.

I looked hard at Paulo. My hands rolled themselves into fists without my permission. Every time I hadn't slapped him in the past when he so richly deserved it for being an insufferable, arrogant, preening, pompous ass came flooding back into my mind. My nerves tingled. Mocking me for 'not doing what I should've done', reminding me 'what he'd earned a hundred times already' with his contemptuous, smug attitude. I took a long, slow breath, staring him in the eye, and said in a whisper

> "What the fuck was that?"

He was trapped by my gaze and after a long silence he said, weakly

> "I don't know. I think that was just some old resentment I had inside me."

This was what passed for 'an apology' from him. He had crossed a line in front of everyone and he knew it. Only my youngest brother had the good grace to remain quiet through this bloodletting. He sat in his chair and just watched on – mute.

After a moment, the meeting reorganized itself, shaking off the tension just enough to resume the talking. The significance of Annabel's opening comment was crystalizing in my mind now. As this absurd family drama progressed, I had a sensation of one link of misplaced loyalty after another disconnecting between them and myself. With each separation, the truth became clearer. Whilst I could manage without them, I also craved their acceptance. The answer to my most fundamental question had been on the other side of the curtain all along.

As this realization was unfolding inside of me, I'd only really been listening with one ear to what was going on in the room. That is until my sister said

> *"And I have an idea of what we can do to support you right now, to help you while you deal with this."*

That got my attention, especially after all that had just transpired, both in the room and inside of myself.

> *"I'm listening," I replied.*

Magnanimously, my sister went on

> *"We've decided that Tobin can stay with us...We'll make sure he gets to school, take care of all of his needs, food, clothes and everything, while you figure all of this out."*

Before I even had a chance to let that sink in, like tag-team wrestlers, Paulo continued with the killer blow

> *"Yeah, you can do whatever you need to do and we'll make sure Tobin is OK. I've even talked to a lawyer and had him draw up some simple visitation papers so we can all be on the same page about when you can come and see him."*

Well that was it – I flipped.

> *"What the fuck did you just say? Did I hear you right? You had a LAWYER draw up 'VISITATION PAPERS' to decide when I can see my OWN SON? ARE YOU FUCKING KIDDING ME!!"*

Mom chimed in

> *"Now don't get upset..."*

"Don't get upset? Really? This is your idea of 'helping?' Who the fuck are you people? VISITATION PAPERS!!"

"Honey... calm down..."

"Calm down! Fucking calm down!! Oh my God, you people are insane! Let me tell you how this ends. You can take your help, your smug, self-righteousness and your fucking 'visitation paper,' and you can shove them up your ass. You can go fuck yourselves! And for the record, if any of you were in the situation I am in, here's what I would've done. I would've told you, not asked you but TOLD you that you were staying with me as long as you needed, no questions asked..."

I was screaming now. I could barely control my rage.

"That's what I thought family did for each other, that's how I thought we were raised. I thought we looked after each other... FUCKING VISITATION PAPERS? FUCK YOU!!"

I got up and walked out of the room and out of the meeting.

My head was spinning. As much as I felt furious at them, I also felt such an amazing clarity, like I'd been living under a lead blanket for the last few years and had it finally been lifted off of me. As I was walking home, I was connecting the dots rapidly. Never again would I bargain off pieces of myself, of my integrity, for the possibility of acceptance of others. The clarity and understanding came crashing in on me like a tidal wave. From here on out, I was 'Frank fucking Sinatra' and win, lose or draw, I'd do it 'my way!'

I saw it all as if it was on a movie screen in front of my eyes. All of the confusion, doubt, the frustration of not being able to identify why I'd been struggling so hard for so long had become clear as day.

All the way home, my phone rang off the hook with work calls. By the time I got back, I'd booked three jobs.

The sudden clarity that I was experiencing brought certain questions with it however. The biggest one among them was, 'how did I, being a strong willed, aware, and generally highly capable and proactive person, ever let myself come to this place to begin with?' Obviously, the economic crash that was rocking the entire world played a huge part, but in addition to those immutable challenges that we all faced, the crash also amplified many of my own personal issues.

To understand how I came to this situation in the first place, we need to go back in time...

CHAPTER 2

PREMATURE ENLIGHTENMENT

I

November 23rd, 1994 is a day that sticks in my mind. Why? Well, it was the day I got sober.

I'd been living in Chico, California for about seven years at the advice of my extended family and with the approval of mom.

I'd fooled a psychiatrist into thinking I was crazy but not so crazy that I needed supervision or medication. I was just 'crazy enough' to convince them that I was mentally unfit to hold a job and I needed to receive government handouts, welfare, for the rest of my life. (I'll talk more about this in due time, but for now, suffice to say because of this 'little white lie', I was free to live the life of a gypsy.) Every month, I'd receive enough to pay a little rent, buy and consume lots of drugs and carry no responsibility whatsoever. This worked out fine with me because until I was fourteen, that's how I was raised to behave – again more on that later.

About five years through my tenure in Chico, I began to feel the money I was receiving every month was not quite enough to support my ever-expanding appetite for drugs, booze and partying. At the time, I felt a natural solution to this problem was to try my hand at selling drugs. It made perfect, addict sense. I loved doing the drugs. What's more, I hung out exclusively with other people who loved doing drugs. They would be thrilled to have one of their buddies also be their dealer. It was a 'win-win.' I began in earnest.

For a while, it went great! Before I started being a dealer, my friends and I frequently partied all day and all night. Except now, when we wanted 'party supplies,' they came to my place. No more inconvenience of running across town late at night to cop a bag, I had it. If it was time to smoke out, I had it covered, no need to interrupt the festivities. Hand me the money and the party doesn't need to stop. 'Easy-peasy-lemon-squeezy.' I was the belle of the ball.

Slowly, though, problems stared to seep in. Like when I'd push the envelope too far and black out, trying to start fights with strangers or staying up for several days straight, until I couldn't think clearly. (Come to think of it, all of my drug-related problems orbited around not thinking clearly. How about that?)

Little-by-little, things began to change for the worse. Some old friends stopped coming around anymore. New friends – dangerous friends – began to replace those old ones. I found myself doing things I really thought I'd never do, with people I never thought I'd do them with. Gang-bangers and guns became increasingly common features of my day. I consider the true low point for me to be when I found myself living with a hooker, buying and selling drugs with white supremacists that lived up the hill from Chico. Plus, having an O.G. blood from the Sacramento ghetto as a best friend and mentor... things had definitely taken a turn for the worse.

One morning my sex-worker girlfriend, Elouise and I were heading out to breakfast after staying up all night partying. She'd just gotten back from a 'date' a little while earlier and I remember I could still smell sex on her. She was upset with me because I refused to kiss her. I let her blow me to apologize for blowing the guy she'd just been with – but I didn't kiss her.

This didn't sit well with her at all. So there we were, around five in the morning, strung out for Jesus, driving down the main road through downtown Chico. Both of us were angry at each other, sitting in silence on opposite sides of her little grey, piece-of-shit Fiero sports coupe. I took a hit from a glass pipe, full to overflowing with melted crank, when, in front of us about a block away, we saw a sheriff's patrol car.

There was no way they could have seen us in any sort of incriminating detail from so far away. Nevertheless, Elouise, panicked. I don't mean 'oh shit, be cool, cops up ahead' panic – oh no. I'm talking about 'full-blown dope fiend, lose your shit' panic. She began swerving wildly across the lanes of the road, back and forth, whispering to me

"What are we going to do? What are we going to do?"

"Jeezus fucking Christ, El, you can start by playing it cool. Stop swerving! What the hell are you doing?"

"They know we're high, they know it!" her voice escalating to a high panicky screech.

"What the fuck are you talking about?" I shouted in disbelief! "How can they know anything? STOP FUCKING SWERVING!"

But it was too late. She was off the reservation. There was no talking her down. The cow had jumped over the moon. The patrol car up ahead slowed down a little and made a left turn. Oddly, Elouise saw this as us dodging a bullet. I did not share her optimism.

As soon as the cops were out of sight she looked at me again, calming down as suddenly as she'd blown up

"Whew, that was a close one!" she added, now placid again.

I was speechless, just staring at her as the blue and red lights came on behind us with the all too familiar siren wail accompanying them. The wily sheriffs had circled the block, allowing us to pass in front of them, as they came up from behind.

Surprise!

I quickly stashed my pipe, my dope (a big bag of crystal nuggets with its distinctive pungent gasoline and drain cleaner aroma – a smell that made my mouth water back then,) my little zip-lock distribution bags and everything else that might incriminate me, under the seat of that little Pontiac Fiero. I quickly checked all of the many pockets in my multi-zippered, black and white Michael Jackson jacket. Good – no incriminating evidence. We pulled to the side of the road.

"Shit! Shit! Shit! What are we gonna do?" Elouise lamented. "What aaaaaarrrre we gonna doooooo?"

"We're going to be pulled over and arrested!"

I looked again at Elouise and said

"Just try to stay calm and follow my lead. It'll be cool, trust me"

II

I'd no 'plan' to speak of but I was very good at talking myself out of being taken to jail. I'd done it more than a dozen times before this particular morning and I figured, with my track record, I had a better than fifty-fifty chance of doing it here. The cops knocked on our window. They were female – a good start. I unleashed a charm offensive.

"Morning officers," I said, not waiting for Elouise to say anything even though she was the driver.

"What seems to be the problem?"

The sheriff looked at me, then at Elouise, then back at me. Both of us must've looked like we were some of Metallica's grungy-looking road crew coming off a six-month tour.

"Are you both high?" the officer asked straight up, skipping the usual formalities.

"Yes... Yes we are..." I responded in kind.

I saw no reason to attempt deception. The officer looked slightly taken aback but quickly composed herself. Smiling just a little, she said

"Step out of the car, please."

"Of course." I replied.

At this point Elouise was open-mouthed watching the exchange between the officer and me.

"Where are you two heading this morning?" she inquired.

"We need to get some breakfast in us then go and try to get some sleep."

I assumed that to the trained eye it was obvious that we were both wired to the teeth.

'Lady Law' smiled at that.

> *"I appreciate your honesty, sir," she came back.*

> *"Please raise your hands out to your sides. Tell me now if I'm going to stick my hand on anything sharp when I search you."*

> *"Yes ma'am. I don't have anything sharp in my pockets." I said, reaching my arms to my sides.*

Elouise did the same. I assumed she had decided to follow my lead and let me do the talking because she was only volunteering grunts and one-word answers to the torrent of questions we were fielding.

We were detained on the curb for about a half an hour while the officers ran our names and social security numbers. The sun was fully up now, lighting the few clouds in the sky in a vanilla ice cream yellow glow. Birds began singing their morning songs. Everything seemed to be going smoothly. Then they began checking the car. A couple of minutes into their search, the officer who hadn't been chatting with me popped her head up.

> *"Got something..." she rang out.*

I could see the pipe and the bag of drugs in her hand. She walked over to us.

> *"Any idea how this got here?"*

> *"No ma'am, I've never seen that stuff before in my life!" I grinned.*

> *"I'm sure that you haven't." she replied.*

> *"What about you ma'am?" she asked, looking at El.*

> *"Do you know how these drugs got in your car?"*

Elouise panicked at this question and blurted out

> *"I've got a ten-year-old daughter. Those drugs aren't mine. I just met him a few days ago. I think he's a dealer. I can't go to jail. I just can't go to jail, pleeeaaase..!"*

So much for following my lead! Besides, her betrayal didn't really matter much anyway – once the car was searched, it was 'game over' for us. If they couldn't get one of us to admit to owning the drugs, we would both be hauled in and arrested. Simple as that.

So, we were taken downtown, to Chico's version of the county lock-up. After we arrived, I didn't see Elouise again until our court date. After I was processed, the sheriff who brought me in had another officer perform a search of 'my person,' which came up clean. Then they put me in a holding cell while they were doing paperwork or something – I'm not really sure. I just know they left me in a large cell with several other guys who were all going to jail for real.

I sat for a long time in that holding cell, ten or eleven hours maybe, coming down off the drugs that had me so chipper on my way in to the police station. After many hours of sitting and trading tall tales with the others, I was called to the front. I was being released. I had no idea why but I wasn't going to argue.

"Manny Wolfe, you're free to go."

(...Really? Shit! How did this happen? Who cares! Get me out of here...)

As it happened, the same lady cop who arrested me was the one walking me to freedom.

"I want to thank you for being so polite and cooperative," she said to me as she walked me to the front of the building.

I could see through the greasy, sliding glass doors in the entry way, the sun was actually sinking again, meaning I could work out I'd been there all day from sun up to sun down.

"Of course." I replied. "After all, we were both just doing our jobs."

She laughed out loud at this.

"I'm going to have a note put in your record stating how well behaved you were today, just in case we ever see you again, not

that that's likely..." she said with a playfully sarcastic edge to her tone.

"Yes ma'am! It's the straight and narrow for me from here on out. No more shenanigans or rambunctiousness for me... I'm a new man," I said, affecting a southern drawl.

Then, I looked sideways at her and tipped an imaginary straw hat to complete the effect.

"Hahahaa, I love it!" she said. "Let's just give you one last search before you leave so that I can feel good about doing my job the right way, O.K?"

"No problem, do what you need to do."

"Alrighty then. We'll have you out of here in a few minutes. Please assume the position."

I leaned slightly over the counter, arms out, so she could frisk me one last time – for old times' sake. She started at my ankles and worked her way up, around the legs, up to the hips, around the rib cage, out the arms and then back down. This time she stopped at my waist. Double-checking, she made a small noise.

"Huh! What's this?" she said, more to herself than to me.

III

She lifted my shirt and there it was. A money belt I'd forgotten about completely.

"What is this?" she asked me.

"I don't know." I said in all seriousness.

I'd not only forgotten it was there, to be honest, I'd forgotten I even had a belt like that! Going days without sleep can make you forgetful, after all.

As it turned out, a couple of days earlier, in the midst of the five-day run of partying without sleep (that led me to this fine mess to begin with) I was with some friends. Someone had produced this money belt in the hope they could trade me for a little dope in lieu of payment. I was immediately intrigued by the slim little hideaway compartment and quickly agreed. I put it around my waist complete with, it seems, a tiny stash of drugs still inside. I completely forgot about the belt in the course of the next couple of days. That is until she, the 'nice lady sheriff', found it again.

> *"No idea, huh?" she asked me, suddenly skeptical and
>   unfriendly.*

> *"Let's take a look."*

> *"Sure. Go right ahead."*

At the time, I had no idea there was anything untoward inside but of course, there was. The money belt which I had initially thought of as my secret accomplice, my stealthy friend, was about to become my betrayer instead. Hidden behind the edge of some stitching, running like a spine across the length of my secret pocket, was another smaller pouch. Inside, was a stowaway of the narcotic variety. A tiny little bag of meth, no more than one good hit if you were a smoker, not even enough for a real bump if you preferred snorting it. However, it was unquestionably a controlled substance and unquestionably in my possession.

> *"What's this?" she asked with no amusement left in her tone.*

> *"Looks like drugs to me."*

She opened the little bag and sniffed carefully.

> *"Yup."*

I was fucked.

After all the bonding and banter, our playful back-and-forth almost to the point of flirtation – and this had to happen? I began to explain 'I had no idea how the tiny bag got there' but quickly realized that, to her, I looked like a grinning Cheshire cat with feathers sticking out of my mouth. I was caught red handed.

I sighed as the handcuffs that had so recently been removed went back on and with very little further ado, I was escorted to a stainless steel room. It was smaller than the room I'd just shared with my purgatory partners – and much less comfortable. It was chilly, blank and dismal. I was left in that room for hours, alone, cold and coming down. I even managed to sleep a bit until a new cop came in and began questioning me. I guessed 'good cop' had gone home or something because this guy was playing the hard guy role like day old bread at a second-rate deli.

I knew when you're being interrogated, if you're tired, it's beneficial for the police. It's how they can wear you down more easily. They try to trip you up with conflicting accusations and lead you around in circles until you get dizzy with it. And at this point, I can testify there is such a thing as being 'too tired' to be interrogated because that's definitely what I was.

As I was sitting there, drifting in and out of sleep, Detective Dick Hardcase walked in.

"Looks like we caught us a cowboy. A real baller."

He looked at me like a schoolyard bully.

"Is that you? A big shot, dealer?"

Exhausted, I said

"Oh yeah, that's me. Did my clothes give it away?"

At that, he jammed his face close, nose almost pressed to mine

"You wanna crack wise with me princess?"

(...do people really talk like this..?)

"Cause we got you dead-to-rights you little punk. We know all about you and your girlfriend."

(...oh yeah, Elouise, I'd forgotten about her...)

"She gave you up... told us everything!"

"What exactly did she tell you?" I asked amused.

If I hadn't been so tired and strung out, I am pretty sure I wouldn't have had the balls to have such a bad attitude with this guy. But I was exhausted. And he was such a cliché.

> *"There's nothing to tell officer. We were out partying. We had been up for a few days. We wanted to crash so we decided to get some breakfast and see if we could sleep afterwards. That's it."*

> *"That's it huh?" he shot back.*

> *"Well, I've got a different story for ya! Tell me what you think? My story is about a 'big-time supplier' who is slumming it with a local hooker. Did you know that your girlfriend is a hooker?"*

(...actually, I did know, not my proudest moment I admit...)

> *"We all gotta make a living" I responded "and what do you mean by 'big-time supplier'?"*

> *"We've had our eye on you for a long time. We know that you supply Flaco Sanchez and Tug Giminez."*

Flaco Sanchez and Tug Giminez were big fish in the local drug scene, reputed to work for the Mexican mob. If you wanted a large order and you knew the right people, chances are your people were going to one of them to get it. I laughed out loud at the idea I was supplying these two guys. Even I couldn't get my own drugs directly from them – I'd have to go through one of their 'street-team' members lower down the food chain.

> *"You've had your eye on me for a long time and this what you came up with?"*

At this point, I realized the detective was obviously grasping at straws, so I relaxed a little. I wasn't sure what was going to happen to me but I thought it wasn't going to be much. Only in hindsight, did I understand the events in my life that would put into motion with all of this. How all of these things happening were laying the groundwork for a turning point for me. A moment which would change every aspect of my life and ultimately set me on a brand new trajectory.

"Officer, if you can prove any of this, then charge me, otherwise, can I please go home? I'm very tired and I'm ready to sleep for like two days."

"Oh I don't think you're going home just yet smartass." he shot back at me.

"Just get comfortable. You're still mine for a little while."

He got up and left the room – and me – not to return for several more hours.

When he did return, it was to tell me I'd be kept while I awaited my court date for the minor possession charge and the other one, the suspicion of possession with intent to distribute. The police could not definitively prove the distribution charge at the time. The problem was at the time of my arrest, Butte County was cracking down on the meth trade. They wanted to make 'examples of people.' Thanks to that initiative, I was to be detained until my trial. Two officers picked me up, put me in handcuffs and led me back through the long hallway and to be processed.

IV

My short spell in jail was surprisingly uneventful. It turned out that I had several friends in there who I hadn't seen for a long time (obviously.) I did sketching to pass the time. Once people discovered I knew how to draw well, my skills were in demand. I traded them for freeze-dried coffee, candy, the occasional cigarette and for custom mail envelopes (used for letters home to loved ones.) Sometimes there were tattoo idea requests and of course, naked women in compromising positions (such as straddling bald eagles or riding topless on motorcycles.)

After about three-and-a-half weeks of waking up early, going to breakfast, then sitting in the dorm area watching TV, drawing pictures, telling tall tales of our exploits on the outside and drinking way too much instant coffee, I got a visit from my public defender (P.D.) Now, many jokes are made in jail, concerning the skill and efficacy of P.D.s – none of them do the real story justice...

To say that my P.D. was useless would be a massive understatement!

When he first showed up to our visit, with his jacket hopelessly crumpled and frumpy just like his hair, I noticed that he'd buttoned his shirt buttons out of sequence. This resulted in the left side of his collar being up one button higher than his right side. He called me no less than four wrong names from no less than four wrong files.

When he finally found my file and established I was, in fact 'me' and not another selection from the 'rogues' gallery' trapped in his faux-leather accordion file, he had to read it in front of me, indicating that he really and truly had no sense of me as a person.

He'd not just not done his homework. He hadn't even cracked his schoolbooks open – opting instead to stay up all night with his frat-house brothers pounding shots of Jägermeister and draining kegs of beer, while devising ways to steal the feigned innocence of some chubby, naïve, sorority girl. In short, he was useless and incompetent. He was the real-life lawyer equivalent of showing up to class in your underwear.

Other than convincing me I was doomed by the sheer force of his ineptitude, not much happened as a result of our initial meeting. I was informed my court date would be a couple of days later and he left like a shot.

My court date arrived. I was brought out to a waiting room off of the main dorm. In it, were seven other guys also due to appear that day. We were all shackled to each other, chain gang style with rusty, silver wrist and ankle restraints over our dingy orange jumpsuits. BCCF (Butte County Correction Facility) was stenciled in big, grey-black letters across our backs.

The waiting area was covered with years of patchy, lead-based paint in different shades of institutional greys and beiges – the result of countless, careless years of sloppy painting and poor workmanship.

We jostled with each other, telling stories of what ballsy, brash things we would tell the judge when our turn came up to go in front of him.

We would make those felons who came before us proud, demonstrating a real American rebel spirit. We would show no fear telling him exactly what we thought about his 'so-called authority' and opinions. He would come to know he was in the midst of true outlaws – real criminals who would not be intimidated by the threat of 'jail time.' We would do it standing on our heads. Fuck the police!

In the middle of this dreamy fantasizing, the guard in charge of us spoke.

"INMATES, LISTEN UP CLOSE!"

In spite of ourselves, we snapped to attention, all of our daydreams rapidly dissolving as we woke up to our situation. Reality just bit us on the ass – hard.

> *"You are about to go in front of a California circuit judge for Butte County. Do not speak! Do not make any gestures with your hands – whatsoever! Do not make eye contact with anyone in the courtroom except the judge! Do not look over to see your friends in the stands! Do not speak unless you're spoken to. Do not speak while awaiting your turn! Sit quietly and wait for your name to be called. DO YOU UNDERSTAND?"*

Silence...

> *"I said – DO YOU UN-DER-STAND?"*

> *"Yes, Sir!" was the weak reply given by some, the others too afraid or unwilling to speak.*

> *"I can't hear you inmates. Do you understand the directions I have given you? ANSWER ME!!"*

> *"YES, SIR!" we all shouted together.*

(...where had all those 'rebels' evaporated to..?)

> *"When that door opens," he pointed to his left, "you will enter, single file and silently. Do you understand?"*

> *"Yes, Sir!"*

> *"Wait at attention, inmates!"*

> *"Yes, Sir!"*

We had definitely lost our 'true outlaw' disposition! Speaking only for myself, I can tell you when the guard started shouting at us, I realized I had a simple choice. I could hold onto my bad attitude OR the urine in my bladder. I chose the latter, not wishing to walk into court wearing a urine-soaked jump suit.

The appointed door opened and the reality of my situation flooded down on me. I was going to court to await sentencing for possession of and intent to distribute narcotics in the State of California.

This was not good.

In our chains, we shuffled through the door, suddenly sullen and desultory, looking utterly dejected. Despite the earlier instructions, I glanced up quickly and to my great surprise, one of my best friends was sitting in the stands. He caught my eye immediately and discretely gestured to me. Daringly, I returned his signal and he smiled. I was genuinely overwhelmed by his presence in the courtroom. I tried to smile in return but started to cry instead. I don't know why but tears began to roll quietly down my cheeks.

What the hell was I doing here? How bad was this?

I had always (like most of us, at least those I associated with) foolishly, recklessly thought of myself as too smart to be caught, too good somehow, to be arrested and brought to trial, to do 'jail time.'

I sat in my hard, little wooden seat and watched. I watched as one by one, the people I came in with – chained to – were sentenced. First, the drunk driver, twice before arrested for the same thing. This time his luck ran out and he was sent to the infamous San Quentin State Penitentiary for twenty months for drunk driving and reckless endangerment. Next, the dim frat boy, too stupid to understand when the judge was being coy and vague in an attempt avoid saying 'date rape' in reference to the young man's crime.

> *"Do you understand the charges that are being brought against you today, young man?"*

> *"No, your Honor, I don't."*

There was a palpable frustrated sigh from the judge and the bailiff at this. I watched any remaining sympathy leave the judge's face.

> *"Young man, you are being charged with rape. How do you plead?"*

Sheepishly, the young man answered.

> *"Guilty, your Honor."*

I stole a glance at my friend in the audience. He shook his head gently in disbelief.

As the college boy was being escorted back into custody, the guy next to me leaned over and whispered

> *"He won't last a week inside... They don't take too kindly to*
> *rapists."*

(...that explained the black eye he came to court with, then...)

One by one, those ahead of me were dealt with, until my turn arrived.

> *"Next the judge calls Emmanuel Wolfe, for charges of being under*
> *the influence of, in possession of and intending to distribute*
> *methamphetamine in the State of California."*
>
> *"Here, your Honor." I said instinctively.*

The judge looked at me.

> *"I am glad to see that you are here, Mr. Wolfe, however I am*
> *wondering if your lawyer is present?"*
>
> *"Yes, I am, your Honor." answered my P.D.*
>
> *"Your Honor, my client is a first-time offender, with no past record.*
> *In my opinion, he is repentant and not a risk of repeating any*
> *crimes of this nature. Therefore, your Honor, I ask for his charges*
> *to be dismissed and considered as time served."*

The judge looked down his glasses at my P.D., took a breath, then replied

> *"Perhaps you and I have differing views on the inherent severity of*
> *our collective drug epidemic, counselor? I am ordering Mr. Wolfe*
> *to serve a sentence of two years in San Quentin. If he successfully*
> *serves this sentence, he will then be eligible for three years'*
> *probation – which I feel is very lenient considering, as I have*
> *alluded to today, my feelings about the severity of our current drug*
> *epidemic."*

My heart jumped into my throat, then, changing its mind, it went to hide in my bowels.

> *"Two years in prison?" my P.D. answered. "Sounds good to me!"*

I shit you not, dear reader, he actually said

> *"Sounds good to me!"*

He then turned and began to leave the courtroom. I was in a full-blown panic.

(...c'mon God! Don't you think this is a little fucking stiff? Just a bit of an overreaction..!)

As the bailiff moved to pick up my file and bring it to the judge, he paused.

> *"Your Honor, Mr. Wolfe's counselor seems to have a conflict of interest here."*
>
> *"What do you mean, bailiff?" asked the judge.*
>
> *"Mr. Wolfe was arrested with one 'Elouise Jamison' and it seems his counsel is also her counsel."*
>
> *"Hand me the file, bailiff."*

The judge took the file, looked over it for a moment, then said

> *"We will continue Mr. Wolfe's sentencing ten weeks from today, at which time he will show up back here, with appropriate legal representation, is that understood bailiff?"*
>
> *"Yes, your Honor."*

Just like that, I was snatched back from the abyss! My head was all over the place. My body was still light from the adrenaline surge that had been coursing through me as I pondered doing a two-year stint in San Quentin!

I felt both sick and relieved all at once.

I couldn't believe the judge could be so impassive while first giving me a sentence that was far too extreme for my crime and then simply postponing it, like it was nothing. He never even flinched.

From the courtroom, I was taken back to the side room where I'd lately commiserated with my fellow brigands about what rebels we were and how we laughed at the law. I didn't feel that sense of foolish bravado now. I felt beaten.

Though, thankfully, I was not to be shipped directly to prison that day, still I felt like I'd been flayed. I was naked and exposed, like a raw nerve in a salt bath. I was escorted back to the county jail where I was released into my own custody to await my new court date.

As I stood there at the window where the cantankerous old guard gave you back whatever you'd been brought in with, I began to notice how much of a toll the preceding hours, indeed the last few weeks had taken on me. By the time he got around to my black and white, multi-zippered popstar jacket, the memories of the evening of my arrest came back to me.

Me, Rob and our friend Tony at Ladd's Marina

It had all been so surreal, so outright bizarre. I don't know why, but in front of the guards, the clerk and everyone else who was present, I began to laugh out loud. I laughed at the improbability of the events leading to my arrest.

The money belt, forgotten until it surfaced to betray me, the erratic swerving driving of my hooker girlfriend Elouise as she comically tried to avoid capture on Main Street at sun up. I laughed at my attempts – almost successful – at charming my way out of incarceration. I laughed at being sentenced to two years in San Quentin. I laughed at the ineptitude of my useless 'sounds good' P.D. – at least, because he was so useless I had garnered a few more weeks of freedom. I laughed at all of it – until I cried.

I cried as I walked out to the parking lot and I saw my friend, the one who had come to court to support me during my sentencing, waiting for me with a ride back to town. I cried at the sight of him and I cried in the car on the ride home. I cried until I fell asleep.

V

When I finally woke up, two days later, it was to the sound of my friend and his girlfriend arguing about me. They were trying to figure out what to do with me. You see, before I went to jail, I was, essentially, homeless. I always had drugs and money so I always had somewhere to go or least others with whom I could spend the wee hours. In truth, I'd not had a place of my own for about three months. During the summers in Chico, this wasn't so bad if you had friends who were 'partiers.'

The nights were warm and there were lots of us who were fans of staying up all night, partying hard. You could always find a partner in crime. Usually I'd just crash at Elouise's house if I wasn't out partying but after the arrest, that option was no longer on the table. So, when my friend's girlfriend decided that I had to go, literally, I had nowhere 'to go.' I had no drugs and only a few dollars to my name.

Once thrown out into the street, I headed to the apartment of another one of my partying friends, seeking a place to regroup for a bit and come up with a new plan of attack. This particular friend was one of a couple of people with whom I had an informal agreement. I'd make sure they were included in my partying and earning. In return, they would store my things for me – cardboard boxes of clothes, the curious collectibles one accumulates through being a speed freak, a few out-of-tune guitars and other bits and pieces.

With the expectation of a shower and a change of clothes, I made my way to his place.

When I arrived at his front door, I knocked a few of times. As I stood there waiting for an answer, I took a deep breath in and reflected on how good it was to be free again – if only for the few weeks until my new court date. ('Out of jail' beats 'in jail' hands down!) After a minute or so, he answered the door. When he saw me, he looked like he'd seen a ghost.

> *"Hey man, what's happening? Did you miss me?" I asked, jokingly.*

He just stood there, agog. I could see a mix of confusion and nervousness in his eyes.

> *"What's up, man? What's going on?"*

> *"How... How did... What are you doing HERE?"*

> *"Man, I just got out of jail like a second ago, bro. Can I come in and grab a change of clothes, maybe a shower?"*

> *"...I don't understand? How... How are you here?"*

> *"What the hell are you talking about?" I demanded, beginning to sense there was something wrong.*

> *"Where else would I go? You've got most of my clothes, man."*

> *"I don't... I thought... you weren't coming back... how come you're here at my place?"*

He was sounding very nervous, almost hysterical. His eyes kept darting back and forth, looking at me then behind me, then back at me again, as if he were waiting for the hidden cameras to burst out any second and yell

> *"Surprise, you're on candid camera!"*

He just stood there twitching, looking at me as if I was back from the dead or something. Finally, he said

> *"I don't have any of your clothes man... everything's gone. It's all gone."*

> *"What are you talking about? Where's my stuff, bro? I've been in the same clothes for three days. What the fuck is going on here?"*

His eyes lowered slightly and he said

"Sorry man, but I can't let you in."

He closed the door in my face.

I was blown away. Events beyond my comprehension just kept on happening to me, one after the other. This was unbelievable. I knocked again but he didn't answer. I stood a few minutes more, puzzled and speechless, then left. As I looked back one final time, I saw him peek out from behind one of his curtains.

When I had visited three 'bros' places and the exact same thing happened, I was starting to get pretty upset. Obviously, I was not privy to some important piece of new information about me and my doings. Everywhere I turned, friends were acting as if I was the 'King of the Leper Colony,' closing doors in my face, offering no explanations as to why they wouldn't let me in. I couldn't put my finger on why but they were acting like there was a big, obvious secret I was not in on.

Finally, I decided to look up a couple of old friends – two big farm boys I used to drink with before social drinking was replaced by anti-social speed (ab)use. I enlisted them in my quest for answers. Together, we made our way to yet another friend's house and knocked on his door.

Predictably, he reacted like the others, nervous, sketchy and dismissive, trying to get as much distance between himself and me as possible. This time when the now familiar behavior started, I kicked in his door and my two friends who each took up most of the doorway, entered.

"How's it going, Mickey?"

Silence...

"You wanna tell me what the fuck is going on around here? I've been in jail for less than a month and when I return all my friends are acting like I'm the boogeyman! Care to explain?"

At the sight of me and my two large friends, Mickey caved

"We thought you were going away for a long time, shit, you made the papers man. You were in the fucking papers!"

He backed away and began shuffling around in the mess of his apartment until, at last, he produced a month-old copy of the Chico Gazette. He pointed to the lower-right corner. The headline read 'Possible Drug Kingpin Seized in Routine Traffic Stop.'

(...what? What the hell was going on here? There was even a traffic camera shot of Elouise's piece-of-shit grey Pontiac Fiero as it crossed lanes of traffic erratically...)

>*"Everyone was spooked by this shit." said Mickey.*

>*"You know how these motherfuckers can talk? Then [that gangster] Ray Ray started telling everyone that you were an undercover narc or some shit"*

Ray Ray?

Shit!

VI

Ray Ray was a self-described O.G. black guy, about five foot eight. He weighed maybe a hundred and forty pounds and he was all bad attitude and thug disposition. He liked guns, had a ten-foot-tall chip on his shoulder and he liked dirty pool. In short, settling a score with Ray Ray, even if it was a score he started, would never be a simple 'meet me on the playground at recess' type of squabble.

No, if you fought and you won, he would come back for more. I'd seen it personally more than once. The little fucker held a grudge like a possessed pit bull terrier.

Even if he won, you couldn't say it was over because then you were his bitch and in his mind, he'd license to fuck with you at will.

>*"So Ray Ray came over here and told me you told him to collect all of your shit from everyone if you ever got busted."*

>*"Jeezus! What the hell is all this about?"*

Now, I was unaware at this time one of the good old farm boys I'd brought with me for muscle was pretty deep in with the white supremacists up in the hills above Chico. I knew these white supremacists too. We had bought and sold drugs to each other many, many times, making us 'friends.' These 'friends' would definitely take a distinctly 'racial view' of the things unfolding.

A few hours after I got the news Ray Ray had been responsible not only for taking all of my worldly possessions but for turning all my friends against me, capitalizing on the vague and misleading article in the paper about me and my arrest, I was laying low at the apartment of one of the good old boys.

My beeper went off.

> "Can I use the phone?" I asked.
>
> "Sure, right over there," he pointed to the corner of the living room.
>
> "Cool."

I dialed the number.

> "Hey, this is Manny. Did you page me?"
>
> "Hey man, this is Robbie. What's this shit I hear about some nigger taking all of your shit?"

Even as a kid, when I was in the ghetto, I always found the word 'nigger' just like any aggressive racial slur – highly disturbing. It's one of those words that makes my skin crawl. Even now, it is difficult for me to stay calm when I hear it used. However, given my circumstances, this was neither the time and place, nor the guy to reveal my take on what 'nigger' meant.

> "What did you hear?"
>
> "I heard that you went to jail and some fucking toadie stole all of your shit!"
>
> "That's about right," I replied. "I'm working on a solution as we speak."
>
> "Well I'm coming down the hill right now and you and I are going to work on that solution together, got it?"

(...I got very tense hearing those words but thought it best to keep any feelings like that to myself...)

"Sounds good, I'll be waiting."

"Alright. See you in a bit."

At this point, I knew bad stuff was happening – for sure. That's the funny thing about the mythical 'moment of clarity.' Even when it's right in front of your face, staring at you with all the subtlety of a neon, flaming jackhammer, you just don't see it clearly until you 'see it.'

As I paced the floor, wondering what was going to happen when Robbie arrived. I didn't see it. As I connected the dots about the added 'racial' level that had just been introduced into the proceedings, I didn't see it.

As my friends were there with me, the guy had called Robbie in the first place, the other good old boy and a couple of others I didn't know very well began to get riled up at the inevitable confrontation – yet I still didn't see it.

While my mind was working double duty trying to navigate the narrower and narrower options left to me – still not fucking seeing it. I did, however, see it – clearly – when Robbie arrived.

"Hey man, come on out to my truck with me. I want to show you something."

"Ok, sure. Let's go"

"Look at these, bro!"

He produced from out of an oily rag, two handguns.

"What are these for?" I asked idiotically

"These are untraceable. I got them from someone who, well, let's just say that he's sympathetic to your situation with the 'nigger.' You and me are going to go and find this fucker tonight and were going to 'handle your problem' – once and for all."

Right then, I fucking saw it – the 'clarity moment.'

It's difficult to describe my personal experience standing there, my hand on the rag, wrapped around the gun brought to me – unsolicited – to help me with 'my problem.'

Robert de Niro himself would have been proud of my superb acting abilities as I stood there, on the outside unflinching and cool as the proverbial fucking cucumber, while inside it utter chaos.

Here's how it felt. You know that action scene in a thriller movie, when there's a problem with a plane and a door suddenly gets whipped away – whoosh. There's now a big gaping hole in the fuselage. The change in pressure makes trays and cups to launch up and vanish out of the doorway. The onlooking passengers and crew desperately hold onto seats to avoid being dragged to oblivion.

Well, imagine that taking place inside you, but worse – and better – all at once. That's what it felt like. Time slowed down and suddenly, I was aware of my outer calm and simultaneously aware of the fucking chaos inside of me. That chaos raged as all of my ridiculous notions of being able to keep this charade up were stripped away from me and dragged away into oblivion. It lasted a lifetime yet only took one second on the clock.

So there it was. The 'moment.' I saw it.

I REALLY SAW IT.

I was done with this shit. I let go of the controls all at once, as the clarity came. It came like the fucking voice of God, assuring me that I'd be O.K. I'd get through this. The steps I needed to take would simply revealed themselves to me. A sublime catharsis. (...I once was blind but now I see...)

I calmly looked at Robbie and said

"Let's get it done. Can you meet me back here at midnight?"

"I can do that. Are you good right now?"

I knew from his tone that he was referring to whether or not I'd any dope on me.

"No, but I'll make it to midnight."

"Here you go, bro."

He handed me a small, stinky, zip-lock bag of gear.

"Meet me back here at midnight. We're going hunting."

"All right brother, see you then."

Robbie left and I went back inside, broke out the drugs, chopped a few lines, enough for all of us in the apartment and got good and loaded for one last time.

As soon as I'd done that, I grabbed the phone, walked outside and began calling people who might still be friendly. After a few calls, I reached Kevin. He was glad to hear from me.

"Kevin, I need a ride to Stockton, buddy. What are you up to?"

"I'm going out of town for the Thanksgiving holidays so I'm going the opposite direction from Stockton. Let me make a couple of calls and I'll ring you back."

In a few minutes, he did just that.

"I got you taken care of, man. My niece and her friend are going to L.A. for the week and they will pass right through Stockton. They'll pick you up in an hour."

"Amazing, bro! Thank you so much. I'll see you when you get back."

I lied. I knew, for certain, I'd never see him or any of my other friends ever again.

One hour later, I was in squashed in the hatch of a Honda CRX with two girls I'd never met before. I had nothing but the clothes on my back and two small boxes of belongings I'd cobbled together on my way to mom's house in Stockton. I'd not even set foot in Chico again until ten years later.

It was November 23rd, 1994, the evening before Thanksgiving and it was indeed the last time I saw anyone from that life.

As I lay there, stuffed into back of that CRX, wired to the teeth, I found myself reflecting on how the hell I could have come to this in the first place.

Hunched up in the back of the tiny little car, reduced to nothing but the clothes on my back, heavily under the influence of what proved to be very strong narcotics, I found myself drifting back into memory.

How did I end up here?

I had always, even during the darkest of times, considered myself a person with a 'moral code.' This code consisted of lines I told myself I would never cross – the things I considered unacceptable. Man, in the last few years, I'd crossed most of these without even slowing down!

At times. I had stolen from strangers and friends alike. I blithely seduced other men's girlfriends and even the occasional wife. I'd justified all manner of deception and fraud. I found myself squatting in unoccupied apartments and foraging through dumpsters. I'd taken up with a prostitute who kept me in drugs, money, food and shelter, in exchange for which I let her 'service' me with her mouth and occasionally gave her my cock. I sold drugs to homeless people and had even became homeless myself.

I had allowed myself to cross those lines. I had become a thief, a cheat, a liar, a womanizer and a drug addict.

It wasn't until I was faced with the prospect of killing another man in cold blood that I woke up to what all those transgressions of my code meant. I was disgusted with myself. I felt unclean to the very marrow in my bones.

I did all of those things, crossed all of those boundaries, while buried inside me, watching helpless, was a deeply 'Moral Man.' This moral part of me hungered to keep his word, demonstrate honor, integrity, principled action and character in all things. A man who valued and desired a spiritual life. A life of service to others and to a higher level of accountability. For many years, my out of control rebellious side mocked this Moral Man with the way I conducted myself. All the while, 'rebel me' was very aware of his presence. It felt like a child rebelling against a nurturing, loving parent.

During the quiet times, the times when it was just he and I, Moral Man would plead with 'rebel me' but to no avail. My addiction and the pain it was spawned from were too powerful for him to override until then. And so, he sat and watched horrified as I took my life to its last and final low.

Looking back now, I can see that I was engaged in an end-game struggle for survival. The only possible course of action I knew of was to run my addiction to its limits and see if it would kill me or I'd kill it. Live or die. Kill or cure. Only one of us was going to be left standing.

During that car ride to Stockton the Moral Man and I got our first ever chance to spend some real 'quality time' together. I'd known of his existence of course but I was always so deep in the habits and behaviors of my addiction and trying to hide from all that internal pain that we never really connected. He was always something of a tag-along, fruitlessly attempting to lend guidance and offer less destructive options to me during the years where I ran amok.

The moment of clarity that came from how I reacted to the proposed 'Ray Ray solution' made him more powerful. Moral Man suddenly commanded more presence – more authority. I was totally and completely ready to give him a seat at the table. In fact, I was utterly depending on him to save me. Together on that car ride, we went back to the very beginning in an attempt to understand how we came to this crystalline moment. We flipped through the mental files together, back through the years and experiences, the near-death encounters, the drug-addled wasted days, the women, the friends, the violence and the rebellion, until we stopped at the start – the end of the 'Summer of Love' in a house at 60 Webster St. in San Francisco. The place of my birth.

CHAPTER 3

THE SUM OF MY PARTS

I

To make sense of why I, in spite of all the gifts I'd been given, could not go out into the world, provide for myself nor experience any success or fulfillment, you must understand the context of my upbringing. Bizarre values and crazy ways of thinking were imposed upon me, both within my family and in the larger social environment of my youth. These wacky values were useless in the world I would be thrust into as a teenager and a man. I was taught to be an outcast, addict, rebel and a criminal from birth.

I was the first child born into a new age cult known as the 'One World Family Commune.' It was a founded by a man named Stephan. He was known as the 'Messiah' by the cult members. We followed him without question. Every far-reaching corner of his doctrine was obediently obliged by our members, from group sex, to the absolute belief in UFOs, to rampant drug use, to our desire to overthrow the entire capitalist system due to our view of money as the chief tool of Satan in his war to destroy the world.

Group members got high, had indiscriminate sex, made staggeringly bad choices in the raising of children, dropped out of society and even tried to spark a revolution. I was expected to embody the spirit of this doctrine and was strongly encouraged to behave accordingly. The members of the commune, mom included, downloaded all the ideology and beliefs the cult stood for into the virginal little hard drive of my psyche from birth.

Here's an example of some of the things that were considered 'normal' for me as a child.

We had something called 'Natural Selection' every Tuesday night and some Sundays. This was when all the adults had group sex, leaving the children to look after each other elsewhere in the house whilst they were 'selecting.' They were assigned a partner and told to 'get it on.' Everyone had multiple partners within a given night and, of course, there was plenty of pot smoking and wine.

Life in the commune

There was almost no effort made to keep their sex lives from us kids. Some of them would take photos during 'Natural Selection' night that would mistakenly find their way into the family slide shows we would have from time to time. The collective attitude about the 'Natural Selection' nights was so cavalier and out-in-the-open, it was easy for the kids to spy on those meetings – which we often did. To the best of my knowledge, every kid in the commune watched their parents take part at some point.

Another everyday occurrence was the obsession with UFOs. You could always find people talking about them. 'Who has seen them recently?' (Everyone had seen one recently.) 'Who had been contacted by one?' (Many of them boasted this prestigious honor.) 'Who had actually seen the inside of one?' (Yes, you guessed it, many made this incredible claim too.)

On the walls of our houses, images of flying saucers were everywhere. We painted huge canvasses with them, made woodcarvings of them, airbrushed them onto our clothing, even the occasional tattoo surfaced.

(...on a side note, I'm not here to say that UFOs do or don't exist. In fact, by sheer probability, I'd guess they do. But the likelihood of an entire group of people having not only seen them but most having been beamed aboard them making contact with aliens, just seems, well... a bit far-fetched...)

Another of my favorites were the large, slogan-covered campers and school buses. There were messages such as 'WE CAN ALL SHARE THE WORLD', 'GET RID OF MONEY' and 'UFO-ETI' (which stood for Extra-Terrestrial Intelligence) and 'GALACTIC COMMAND.' Each vehicle was done up in ten-inch tall, full-color circus sideshow letters across the sides and hoods and colorfully announced our arrival (and beliefs) everywhere we went.

Other common features of my childhood were our 'Family Sunday Meetings.' They were pitched as an opportunity to air our grievances with each other in the commune. It was also where we would gather, drink wine and smoke massive amounts of pot. The children were welcome to participate in this part if they wished. The messiah, Stephan would make public rulings then, wait for it, smoke a lot more pot and sing songs as a group. These meetings would often take the entire afternoon. Looking back on the levels of excess, it's a wonder my brain can still manage to complete sentences.

Since we were against money but obviously needed some money for our day-to-day lives, we were given a 'personal needs allowance.' This was a very small stipend doled out once a week to individuals and blood families within the commune. It amounted to about five dollars a week per person. If you needed more than that, you really needed a good reason. You had to plead your case with a line of other people behind you waiting for their money too. The money for this flowed from one of the requirements for entry into the commune, namely that new members had to surrender all of their money to the commune and get themselves onto some form of government assistance – welfare and supplemental security income (S.S.I.) being the big two.

Everyone contributed in this way. We romanticized this action by telling each other tales of how the entire government would come crashing down if only the rest of America would follow our lead. The theory was that if everyone in society would follow us, the entire government would run out of money and be forced to grind to a halt. We were nothing if not grandiose.

II

Children don't have filters in place when it comes to those they consider caregivers. From a child's perspective, it is a matter of life and death to be able to relate to and connect with those you perceive to be your caregivers. This is a biological imperative. It is literally a cornerstone in human survival strategy. It is how we survive such long adolescences. Only when we are older and learn to take care of ourselves do we begin to question the ideas we were raised with and sometimes not even then. So, it doesn't really matter to a very young child what kind of environment they are raised in. They will try to make it work. They will employ strategy upon strategy in an effort to connect and normalize. Sometimes, however, it can be too overwhelming.

From my youngest memories, I can recall undercurrents within my expanded family of suppressed hostility, duplicity, hypocrisy and a deep, deep incongruence between the ways we were required to behave and what was felt appropriate by many of the adults of the commune. There was subtext everywhere. One of the things my early years Moral Man always sensed was how it seemed as though so many members of the commune were hanging on by a thread, struggling to fit in, to walk the walk.

Witnessing this sort of disconnect between the words being spoken, and the much more real and easily understood emotional dialogue being expressed by peoples' body language, vocal tonality and other 'tells', on the scale I witnessed it on, enabled me to read people and situations with ease. It trained me to become an extremely accurate bullshit meter.

On any given day, there were about fifty of us, all under the same roof. As a child, I could sense there was something wrong – very wrong – all the time. I could actually see it in the faces of the members and hear it, barely restrained by the speech. It was palpable to me, even as a boy. It was as if we were living with a beast in our midst and the only way to keep it at bay was to keep the facade going. Keep smiling and make it believable. If the beast smelled your fear, it would rip you apart. 'Tune in. Turn on. Drop out. Everything is groovy so keep on trucking.'

Sometimes, when I hear people talk about the way the currents of dysfunction and co-dependence ripple within normal-sized families and the damage it does, I feel a perverse sense of 'survivor's pride,' like a man who has been on the front lines of life and death combat listening to children talking in earnest about a school yard fight.

That was life inside the commune. Outside those confines, the rest of the sixties and seventies raged out of control. Chaos creating order creating chaos, folding in on itself then subdividing and surging outward again and again, in patterns too complex to know. Living, as we did, in San Francisco we were in the West Coast epicenter of the drug-fueled, music revolution known as the 'hippie movement'. It was a full-tilt, swirling, paisley-drenched, tie-dyed torrent of experimental ideas, rebelling against (to paraphrase Marlon Brando) 'whatever you've got.' We really were all trying to change the world. How we would achieve that was another matter. We utterly lacked any focus, any kind of specific ambition, worthy leadership, goals or any of the other prerequisites (with the exception of sheer numbers) to make it happen.

That time and place in history was like a field of pure potentiality. The living, breathing combination of drugs, masses pushed to the point of action, the raw creativity of hundreds of thousands of people all wanting something, anything different than what came before, creating a type of critical mass. Generating outcome after outcome with no regard to viability, it's easy to see how a group like the One World Family Commune could come forth from so fertile an environment of anarchy and rebellion. And it's equally easy, for me, to see how I could be spawned from a group like that. Just as they were a microcosm of the larger social unrest and upheaval, so was I a microcosm of the commune's unique mixture of dysfunction, idealism, drug use and co-dependence – a tempest in a tea pot as it were.

But funny things can sometimes happen when you play with scale like that. It's as though that time was too big for any one man to embody. Things that started as irreducible at the greater scale of the commune or the Bay Area hippie movement, didn't play out so well when they were crammed into the size of a single human body. Rebellion, for instance, looks very different when tens of thousands of people are doing it. It's very easy to romanticize something when it's at that scale than when one anachronistic young man is doing it, trying to justify his behaviors through the lens of an entire movement.

Another place where scale really lends credence is with sexual partners. It's one thing for fifty or so (or fifty thousand for that matter) people, under the sway of a charismatic leader to have open sexual relationships and multiple partners. It looks very different and not so charming when it's one skinny, emotionally retarded teen discovering early on that the opposite sex finds him irresistible and recklessly sleeping with any woman that throws herself at him – regardless of which best friend or even enemy she might also be seeing at the time.

The utter lack of conventional social boundaries that the commune was striving for might have made me into some kind of rockstar if the hippies had won, if we all really did live in a 'Yellow Submarine' with 'Lucy in the Sky with Diamonds.' I might have been perfectly well adjusted in that hypothetical outcome but as we know from my earlier courtroom story, it did not turn out like that. As a result, like an entire generation, the influences I was exposed to early on in my life in that environment would wreak havoc on me (and others) later instead.

I didn't realize it until many years afterwards but there was another way I was being influenced during my childhood. In addition to the cripplingly counter-cultural ethos being instilled, there was another set of messages being piggybacked into my subconscious. These messages came from Moral Man who introduced me to the ideas of many of the great thinkers, Aristotle, Jesus, Buddha, Lao Tzu, Plato, and Kant along with Kafka, Proust, Dante, Kierkegaard and more.

In the way a child whose father is a carpenter might grow up knowing about the properties of wood and woodworking tools, so I grew up knowing about religion, philosophy, spirituality and self-improvement. All of the great thinkers and teachers of history were bandied about liberally in the place I called home. Granted, they were most often quoted in the service of one of us sanctimoniously 'besting' another in some insipid, passive-aggressive debate but at least within me, these great thinkers and their teachings stuck and took root. I guess that sometimes, one generations lip service and platitudes can become the next generation's 'true north.'

Fake it until you make it.

Additionally, I was exposed to many other ideas society would not catch on to until many years later. Ideas such as eating a healthy, life-sustaining vegetarian diet, practicing peace and compassion, the health benefits of yoga and meditation, to the openness towards different healing modalities, to name a few. These were all commonplace concept in the commune. When I was going to grade school, I had to fight often, because I was a vegetarian and the other kids would ridicule me for it. Now, it's not unheard of for a kid to be singled out for eating meat.

These wild and varied influences from the commune were stuffed into me from the moment I opened my eyes and they would create the lenses through which I'd interpret the world for many years to come.

Now, let me tell you a little bit about some of the potential developmental effects of being raised in a cult environment. One of the most common, and devastating emotional traps created in those circumstances, is called the 'double bind.'

III

A double bind happens when a child is forced to choose between the secure connection to their parent or caregiver and the normally occurring process of emotional development and differentiation from the parent. The rub is that as long as the adult caregiver is under the influence of the cult leader, they can't provide a secure attachment for the child because they themselves are in a semi-regressed emotional state. This happens because, in order for the leader's influence to be effective, the adult is required to engage in a parent-child dynamic with the cult leader and therefore can't function in an adult capacity in any other areas of their lives.

There is an abdication of maturity on the part of the compliant member. Emotionally, they regress and become stuck somewhere in their teens, even if they joined the cult in their twenties or thirties or beyond. In effect, this dynamic makes the adults and their children dependent on the leader figure. Faced with this type of behavior from their parents, children automatically begin to assume grown up responsibilities out of an instinctual need to protect their parents. In a very real way, 'someone' has to be driving the bus.

So, if there is a significant blank spot in the role the parent is naturally supposed to step into, the child will do it instead. You get children parenting their parents. A kid, quite literally can't be a kid while they are busy being a grown up. In other words, the child who has a double bind situation is being forced to choose, day-by-day, hour-by-hour between the natural emotional imperative of developing their own identity and trying to develop the secure attachment to the parent every child needs for emotional wellbeing. This means it's an attachment that isn't possible to attain in that situation in the first place.

This creates a 'damned-if-you-do, damned-if-you-don't' scenario that is crippling to normal emotional development and left unresolved will play out over and over in every adult relationship the child goes on to have. Long before the child can articulate or understand what is happening, they experience a conflict between two things that have survival level importance to them. They live their lives stuck between a rock and a hard place, unable to pursue either imperative for the damage it will do to the other.

I have uncovered and identified no less than three individual double binds within myself (with the help of an amazing therapist.) One caused me to feel like I had to choose between the love and acceptance of mom or living a life outside of the narrow, restrictive limitations of the way I was raised. Another bind caused me to be utterly self-destructive with my behavior around money, which kept me from becoming financially successful for years, in spite of knowing how to earn a good income. The third bind has led me to the same empty, unfulfilling relationships with women, over and over, as an adult.

Even one sufficiently deep double bind can totally dictate the course of a person's life. Psychiatrists can predict with shocking accuracy how a person's relationships will play out, what some of their behavioral quirks will be and, in general, how their lives will be adversely affected by the trap they are in. A single double bind is no laughing matter – and I had three of them!

With the proverbial deck stacked like that, it's hard to say exactly why I refused to just lay down and die during the most difficult periods of my life. There were so many times when I just wanted to give up, to throw in the towel.

Why keep fighting? Why keep pushing?

I can't really say, but I did keep pushing. I refused to roll over.

Mom has speculated on occasion perhaps I inherited this tenacity from my dad. He was descended from a long line of extraordinarily tough sons-of-bitches. He himself was a pacifist and a hippie. That said, it's known within dad's side of the family that both my grandfather and my great-grandfather had allegedly killed men with their bare hands.

I certainly didn't learn this kind of perseverance from mom or any of my so-called role models within the commune. It was never modeled to me there but it was in me. There is a fighter inside me, a warrior who didn't make many appearances while I lived in the Bay Area but if you knew what to look for, you could tell he was there.

It was little things mostly, like getting in a fight at school and kicking another boy in the chin so hard that his two front teeth flew out. Or even earlier on, having another kid in the commune take a toy from me and throwing myself on him, teeth first, and shaking him until I ripped flesh. These events were not commonplace but there was a theme of me over-responding to aggressive behavior, real or imagined, from others.

IV

When I was nine, the entire commune, for reasons I've never had sufficiently explained to me, up and moved to Stockton. For those that don't know, Stockton has been on the top ten list of most violent cities in America for over forty years. While South Central and Compton, Watts and Crenshaw got all the glory, Stockton has been holding steady – quietly defending its crown. We moved not just to Stockton but literally, into the center of the worst neighborhood it had to offer. This skinny little hippie kid found himself living on the corner of Clay Street and Charter Way, in the middle of the 'Mexican ghetto.' This was when the fighter in me came out.

This move was more than just culture shock, living on the south side of Stockton would hone my senses and shape the way I saw the world for the rest of my life. I don't remember packing to move, or even discussing it. I don't remember the drive there, or saying goodbye to San Francisco and Berkeley. There is a blank spot where all of those memories should be. I do remember pulling up to our new house, a caravan of hippies in our slogan emblazoned buses and camper vans, driving naively straight into the mouth of what would prove to be 'hell.'

As we rounded the corner to our new home, I was looking out of the window of the camper I was riding in, a Chevy Chinook with 'WE CAN ALL SHARE THE WORLD' painted across one side and 'GET RID OF MONEY' across the other. From my vantage point, I could see the natives watching us, circling in behind as we drove by. They looked restless.

I remember the dirty looks as we drove deeper into the neighborhood, young men 'flipping us the bird' sign and standing up on their dilapidated front steps to get a better look at the 'freaks' who were moving in across the street. The neighborhood we had so recently left was also full of freaks. But they were the kind of freaks I was used to, hippies, hopers, street-corner prophets. The houses were all Technicolor and the streets were lined with little tables and booths where long hairs would sell their wares. There was dancing and singing. Everyone was high and happy and it felt safe and familiar.

By contrast, the neighborhood we were moving into was run down beyond belief. Instead of paisley and tie-dye, it was pinstripes and candy apple. Chevys and Chryslers were parked on front lawns with huge dogs standing next to them. Everywhere were brown and bronze men with slick, oily hair and dangerous eyes. Instead of the Technicolor I'd just left, everything was faded and peeling. The sound of music with a thumping heavy bass line was always present, and as it turned out, so was the sound of gunshots.

Somehow, when someone decided we should move here, it escaped their attention our neighborhood, our street, our house, was located in the heart of gangland territory. Everywhere I looked, the young men and even the women wore bandanas of the same color, flannel shirts unbuttoned except for the top button. Jet-black sunglasses hid their eyes and matched their dark hair. Often times, they made no effort whatsoever to conceal the gun handles that stuck out of their belts. They would stand as I passed, lifting their arms up high so that their shirts would rise and reveal their weapons.

"What the fuck you looking at 'homeboy'? You want my little brother to fuck you up, homie?"

And, as if we didn't stand out enough already, we somehow found a three story, Victorian-era brothel, right smack in the middle of that ghetto. That's where we all lived – and you can't make this shit up – it was bright yellow. So, in a way, the hippies really did live in all together in a kind of 'Yellow Submarine.'

I can't imagine what we could have done to draw more attention to ourselves if we had wanted to.

From day one, we had to fight. We fought hard and often. These were no lightweight schoolyard scuffles – these were fierce encounters with other kids who truly despised us. Most of the time there were more of them than there were of us and usually they were bigger and older too.

In the beginning, most of the time we lost those fights.

V

But something began to happen as I adjusted to the stark realities of my new life. Something inside me began to come to the surface. The way I fought became more and more savage and, ultimately, I discovered I could surrender to the combination of fear, rage and a primal need to inflict pain on those who threatened my safety and wellbeing. I could just step into that 'zone' and let it take the reins.

Earlier, I referred to this as the 'fighter' in me. I'm not sure that's exactly accurate. It was more like the 'berserker' in me. A fighter becomes more polished and smarter the more they fight. I was not like that. For me, it was more Jekyll and Hyde – more blindly violent. The adrenaline rush building up pressure inside me during those conflict moments gave me only two choices. One, give in and let it take over or two, freeze up. I began letting myself give in to it, stepping through the outer wall of terror and into the middle of that rage where it was out of my hands. I'd see everything in shades of red with a white outline around whoever I needed to hurt. All I cared about was causing pain to that white outline.

It was no easy task to learn how to surrender to the berserker inside of me, the savage protector, dark and vicious. Like trusting a snarling beast who is staring at you and salivating while backing you towards a cliff edge, I could always sense the deep well of rage there inside me but I'd always been more afraid of it than of my attackers. As the fights continued, I'd come closer and closer to it, scared of letting myself reach out for it. Ultimately, it would prove too much for me in my waking state, so, prompted by my subconscious, it happened one night in a dream.

In most cultures throughout the world, there exist rituals for just this purpose. These rituals put men in touch with the primal side of themselves. Hunter-gatherer and warrior cultures from the Spartans to the Samurai to the Native Americans use this technique. Each culture had developed methods to help connect the man with this power source. For me, it happened in that dream.

Me aged 15

When I moved to Stockton and the fights started, I was haunted by recurring nightmares where those I loved were being threatened by overwhelming attackers. Full-grown adults would corner my family and me, sometimes carrying off mom and my sister, other times beating us with sticks.

Always I'd try to fight back, to defend my family and I was useless against them. I'd throw punches as if I was under water, slowly and with terrible aim – utterly ineffectual. These dreams continued for months. I'd wake up rattled and weak, as if my soul was somehow diminished.

One night, the pattern of the dream changed. Something amazing happened. I was on the street corner out in front of my house surrounded by my attackers as usual. This dream was different. For one thing, I could tell I was going to die. I just knew it. Right in the middle of it, I thought to myself 'I wonder what happens if you die in a dream? Do you die in your waking life too?' I'd never before been able to 'understand' whilst dreaming that I was actually dreaming. At that moment, something sort of clicked.

I now know this phenomenon is 'lucid dreaming' but at the time I only knew something changed. I felt able to connect myself to that primal rage. I stepped in to it and I was strong. I was still surrounded by all of my dream attackers but now when I threw punches, they connected! Suddenly I was faster, stronger and smarter than the phantoms that circled me.

I began to cut through them like butter. There were more of them than I originally realized and I mowed them down one after another. They began folding over when I'd hit them. I was moving faster and faster around them, ripping them in two and tossing them aside.

Then something incredible happened. The entire dreamscape transformed into a white soundstage and all my attackers turned into cardboard cut-outs. I began to fly! All the while, I was aware of what was happening from a conscious perspective. I laughed out loud and flew off over the rooftops of my city. I felt fearless and supremely powerful.

The very next day I found myself cornered at school, alone with four Mexican boys who were all older and bigger than me. They were rapidly closing in. They were throwing small rocks at me and calling me names while my back was up against a wall.

It was right out in the open and no one was doing anything about it. I could actually see adults from where I was standing. In the past, I'd have cried out for help or tried to talk my way out of the situation, babbling and making excuses and apologies. But thanks to last night's dream, something changed inside of me. I was still scared but I was not backing down. They were still taunting me, laughing and acting sure of themselves. But, inside me I could feel the anger rising.

I kept quiet and let them continue, all the while, feeling the building pressure inside. Then it happened, just like in the dream, I stepped inside of the rage. Time slowed down. I felt as if I was in the eye of a hurricane, calm and placid, whilst chaos whirled around me.

I could see the outlines of the four boys in front of me. I picked up a rock that was bigger than my fist and marched forward with slow purpose, grabbing the boy directly in front of me by his oily hair. I slammed the rock into the side of his head. I felt his knees buckle as the rock made impact.

I smiled.

I wouldn't know what else happened until someone pulled me off him. Apparently, I hit him several times as he was collapsing, never letting go of his hair. I didn't speak while this was happening. He and I communicated nonetheless, my snarling and screaming was clearer than words could ever have been. I made him and all the onlookers understand I was no longer willing to be a 'whipping boy.' I thought, 'if you want to come at me, you had better think twice and be sure motherfucker because I'll split your fucking head open!'

I think I was ten.

Every time I was forced to access the rage inside me, it became easier and easier. I began to get a reputation. I'd like to say after a few times where I publicly went berserk, people started to leave me alone, to think twice about messing with the kid who would lose his mind and try to rip your head off your body if you messed with him.

But that's not how it went.

I did get a reputation for being crazy but it made everyone want to try all the more to get a piece of me. I hurt a lot of people and got hurt a lot too during those days. My strategy was always the same. I'd simply let whoever it was wanting to fight antagonize me until the red rage boiled over, then I'd focus on causing as much pain as I could to the white outline in my field of vision.

When the sensation passed, it was like coming back to consciousness from a drug trip. I'd suddenly 'wake up' and be aware of my true surroundings. More than once, I snapped out of it while still fighting. When this happened, I'd find myself in the strangest situations.

One day, a boy from my school, Dennis, decided that he was going to kick my ass in front of all the other kids during recess. He cornered me and began taunting and pushing me, saying things about mom and her sexual preferences. I sat there taking it, knowing it was only a matter of time before the anger would rise to a sufficient level and then, 'surprise!'

I don't remember getting mad enough to engage him. I only remember coming to from the rage. When I did, I was holding Dennis upside down, fully off of the ground and pile driving his head into the concrete. I have no idea to this day how we got into that position. His forehead was cut open and bleeding and his bravado had left him. He was whimpering for mercy.

VI

As this new – or ancient and primal – side of me was brought to the surface, the already tenuous and disengaged relationship I had with mom became more strained.

When I fought at school, it would invariably be because I was antagonized by other kids cornering me and shouting lurid, graphic insults about her. I could never put up with this for long and sooner or later, I'd fight back. Afterwards, I'd go to the principal's office, whereupon he would send me home. I'd come home and have to explain to mom why I was fighting and when I did, all she would say was stuff like 'Why can't you just turn the other cheek?' or 'I don't want you to fight just because other kids say mean things about me.' The rage and anguish caused by these bullies using her to get at me brought forth from her no compassion. It would have been so nice, if just once she said, 'I really don't want you to be fighting but I totally understand why you felt like you had to defend my honor, thank you.'

It was as though she was so completely unaware of the realities of my day-to-day life she didn't even comprehend the surface layer of my experience –

much less any of the depth or complexity of the waters beneath. I was, for all intents and purposes, a child completely alone in hostile territory.

It was not just mom either. Everyone in the commune was so caught up in the platitudes and the veneer of being 'peace-loving hippies,' desperately trying to live that warped, pseudo-utopian dream, that all of the children were emotionally abandoned in a fundamental way.

Our parents, our caregivers, our protectors were there but not there – asleep at their posts – while we were left to fend for ourselves, flanked on all sides by the enemy. The jungle drums were swelling around us and our torches were guttering.

I remember sitting in class one day with two boys, one behind me, one in front. They began whispering messages to each other deliberately in my earshot, making plans to jump me.

"Hey Ricky! Let's find Manny after school and kick his ass."

"Hell yeah! I hate that fucking freak."

"Me too. I can't wait to get my hands on him, fucking weirdo."

"Did you ever see the car he gets dropped off to school in? It's got weird shit painted all over it, like flying saucers and shit. What a goddamn freak!"

"I know... and what about those clothes he wears? It's like his mom doesn't even know how to dress him."

"I heard that his mom is a whore anyway. Everyone who lives in his house is a fucking weirdo."

"When we get him after school, you hold him – I'm going to punch his face in."

I sat there in silence, feeling the red rage starting to boil up. I gripped the edge of the desk, tensing up.

"As long as I get a turn, just like everyone does with his mom."

"Hahahaa! I heard she stands around on the corner and waits for bums to walk by so she can suck them off."

Well that was it. I got up in the middle of class and walked over to the boy behind me. The teacher asked

"Manny, what are you doing? Get back into your seat!"

Ignoring her, I looked this little fucker in the eye and growled

"You want a piece of me? Say that shit again! I dare you! Say it again! Why wait until after school?"

He began to speak

"Shut up, freak, we're going to kick your aaahhh..."

Before he could finish his thought, I grabbed his hair with one hand and the edge of his desk with the other and slammed his head down as hard as I could. I was seeing red now. I could hear the gasps from the other children watching but all I could see was the white outline of what I needed to hurt. I kept slamming him into the desk until the teacher pulled me away.

I spun around and bit her in the arm, snarling as I did so. The other kid was laying back in his chair, bleeding and confused, crying in pain. There was blood all over his desk and his hands. The teacher dropped me when I bit her and shouted

"Get to the principal's office, NOW!!"

I suddenly regained consciousness, quicker than a soapy bubble bursts and made my way to the principal's office.

As I was waiting in the lobby for my turn to talk to the principal, my teacher came storming by, holding her arm where I'd bitten it. She swept past me giving me the best death stare she could muster and disappeared through the principal's door.

If looks could kill!

A few minutes later, I was called in and told to sit down quietly. The principal, my teacher and a couple other people were in there, all talking about me as if I was not there. The discussion was about what had just happened.

"I've never seen anything like that..."

"He just went crazy. The other boy is going to the hospital..."

"It was like he just went berserk or something..."

"Did you call his mother?"

I just sat there, listening, somewhat dazed, thinking 'I was in a lot of trouble,' wondering what was going to happen. The discussion went on for several more minutes. I was asked the kind of questions adults ask children when they can't fathom the events they are being required to deal with...

"Do you have any idea what you've done?"

(...yes, with any luck I broke his fucking nose... I don't see how the teacher didn't hear him as he was threatening me and saying incredibly offensive things about mom...)

"What kind of kid does something like that to another kid?"

(...the kind of kid who believes in every fiber of his being no one will ever protect him...who knows all adults in his life are barely on this planet, much less paying any attention what-so-fucking-ever to what is going on in his life... or in the hostile environment they put him in against his will... who never check in with him... any other questions...)

"Why didn't you talk to the teacher if other boys were bothering you?"

(...because it's fucking life or death out there you stupid son-of-a-bitch... do you realize I am forced to fight every fucking day at your fucking school... what the hell kind of operation are you running here, anyway... the inmates are running the asylum out there... I get cornered in the hallways or on the playground all the fucking time and I'm not the only one... evil is on the rampage and you're doing shit about it... so yeah, if I feel like my life is in danger, I'm gonna act... go fuck yourself...)

Of course, I was silent during this questioning. Then, somehow, inexplicably, against all common sense and good judgement, I was simply sent home.

The 'plan' was this. I was told to 'walk home and tell mom what had happened.' I swear to you that this is true. There was no note, no phone call home, no help, no nothing. They just dumped me out the front gate to fend for myself. I had to walk home through the same ghetto that wanted me dead because they hated me for being 'different' and tell mom 'what I did at school today.' Great!

If any of this were to happen in a public school today there would be psychiatric evaluations, investigations and possible criminal charges brought up against mom, the school and me. It was unbelievable that everything unfolded the way it did. Yet, there I was, again, walking through the streets of Stockton's most notorious ghetto alone during school hours.

When I got home, I opened the enormous double-front doors to our house. It was dark in the entryway due to the way the building was designed. It took a few seconds for your eyes to adjust to your surroundings but I knew where the stairs were by memory. I headed straight up to mom's room to see if she was there. I knocked quietly, hoping she wouldn't hear me but she did.

"Come in."

"Hi mom... I got sent home from school today."

"I can see that, what happened?"

"I got into a fight."

"Why were you fighting?"

My shoulders were slumped forward and my head was hung low.

"Because these boys were talking about jumping me after school and I just got really mad. Then they started saying stuff about you."

"How many times have I told you that I don't want you to fight?"

"I know..."

"Why do you let other kids get the better of you like that? Why can't you just turn the other cheek?"

(...because I fucking can't... I just fucking can't... I can't just sit there and let people say those things about you or me...)

"I don't know..."

"Well, I don't want you to fight anymore"

(...why don't you try going to school in my place for just one goddamn day, mom... then you could see what it's like... they hate me there... no one ever leaves me alone... if I don't fight, I'll just get beat up all the time anyways... besides, it turns out that I've got a fucking primeval monster living inside me and he's the only one who will protect me since you obviously won't...)

"I know. I'll try not to"

"O.K. Well you're grounded for the rest of the day. Stay in your room."

(...like I want to go outside anyway... I'll just wind up fighting again if I do...)

"O.K."

I walked to my room. I couldn't believe the punishment for grabbing a boy by the hair and smashing his face into the desk until he needed to go to the hospital from the injuries and then biting a teacher on the arm, was a trip to the principal's office to listen as other people talked about me. Afterwards, there was the 'joy' of being sent home, unchaperoned, in the middle of the day through a thoroughly unsafe neighborhood, only to be gently reprimanded by mom when I got in. No wonder 'Lady Justice' wears a blindfold.

CHAPTER 4

INCANTATUM

I

'Honor the primal, seek the divine,' is my family motto. These are the words I posthumously bequeath to my dad, the broken genius whose own father's abuse, both emotional and physical would set the course of his entire life and ultimately destroy him. I send these words back in time to all the Wolfe men who came before me. Settlers, hustlers, workers, killers in some cases, bastards. My kin.

I send them these words in the hope they provide some kind of context to our existence. Some sort of nobility. Mostly I send them to a younger me, to the innocent little nine-year-old boy walking down the stairs, watching the dust in the air twirl and caper in the afternoon sunlight streaming through the window. The little boy wearing a three-piece polyester leisure suit to Sunday breakfast, not because he was made to, but because, goddamn it, it looked good. The little boy who was larger-than-life and misunderstood even then. The little boy with the beast inside of him who shared the space with the philosopher, the artist, the addict and all the others. The little boy who would not be broken by the situation he found himself in that others had chosen for him. He who couldn't help but strive for something bigger, even when his mom no longer understood him, even when the very same traits used to garner him love and approval from his mom turned inside out and began to drive a wedge between them. He couldn't help but live big and loud.

For him, I crafted those words, 'honorem primum, quaritae divinea' – 'honor the primal, seek the divine.' Though you may be unseen, misunderstood by those closest to you, be true to yourself. You really have no choice. You see once you stop, once you begin to trade your authenticity for others' acceptance, a poison begins to accumulate inside you. It creeps in one justification at a time until you're paralyzed by it.

When you begin modifying (by which I mean minimizing) your natural sense of vision, of scope, of sheer, reckless imagination in the hopes of hitting some sporadic moving target of familial approval, chasing a phantom, a 'Will O' The Wisp,' living in the shadow cast by the judgement of those not fit to judge you but who's approval is like manna from heaven none the less.

Then the little boy starts to lose his innocence, begins to conform under the pressure of emotional extortion. To shrink to the dimensions of their narrow expectations. To die.

If I could whisper into the hearts of all children or shout from a mountaintop so the entire world could hear, I'd do it. I'd gladly suffer the 'slings and arrows of not outrageous but infamous fortune' if I could spread this one message, 'honor the primal, seek the divine.' Boldly follow the unfolding truth of who you are. Be grateful for every misstep, every wrong turn in the pursuit of your authenticity. Never, ever pay with your dreams for the right to a seat at the table of the bland masses, the grey, muted horde who would stone you for your uniqueness. You are creativity made manifest – stardust experiencing itself subjectively. You have a duty to all mankind to become the fullest manifestation of yourself you possibly can. Go now and be fearless in pursuit of your truth.

You see the truth about pursuing your truth matters. Any time one of us has the courage, the audacity, the sheer balls, swinging low and mighty to quest after our own authenticity, to fly boldly in the face of social convention, it makes the path just a little wider for the next person. It wears the crags and potholes a little smoother and casts a bit more light on the path.

When you do this, you help to blaze a trail. A trail I can then follow and others after me. And the more of us there are seeking to uncover, to reveal our real, authentic selves and live lives in accordance with what we find, the more momentum is created towards a 'leveling up' of our collective consciousness. And continuing to level up our collective consciousness is our only chance for survival as a species.

It is the very essence of why we are here.

II

What you've just read above is at the very core of my power. It contains many of my most closely held convictions and beliefs, beliefs that have given me the strength to rise above. Beliefs I have carved out and developed on my own, without help from – even in spite of – parents or family. Because I am more than my upbringing. Because somewhere along the way I discovered I have the power to choose my life – my destiny.

It would be many years before I put this all together but it all started with the dream I'd had where I was able to step into the heart of my power and learn to defend myself. I believe this dream was a sort of divine spark. A push from God or the universe or whatever you want to call it. It was the starting point from which I'd slowly build the self-esteem I could not otherwise have ever hoped to develop. The self-esteem that is my birthright as it is all of our birthrights but that circumstances seemed determined to keep from me.

When I was twelve, the plight of the children in the commune became too serious to ignore. The adults who were supposed to be watching over us finally began to pay attention to what we were going through. Between my fights and those of the other children, the constant and escalating harassment from the people in our neighborhood, they finally took notice. This is when my blood family was granted permission to move into a smaller, single family home on the west side of town.

We were moved to the Victory Park area of Stockton, not nice, but not nearly as bad as the South Side area we had just left. This area would prove to be the fertile soil where all of the toxic seeds of my life so far would begin to break the surface and sprout. It was at this house I hit puberty and with it came sex, drugs, rebellion and law breaking.

Once I was in an area with a little bit more cultural diversity, I began to make friends. This was something I'd not done before in my life. While I lived in San Francisco and Berkeley, I was too young to really have friends. I just played with whoever was handy. When we moved to Stockton, everyone hated me simply for the color of my skin and the length of my hair.

Me aged 11 in the local park

Making friends wasn't even an option outside of the commune walls and within our walls, I was a loner anyway – too young to play with groups of kids who were older and too old to play with the younger ones.

That all changed when we got to the new neighborhood. There were lots of kids who would play with me right outside my front door. We would play street hockey and ride our BMX bikes over the huge jutting cracks in the sidewalk caused by the gnarly old cypress trees whose roots had broken through the asphalt. We made forts and played in each other's back yards.

Slowly my comfort zone began to expand, block by block until I knew the whole neighborhood. These kids were all discovering girls and smoking pot – which I was already experienced with – and I fell right in line with them.

We all spent our days riding around the neighborhood, practicing our cussing and trash talking, fantasizing about which girls we liked and what we would do with them – if only they'd let us. In those days, we actually did stay out until the streetlights came on and our moms would call us in for dinner. There is something so precious, so utterly fleeting about the period in a child's life when they are on the threshold of puberty.

All of the naiveté of childhood balancing impossibly against the oncoming surge of 'teen-ism.' It is a time when we can reconcile two utterly disparate worlds with ease. In my room at that time, I had posters of the actress Farah Fawcett posed suggestively, in her tiny bikini, her finger wrapped playfully around one side promising to pull it off entirely. Next to her was to a close-up of the singer, Linda Ronstadt, her mouth glistening impossibly, gently opened to show just a hint of perfectly white teeth and the promise of her tongue behind them. Below the posters was my collection of stuffed animals that populated my bed. It was the closest thing to a truly innocent time that I'd ever have in my life.

This age of innocence would prove to be short lived. Though I was away from the violent unpredictability of Stockton's South Side and had some distance from the direct influence of the commune and its freewheeling doctrine of blind faith, the fox had already gotten into the proverbial hen house. I was primed and ready to go, my upbringing behind the communal walls, with the sex, drugs, and the rest of it, mixed with the intense violence and utter terror of the South Side had seen to that.

Fighting for my life all the time while my parents went about their own lives oblivious, seemingly unconcerned about my problems had a 'Jack-in-the-Box' effect on me. I was wound so tightly without even knowing it, by the time I reached the West Side and puberty, it was like the lid just sprang open and out I popped, grinning like a maniac, complete with a hard cock and a wild manifesto.

In no time at all, I managed to locate the other damaged children in my neighborhood – my people – and together we formed a little tribe. You needed to have a 'tribe' in those days, others who had your back, because even though it was nothing like the South Side, all of Stockton was a war zone. You couldn't raise hell without raising the ire of others who lived nearby. All of the places where the lost children would congregate – behind the schools, in the tucked away corners of parks, behind liquor stores, at dead ends on levees – these places were volatile and you needed someone watching your back.

The other 'lost boys' with whom I found common fraternity were Eddie, Chris, Rob, and Charlie. Only in bittersweet hindsight would I realize what they truly meant to me. They were my surrogate family. In many ways, we closer than blood. If I'd really understood this back then, I'd have tread so much more lightly with the unspoken, but nonetheless real bond that we all shared.

But that's not the way I was raised.

CHAPTER 5

BROTHERHOOD

1

(EDDIE)

First of these friends was Eddie. He was squat, barrel-chested and devious looking. His curly auburn hair, he usually wore short. Naturally stocky and strong with a twinkle in his green eyes, he was unbelievably charismatic and relentless in pursuit of the things he wanted. He was a visionary, a true dreamer of dreams. He was also the consummate troublemaker and he did it with a flair and style that you just can't teach. He was Tom Sawyer, Huckleberry Finn, Johnny Rotten and P.T. Barnum all rolled up into one.

It was Eddie who first taught us to smoke cigarettes and other essential life skills, like cutting school, smoking pot out of a bong, hallucinating on L.S.D. and taking speed. Truthfully, with our backgrounds, these things were bound to happen to us at some point but Eddie was our liaison to that world – not to be blamed, but not entirely innocent either.

If not for Eddie, we learned the pleasure of smoking Chesterfield non-filters and quaffing a double espresso whilst sitting in front of a sidewalk café. We discovered the thrill of getting someone to buy some cheap beer, for you and your friends to drink furtively behind the school, and sitting on the levee at sunset, watching the light turn the sky into a painting.

Eddie was the one who took the time to give certain buildings and landmarks in our neighborhood code names so that if we ever needed to run from the police and regroup later we could shout things to each other like

"Meet at the 'Jones house'" or

"Cut through the 'Hall of Evasion.'"

It was nonsense to the uninitiated but perfectly clear to us. Thanks to Eddie, we had a secret map in our minds that we superimposed over the city landscape giving us escape routes and rendezvous points all throughout our neighborhood and beyond.

Also, Eddie first introduced us to 'ninjutsu' – the way of the ninja (at least Eddie's version.) He taught us how to use shadows to avoid detection, plus how to move silently and how to avoid tripping motion detectors. He shared other elements of what he called the 'shadow arts' with us. This included 'ninja practice' where we would all dress in black, armed with wooden weapons strapped to our bodies and practice cutting through people's back yards and running across rooftops at night. The goal was to see how many routes we could find through our neighborhood without using the sidewalks. With Eddie's help, we learned many secret routes between our houses and the parks in our area.

When we were about fourteen, we were all out one night doing 'ninja practice,' black outfits, wooden weapons at the ready. We were practicing 'hiding in the shadows' at the top of a freeway overpass and silently watching the homeless people and other passers-by down below on the sidewalk. Eddie came over to me and tapped me on the shoulder. I turned and he signaled me to follow him.

Silently, we crawled over to where he'd just come from. We were at the top of the embankment the freeway rested on, roughly twenty-five feet up from the sidewalk. He pointed up and under the bottom of the freeway to where, tucked away in the shadows, there was an entry point to a small catwalk that ran the length of the right-hand side of the raised freeway.

The traffic above was providing noise cover so we risked talking.

"Check this out! What do you think it is?" asked Eddie.

"Let's check it out. It looks cool."

"Should we get the other guys?"

"Yeah. I'll be right back."

I scurried back to where the other guys were hanging out and signaled them to follow me. Soon, we were all gathered at the mouth of the catwalk.

"Should we do some exploring?" asked Eddie.

The consensus was unanimous. We should definitely do some exploring. One-by-one we climbed up onto the rickety two-by-six scaffolding planks that ran the foreseeable length of the catwalk. The catwalk itself was constructed of steel 'L-shaped' hooks placed every four feet or so along the underside of the outer edge of the actual freeway, presumably left there for maintenance reasons.

The walkway itself was shrouded in inky black darkness and it took a minute or so for our eyes to adjust. Once they did, we could see twenty or so yards down the walkway but no more. Once we were up, we had to stoop over slightly to avoid hitting our heads on the bottom of the concrete slab as we shuffled along the planks. We proceeded single file along the obscured path, walking face-first into cobwebs and other debris as we travelled. After a few yards, we began to use our little cigarette lighters to help us see the way.

If anyone had bothered to look up as we passed overhead, it would've looked like a small group of confused fireflies hovering just under the edge of the freeway, blinking in and out of sight. As we continued our journey, the freeway climbed higher and higher above the city until we were forty or fifty feet above ground level.

In some places, the several planks were deteriorating and splintering. In others, there was just one crumbling plank to a section. The underside lip of the freeway was on our right. On our left was only air with an occasional stretch of chain between twelve-foot sections. We all had to travel with our right hands on the wall. We reached the point where the freeway stretched over the port and the delta.

We could see we had only water beneath us and it was probably sixty feet down before you would even reach it. That's when Rob's foot suddenly slipped on a splintered plank.

He wobbled down to one knee and tried to grab a protective section of chain only to find air. Eddie spun like a cat and grabbed him as his leg and one of his arms hung precariously over the abyss that lead to the river below.

We all felt the plank beneath our feet shift abruptly.

I reached over and helped Eddie as he pulled Rob back up to safety. All of us stopped and let our banging hearts slow down for a few minutes. The splinters and debris Rob knocked off the plank took a very long time to hit the water below. At this point, we should have turned back but there is something about the immortality of teenaged boys bolstering us to press on.

Soon after we crossed over the river and had land beneath us once more, a renewed sense of calm and self-assurance possessed us again. None of us stopped to think falling sixty feet onto land might hurt more than tumbling onto water. A few more yards and we heard the sounds of music and people with raised voices, though we couldn't make out what they were saying. We came to perch over what looked like a junkyard or industrial lot lying below us. There were perhaps thirty-five low-rider custom cars all parked around a huge bonfire. I estimated a hundred or more people there all told. They were having a good old time.

Off to one side, there were two men fighting in a circle of cheering onlookers, fists raised in the air, screaming and yelling. In another spot, we saw what appeared to be a girl on her knees, in front of a man with his pants around his ankles, his hands on her head. Even from our outlying vantage point, we could tell he was enjoying himself. Everywhere there were people with bottles in their hands and little wisps of smoke from the joints being passed around. Whoever these people were, they were doing it right!

After a few minutes of watching, Eddie said

"Does anyone have any change?"

"What for?" asked Chris.

"Do you have any or not? You'll see what for."

"Let me check, hold on."

I too checked my pockets for change, coming up with a small handful. I looked over just as Eddie tossed a coin into the crowd below.

"What the fuck are you doing, Eddie?" I demanded.

"Relax, there's no way they can see us up here, even if they thought to look up."

The coin made an audible 'Tink!' as it hit the hood of one of the low riders. A couple of guys standing near the car looked around then seemed to dismiss it. Eddie threw another coin, 'Tink!'

I heard one of the guys down below

"What the fuck, man? What was that shit?"

I launched a quarter, watched as it travelled for about a second or two, then, 'Tink!'

"Hey man, what the fuck is going on?" asked one of them.

He turned down his music and looked around some more.

"Did you throw something at my car, motherfucker?"

"Fuck you, Bro! I didn't throw shit!"

We let more pennies rain down from heaven, 'Tink! Tink! Tink! Tink!'

"Somebody is doing something. Shit keeps hitting my car, motherfucker!"

We aimed at another car, 'Tink!' Now more of them were looking around confused. From up above, we could see a general level of agitation was reaching fever pitch as we watched. People started buzzing around. Accusations began to fly. A couple people pushed each other, stereos were turned down. People were pointing and shrugging. It looked like a hornets nest coming to life as the temperature arose.

Up above, we were laughing as quietly as we could, the wind blowing full in our faces, creating a mix of cold skin and warm laughter. We threw more pennies.

Soon the entire party was disrupted. People were fighting and arguing with each other about what was happening,

"I saw you throw shit, bitch!"

"Fuck you! I didn't do shit. You wanna get your ass kicked?"

"Look at my car. Fucking paint is scratched! What the fuck?"

"Too bad for you but I didn't do that shit."

And then we watched as one of the men reached under his shirt and produced a small black rod which he held in his hand like a gun. We were transfixed. We sat perfectly still, then 'Crack!'

We heard a loud pop and the other man bent at the hip, clutching his side

"You fucking SHOT me, motherfucker!"

"You still gonna kick my ass?"

"You fuckin' shot me! What the fuck?"

Suddenly, cars started to leave. The music died, to be replaced by the sound of tires screeching. Dust rose into the air from all directions. We watched as the man who had been shot limped to his car and got inside. The other man walked calmly back to his low rider, got in and drove away.

Still high above, we watch as the injured man started his car and backed it up, accidentally hitting the base of the freeway column that stretched from the ground to just in front of where we were hiding.

Something about watching him bump into the column acted as the signal for us to go. We all moved silently as one, back the way we had come. As we made our way sirens filled the air.

That was my best friend, Eddie.

II

(ROB)

The next of my best friends was Rob. Rob was possibly the closest friend I ever had. I think this was partly because we had so much in common and were very compatible as friends. Also, I think we both just desperately needed to feel a kinship with another person. Rob's life was every bit as fucked up as mine although in a totally different way. He lived with his mom, his Philippino stepfather who couldn't speak English for more than a few words at a stretch and his three stepbrothers and stepsister, all younger, all of a different ethnicity and all out of control.

In our little band of brothers, Rob craved some sense of normalcy the most. He was desperate for it. You could see it in his eyes. In the desperation behind his gentle smile. It utterly broke my heart and it was why I loved him so much. He and I lived around the corner from each other and from the day we met, our friendship was like two atoms fusing to create a new element.

Rob's house was like a run-down home in a movie. There were literally sections of floor missing – only dirt remained. Wallpaper and paint peeled throughout. Nails had worked themselves free from doorjambs and baseboards. I lost count of the number of times I scratched and scraped myself trying to navigate my way through that place. The only time his living room ever saw real daylight was when the front door was opened because there was ancient filth covering every window. The whole place smelled like old Philippino food and shit mixed with cat pee.

Despite his obvious hardships, Rob was not in denial about his life whatsoever. He knew perfectly well the kind of shit life had dealt him and he was furious. Furious and impotent to do anything about it. For Rob every experience away from that place, every shared time with the rest of us, was enormously meaningful. Both real and deeply symbolic. A sort of tiny pilgrimage of faith, faith that he could manifest something better, however fleeting and delicate, than what he'd been given. Like me, he was utterly broken but where I had strength, for some reason Rob had fragility. Where I fought savagely, Rob clung weakly. I would have given anything to be able to protect him, I love him so much and I miss him dearly.

I never knew anyone more obsessed with the idea of being a man than Rob. But without any role models, his coming-of-age was a comedy of errors. I was with him the day he bought his first car, a 77 Pinto hatchback – undoubtedly a big moment in the life of this young man. It was flat-black primer with big wheels in the back and small wheels in the front meant, I'm sure, to make it look cool or intimidating. Alas, it might as well have had polka dots and been stuffed with tiny clowns for how ridiculous it looked. The one redeeming feature, and I believe the real reason he bought it in the first place, was that it had an enormously powerful stereo in it. I mean stupidly loud.

At the time of purchase, Rob did not know how to drive a stick [manual car]. The Pinto was, of course, a stick. For my part, I considered his decision to buy a vehicle he didn't know how to operate to be madness and I said so. But as I mentioned, Rob was determined to be seen as 'a man.' I'd soon learn to Rob, part of being a man was knowing how to drive a stick, and in the absence of a qualified teacher, he therefore resolved to teach himself – in this car.

On the day he bought the car, we were at Rob's modest house, where the seller had agreed to drop the vehicle off. He showed up, money changed hands, as did keys and a pink slip. 'Hey presto' – Rob was the proud owner of a flat-primer black turd. Undaunted by what I, or the rest of the world might think of his choice, Rob proceeded to jump in driver's seat, determined to 'become a man.' I jumped into the passenger seat, equally determined – except I wanted to smoke copious amounts of Northern California skunkweed with him prior to the Pinto's maiden voyage, guaranteeing a wired Rob to be its captain.

We smoked the pot, put Pink Floyd's epic stoner classic, 'Dark Side of the Moon' into the cassette deck and set off. It was a choppy journey. Three things happened simultaneously upon our departure. The marijuana began to take effect, the music began to crescendo (the song playing was "Breathe" which starts out with a very deep heartbeat then some stereophonic screaming and sound effect work before launching into the main theme,) and Rob began to understand why people said that learning to drive a stick could be 'challenging.'

We chirped, scuttled and stalled our way around a few blocks as the pot continued to kick in. Rob was systematically killing the engine, cussing then restarting it again. Little-by-little, the stalls became fewer and there was a rising sense of optimism in the car. Emboldened by having made it two blocks without the engine dying, Rob and I made our way to a four-way stop intersection complete with traffic lights. This would be our biggest test thus far, to stop, let the car idle until the appropriate time and then proceed through the intersection. As we got closer to the crossroads the lights changed from red to green, but Northern California skunkweed being what it is, Rob stopped dead at the crosswalk anyway. The music was deafeningly loud as we sat there, car vibrating from the bass, sitting still, staring at the green light. I was laughing out loud because I was convinced Rob still didn't know about the green light. I looked over at him, his face a mask of determination and quirky pride at having learned to drive the car as much as he did.

I shouted at him

"What the hell are you doing man, the light is green. GO!"

He stayed still. The light turned yellow. Nothing. I was laughing too hard to do anything else. Rob faced forward, looking right at the yellow light.

"Hahahaaahaaaaaaa!! Go man, Go!! Driiiiiiive!!"

Nothing.

He was stoned – really, really stoned.

The light was now red. I was almost peeing my pants. Tears were streaming down my face.

"What the hell are you doing?"

Still no sign of life from Rob, until he accelerated. Unfortunately, in the time we waited for Rob to suss out the lights situation, he seemed to have forgotten how to drive the stick again, because instead of the smooth travelling that had carried us over the last two blocks to this point, we were back to the chirp, stutter and stall method. We managed to get about three quarters of the way across the intersection when the mighty Pintowski, that magnificent primer-black stallion, that glorious turd, sputtered, choked and died. A little plume of black smoke belched feebly from its hood.

In our current state of mind, and since we had no money to speak of, Rob elected – which I wholeheartedly agreed with – to simply walk away once it became apparent his car would no longer start. And so we did. We simply left the primer-black Pinto to its ignominious end there in the intersection. This was in the days before cell phones and internet, so it took weeks before Rob even had to start avoiding calls or throwing away notices from the city about the abandoned vehicle.

That was my best friend, Rob.

III.

(CHRIS)

The next of my friends was Chris, like Rob and Eddie. He too was fair skinned with curly chestnut hair. Chris was a little pudgy and round-faced, and when we met, he wore his hair short and combed tight to his head. He favored pants with slightly high waists and shirts buttoned all the way to the top. All of these individual style choices had the combined effect of making him look something like a severe but well-dressed egg, not unlike a like a modern equivalent to Humpty Dumpty.

Chris had an uncanny ability to be in the right place at the right time to witness the most unbelievable situations. We would be walking down the avenue on a Saturday night, pass a parked car and it would be Chris who would notice the top of a girls head moving gently up and down in the lap of a guy sitting still in the front seat. Or walking into a bathroom just in time to see two guys coming out of a stall with white powder still on their noses, sniffing and snorting.

It would be Chris who discovered the waitress at our favorite diner wasn't wearing any panties. Dropping a spoon in some corner of the restaurant where she thought she would be unseen, she'd bend over at the waist to pick it up, not bothering to hold down her skirt. This would be in the direct line-of-sight of Chris who noticed as he ate his sandwich. Things like that happened to him all the time.

He also had a marvelous gift for exaggeration. When he did witness some extraordinary event no one was supposed to see, he would treat explaining the subtle nuances of a scene as an art form. He would add in all sorts of lush, exotic details and supporting ideas to 'fatten the story up.'

Every time we hung out together, he would regale us with tales of the perfect scenarios we had missed while we were apart. His stories often involved lavish surroundings, better-looking women than we had ever seen together, better drugs than we could ever hope to get our hands on. He had an odd talent for making you feel like when he was spending time with you he was slumming it away from his regular, fabulous life.

On the night of the party (where the police caught me having sex in the closet while hiding from them,) me, the guys and another friend of ours, Kendon, all decided to go out on a 'Halloween pumpkin kicking spree.' (Kendon fitted in with us well. He was also a nutcase.)

In the state we liked to refer to as 'sufficiently inoculated,' together we set out to destroy pumpkins. Many a 'Jack O' Lantern' fell prey to our killing feet that night. We reigned terror on the urban 'pumpkin patch' that was our neighborhood streets. Lane-by-lane, drive-by-drive our massacre went unchecked until Chris spotted the biggest 'Jack O' the night.' It stood almost two feet tall with wide, blazing eyes and a malicious grin, full of pointed teeth. Drunk on both power and beer, Chris ran up to it.

"Die pumpkin, DIE!"

He shouted as his foot drew back for the kill. He let fly with his Nike Cortez sneakers and 'Smash!'

I watched in confusion as the mighty pumpkin remained intact and it was Chris who crumpled.

"Aaaagggghhhh... oooooowwwwwwwww... I think I broke my foot!"

It took us a second to realize what had happened. The 'pumpkin' was not a pumpkin at all. It was a statue. It was entirely made of ceramic and thus, totally 'foot-proof.'

Just as we were connecting the dots, a man – a grown man – came bolting out of the house.

"What the hell do you think you're doing you little shit!?"

Instinctively, Eddie yelled

"Scatter, meet at the Hall of Evasion!"

We all took off like cockroaches when the lights come on. We ran in every direction. Eddie one way, Kendon and Rob another, Chris and I a third. 'Pumpkin man' followed Chris and I, letting the others escape easily. Our ninja training kicked in and we headed for fences, avoiding the open, obvious routes at all costs.

"On the left, red fence!" I panted through lungfuls of air.

We cut slightly left. This would lose our pursuer for sure. We hopped to the top of the fence and kicked our legs over lightly, landing in the strange yard beyond. Immediately, we glanced around for people and dogs, as we were trained to do. Seeing none, we cut straight across the lawn toward the left side of the house. We got a few strides in when, to our disbelief, we heard the Pumpkin man scaling the fence, a bit heavier than us, but still lithe and quick. We pushed past the trashcans, knocking them down as we did.

"Shit!" breathed Chris.

This guy was still on our tail.

"Split up at the street!" I said.

"Got it!"

We made it to the street. I looked at Chris.

"See you at the Hall of Evasion!"

"Cool."

I went left. He went right. I was perhaps ten strides down the road when Pumpkin man came crashing through the fence from the backyard where we just were.

"You're not losing me that easily!"

I heard the man shout, but I didn't look back. I was sucking in air as a shark sucks in water during a feeding frenzy. My legs were pumping like pistons and so were my hands. I'd no idea which one of us he was chasing until I got back to the Hall of Evasion to rendezvous with Eddie and the others.

"Is Chris here?" I asked between sharp breaths.

"Not yet. What happened?" Rob said.

"We made straight for a fence, jumped it, looked back and that guy was jumping it, right behind us."

"Shit, really?"

"Yeah, really."

"Why isn't Chris with you now?" asked Eddie.

"We separated after we cleared the backyard, just like you taught us." I replied.

'It's the best thing you could've done... best thing." He replied.

We waited for quite a while there, hoping to see Chris rounding the corner, grinning with a wild explanation in hand. After about an hour, we decided it would be best to head back to the party. Chris would undoubtedly make his way back there.

We got back to the party, which was in full swing, we walked through the front doors and lo-and-behold, there was Chris – with two girls that none of us recognized!

"S'up?" he said, barely able to contain his grin as he sat there with the girls.

We looked at each other in disbelief, then back at him. Then all at once, the questions erupted from us like a firehose.

"What the hell happened?"

"Where did you go?"

"Who are these girls and where did you meet them?"

"What the fuck H-A-P-P-E-N-E-D to YOU?"

With an air of nonchalance he must have been practicing the entire time he waited for our return, he looked at us, then at the girls, then back at us and said calmly

"You're NOT going to believe this shit!"

We all quieten down as he prepared to tell his story.

After he and I became separated, Chris had tried the 'fence through the back yard trick.' Again and again, Pumpkin man followed. The final time, Chris had stashed himself between two large shrubs and the fence, sitting still in the deep shadows they offered, desperately trying to control his breathing.

"I heard that guy searching the yard for me, cussing and throwing things around. I was fucking scared man!" related Chris.

"Then he walked right up to the bushes I was hiding between and looked right at me, I thought I was going to crap my pants, I held my breath as he brought his face only inches from mine. He was looking right at me!"

"What happened then? How did you get away?" I asked.

"That ninja shit works, bro. He never even knew I was there. He walked away from where I was after a few seconds as I tried to keep holding my breath. Of course, I couldn't hold it anymore and I let it out with a big gasp. Well this guy fucking turned around and made right towards me again!"

"Then what did you do?"

"I jumped out of the bushes and back over the fence as fast as I could but he was following right behind me. I leapt over another fence into that old lady's house on Maple St. You know the one who always let's her little dogs run after everybody?"

"Oh, yeah. I hate that lady, she..."

"No dude, listen, check this out, I hopped the fence and there were two guys breaking into her back door, they were breaking into her house! Do you believe that shit?"

All of us together said

"What! What the hell?"

"I know right?" replied Chris.

"What happened then?" asked Kendon.

"I was just standing there looking at them when the guy jumped the fence..."

"Holy shit!"

"Yeah, I know, so he sees these guys trying to break into the old lady's house and he just goes straight for them, passing me right by. He just attacked them."

"Holy fuckin' shit!!"

"Yeah! So I stand there for a minute watching this guy taking on two dudes, right? And he's like, totally winning. He's kicking these guys' asses, when it dawns on me I should really get the

hell out of there. So I just kind of walk by out onto the front lawn, and BAM! Three cop cars show up, sirens going, guns drawn, the whole deal. It was crazy!"

"Ho-lee shiiiit, man. Holy shit, are you fuckin' kidding me? You gotta be kidding me!"

"Totally not kidding you in the slightest. So one of the cops tells me to freeze and get my ass on the ground, so bam, I'm down, face down. His buddies all charge by me into the back yard, right?"

"Yeah, yeah, what next?"

"Well, a couple of minutes later they come back out with the two dudes in 'cuffs and the fucking Pumpkin man is walking next to them, explaining some shit or something, because everyone is nodding and everything, right?"

"Dude! This is crazy!" I said.

"So then the fuckin' Pumpkin man points at me and says to the cops, 'He wasn't with them, he ran back to help when he heard the commotion,' I was trippin' hard at that point!"

"Oh my fuckin' gawd! Are you even kidding me right now?" said Rob.

"I swear to God that's how it happened, man!" Chris replied.

"Then Pumpkin man leans down like he's helping me up and whispers in my ear, 'Don't let me see you around my house again kid, I know where you live.'"

At this point, we were all in a frenzy at this story, hanging on every detail when it dawned on me – he still had these two girls with him that we had never seen before.

"Yeah, but where did they come from?" I said, pointing to the girls.

"So, I'm walking back from all this shit and my foot starts hurting, I mean hurting bad, so I'm like limping back to the party when these two call out to me from a porch."

"Hey, are you alright, you look hurt."

"'I think I broke my foot a little while ago and it's starting to hurt real bad now,' I said"

"Are you sure you're gonna make it to wherever you're going?"
They asked.

"I think so. I'm just heading back to a party a few blocks away."

They looked at each other and back at me.

"Do you want us to look at your foot? It might be really hurt."

"Sure, O.K. I hobbled up to their porch and they took me inside. As it turned out, they were home alone because their parents are at a Halloween party."

The girls didn't speak but giggled often during the telling of the story.

"After a while I asked them if they wanted to come to the party and the rest is history."

He grinned again. Chris slept with one of them that night and I almost slept with the other one.

That was my best friend, Chris.

IV

(CHARLIE)

Then there was Charlie. Charlie came from a long line of renegade bikers, true American outlaws. His entire family was dangerous on a level we wouldn't even be able to comprehend until we were much older. To us, they were just Charlie's dad and Charlie's uncles. To others, however, they were men to be feared. Men who would invade your house and take your belongings in broad daylight. Men who would HURT you if the reasons were right and they alone decided what the right reasons were.

In stark contrast, Charlie himself was the smallest and quietest of all of us. He was slight and delicate looking, with large, darting eyes and a pointy, 'foxlike' face. At first glance he looked five years younger than he was and almost feminine. However, if you really paid attention and you knew what to look for, you could see it in his eyes – he was descended from outlaw royalty.

One night, all of us Charlie, Chris, Eddie, Rob and I were out playing pool at one of the local halls when we happened to meet Charlie's dad. On this particular night, we had all taken large doses of magic mushrooms and were very high. We were passing the time playing pool and hallucinating wildly when Charlie's dad, Greg, drifted into our little world.

"Well, what have we here? You boys out getting into... trouble?"

He was grinning like a maniac at the lot of us.

None of us had ever spent much time with Greg in a social context before. With the exception of Charlie, none of us really knew how to act in front of him. We all knew him, of course, but he was more like a legend than a real man in our minds. Add to that the fact that the mushrooms made him look a lot like a malevolent imp or some sort of insane gargoyle you can begin to see why we were all a little tongue-tied in his presence.

"Just out playing pool." said Chris, trying not to laugh as the
  mushrooms worked their magic.

"You wanna join us, Greg?" I asked him.

He glanced at Charlie, who gave a slight nod to the affirmative.

"Sure, sounds like fun."

What started as a simple game of pool began to take a turn for the absurd as the mushrooms took us higher and higher above the boundaries of reality. The billiard balls became more and more difficult to differentiate from one another. They refused to stay one color for very long at a stretch. To make matters worse, or funnier, every time Rob potted a ball, Chris would do some sleight of hand, palm the ball out of whichever pocket Rob had just sunk it into and discretely return it to the table. It greatly amused us as Rob became progressively more bewildered.

Greg was chuckling. He began to tell a story of playing pool with a friend of his long ago, who it seemed, was also a master of telekinesis.

"Every time I'd sink a ball, this fucking guy would levitate it out of the pocket and back onto the table... took me a long time to catch on."

We all watched his face as Rob, in his drug-induced confusion, who never was the 'sharpest tool in the box' anyway, struggled to link the vague story with the events he was currently dealing with. He wasn't quite 'connecting the dots.' The fourth time he sunk the number 2 ball, only to find it back on the table after turning around to sip a beer, he came to me and whispered,

"I'm really starting to freak out man! I could've sworn that I've sunk that ball like four times?"

"It's brobably the 'shrooms man."

"I don't know. It's really trippin' me out though!"

"Well, that's kind of the point of 'shroomin' isn't it?"

I looked at him and I could see all at once, by the panicky look in his eye, it was no longer funny to him. I think Greg picked up on this too because right after I confessed we were yanking his chain, Greg announced

"Hey, you guys want to go and have some real fun? I'm getting kinda bored."

We all looked at each other and then at him.

"Fuck yeah! We do!" we said as a group, minus Charlie.

Charlie, it seemed, was less enthusiastic about his dad's suggestion.

"Sure." he said mildly. "Let's go."

We walked out to the parking lot as a group and Greg said

"Let's take my car, boys!"

He pointed at a tan 1966 Ford Falcon that looked like something out of a hot rod magazine cartoon.

This car was built for speed like only a vintage American 'muscle car' can be. It had a modified hood with a hole cut neatly out of the center. Through that hole a huge chrome air-induction cowl protruded – the kind with three red circles in the opening that fold in half as the air is sucked in. It stood with its rear end higher than the front due to the huge rear racing slicks and oversized rims. There were chrome muffler pipes sticking out of the sides. Each individual pipe came out from under the car and braided together into one big fat pipe with a flared opening. They were the sort of pipes that always had flames shooting out of them in those hot rod cartoons.

The paint was a classic 'Stockton' look. It had rust spots everywhere that had been sanded, patched and primered but not yet repainted. It looked like liver spots were covering it. In the areas where the paint was still intact, there were varying degrees of oxidization and failure of the clear coat, adding to the effect of old, dying skin.

As I stood there looking at it, the mushrooms working their particular kind of magic on me, it seemed to me whatever Greg had done underneath the hood of that car was so powerful, so downright toxic, it was rotting the very sheet metal that was supposed to contain it. It was the automobile version of a man who turns into a beast by shedding his human skin to reveal the monster underneath.

And what a monster it was!

When we were all in, Greg said in his best impersonation of a roller coaster attendant

"Will all children please buckle their seatbelts? Keep all body parts inside the vehicle at all times. Please wait until we come to a complete stop before exiting the vehicle. Thank you."

With that, he started the engine with a roar, slammed it into first gear and smashed the gas pedal into the floor. I heard the sound of tires squealing and could smell rubber as we gained traction. When we did, my head whipped back into my seat, my eyes pulled wide by the acceleration. Before I knew what I was doing, my throat opened and I was screaming

"Yeaaahhhhhhhhh!"

What happened next was a blur.

We went blasting down the street, at least twice the speed limit. Greg put Deep Purple's 'Highway Star' in the cassette player and cranked it up past ten (even past eleven, I think) to face-melting volume. This was timely. The mushrooms were in full effect now and everywhere I looked, all I saw was melting faces and laughing souls. I remember ripping down a one-way street the wrong way, going about sixty-five miles an hour as someone shouted

"Look out for that car!"

The car jerked to one side. Suddenly, we were up on someone's lawn, bass and drums pulsing in my skeleton and brain as we swerved this way then that. We were dodging vehicles, trees, mailboxes and whatever else was in our way. Greg whipped the wheel to the right at an intersection, just as the light turned red. Other cars were slamming on their brakes, horns wailing, lights flashing, all of us pushed sideways by gravity as we corrected our course and made our way down the street. Then out of nowhere, red and blue lights and the distorted scream of a siren materialized. I have no idea where that cop came from, but it seemed like he had his siren on even before we passed him. He whipped out behind us and began to give chase. All the while Deep Purple was pounding in my ears,

"...Nobody gonna take my car, gonna race it to the grooo-uund..."

We cut a sharp left at the next intersection.

"...Nobody gonna beat my car, it's gonna break the speed of sooo-uund..."

Then a right, then two more lefts and with that, the sirens faded into the night. Everything was swirling and dripping with color.

"...ooohh, it's a killing machine, ooohh it's got everything..."

Greg shouted to us

"I think we lost them!"

He turned the music up even louder.

"...All right... Hold tight... I'm a Highway Staaaaaaaaar..!"

Somehow, against all odds, we had lost them. We would not see the police again that night.

After we were sure that we eluded the cops, we made our way out to Ladd's Boat Park and Marina. This was the place where you could party virtually all night. Though the police did patrol it, they were very lax about how they approached it. Some nights you wouldn't see them at all. Other nights maybe once or twice, which is noteworthy when you consider even on a Sunday or Monday night, there would be at least a couple hundred people out there drinking and carrying on. We went on a Saturday this time and it was packed. Cars and people everywhere. We did a few laps around the perimeter before Greg stopped in front of a little scrawny-looking guy. The guy approached Greg's window and they began talking to each other in low voices.

"Are you a cop?"

"No. Are you a cop?"

"Have you ever been affiliated with law enforcement in any way?"

"No, have you?"

"No. Look at me. Do I look like a fucking cop?"

"Do you want to buy any shit?"

"What do you got?"

"It's killer!"

"It better be. I can cook the shit myself, so don't try to sell me any bullshit."

"Are you sure you're not a cop?"

At this point, Greg reached across me, opened the glove box and produced a six-shot, 45-caliber handgun. He showed the guy at the window it was loaded and then set it down on his lap.

"I'll ask you again. Do I look like a fucking cop to you?"

"How much are you looking to buy?"

All of us were completely silent during this exchange. We watched mute, as money and drugs changed hands, as though the way we had always done it was somehow amateurish and crass. We were, unquestionably in the presence of greatness. The scrawny man left the window and Greg looked back at us and said

"You guys aren't done going fast tonight are you?"

"I'm not." I said. (My voice seemed small in my ears.)

"Good, I didn't think so."

He produced a mirror from under the seat and divided up 'the goods.' With a rolled up twenty dollar bill, he inhaled a big, chunky line of cocaine and then he passed the mirror around to the rest of us. One by one, we imbibed. Then, very wired on top of our mushroom high, we all got out and congregated around the front of the monstrous car's hood. We felt like gods out there that night. Somehow we all became more than we were by our proximity to this giant. Everyone knew we had been part of something of a new order of magnitude to anything we had previously done. We knew that our street cred had just gone up tenfold.

The time grew so late the sun readied himself to press reset on the night. Greg took us back to our cars and dropped us off. We tried, foolishly, to thank him for everything. He just smiled and said

"Be safe. Take good care of my boy." and drove off.

We all waited until he finally disappeared then we erupted into a cacophony of awe and disbelief.

"Holy shit! Did that just happen?"

"What about when he went up on that lawn."

"We outran the COPS!"

"That was insane!"

We all looked at Charlie to gauge his reaction to the events of the night, waiting with baited breath to see what he would say, what he would do in the aftermath of that epic adventure. All he said was

"I told you my dad was crazy."

That was my best friend, Charlie.

V

These were my friends, the surrogate brothers I was blessed with. They took the place of my real 'blood family' with whom I had nothing in common.

I had two younger brothers and a sister on mom's side and two sisters on my dad's side. Alas, timing and circumstance saw to it that we never developed any meaningful bonds until much later in life. From mom's children, I was the only one with the last name Wolfe and stood out from the rest. My hair and eyes were dark and smoky, theirs all blonde like sand with green eyes. More importantly, they had very different childhood experiences.

The only one who was close in age was Greg. Where I was violent and rowdy, he kept to the confines of the communal house and to his communal friends. Apart from me, I don't think he ever got in a real fight.

The other two, Annabel and James, no matter how they tried could never hope to empathize with nor relate to the things I lived with on a daily basis. They had no personal frame of reference for me, or the way I behaved.

Then there were my sisters Guinevere and Angeline from my dad's side. Guinevere I met only a handful of times. Angeline I saw only once. If she and I walked past each other on the street today, I'd have no idea who she was.

CHAPTER 6

TEMPEST RISING

I

And so, with the perfect storm of my burgeoning adolescence, the relative freedom of the West Side of Stockton, the influences of my childhood, the group of misfit friends and the total lack of parental supervision from my mom. I exploded into my teen and young adult years.

As a group, my friends and I were more than just 'dynamic,' we were a show stopping number. Although we were all poor kids from a poor neighborhood, the mix of our five personalities was very potent. We became known throughout the town by those you would find at parties and gatherings. Our names were known all up and down the main drag long before we even had our own cars to cruise. The combination of Eddie's mischievous sense of vision, Chris's taste for excess, Rob's humor and my sense of style and gift of gab set us apart from the rest. Charlie was mostly quiet.

We burned through those years so fast, never knowing that we were hurtling down what would prove to be a completely self-destructive path. Nevertheless, out there on the streets was where we found meaning, significance and belonging. Spurred on by the approval of our peers and those we didn't even know but who knew us by reputation, we developed a taste and a talent for outdoing what we had already done.

I began encouraging the others to grow their hair long like mine. We took to wearing sport coats and dress shirts with rocker jewelry and custom-ripped jeans. People constantly assumed we were a band. Our reputations grew along with our egos.

By my thirteenth birthday, I'd lost my virginity to a seventeen-year-old rock goddess and neighborhood legend, Lynn Jackson. I was skinny and had just gone through the changes into a young man only months before. She was in the full blossom of her womanhood. She was all curves, smiles and patience as I fumbled my way through those glorious two minutes that left me shaking and unable to speak.

By the end of that year, I'd gotten Bonnie Benjamin pregnant and, not knowing what else to do, had told mom. That would set the tone for our relationship for many years to come. Bonnie's parents made her have an abortion when they found out. Only a few weeks later, I was caught by the police having sex with another girl in the master bedroom closet of a friend's house that my friends and I'd broken into (at Eddie's suggestion) to throw a huge party, while they were on vacation. This won me my first trip to the police department and my first time having the police call mom, who refused to pick me up.

By the time the police arrived, we had broken seven windows, smashed in four doors and Kendra ripped the chandelier out of the ceiling by doing a drunken Tarzan swing across the room on it. The bill for damages was so substantial that 'friend' was forbidden to see any of us again.

A couple weeks later, my friend Michelle gave me my first blowjob in her bedroom – the door was still damaged from the wanton destruction it sustained at the party. I just finished in her mouth as her mom came crashing and screaming through the house from work. I had to jump out of her bedroom window with my pants around my ankles. Yet again, Eddie's training saved me and I did a tuck and roll, just like a real ninja. I heard her mom smack her as I leapt quietly over the back fence.

While other kids were working to get good grades, playing soccer and baseball after school and having meals with their parents around the dinner table, my friends and I were cutting school, smoking weed and getting drunk whenever possible. We continued refining our unique 'fashion sense' aiming to look as good as we could while raising as much hell as possible.

II

Shortly after my family moved out of the South Side, other parents in the commune followed suit. It wasn't long before another kid I grew up with in the communal house, Ian and his mom found a place a couple miles from where we had moved. If my friends and I made a name for ourselves for being flashy, outgoing party guys, Ian made a name for himself as a genuine bad ass.

He was less than two years older than I was but he soon had a loyal crew of thugs and outlaws surrounding him. They were all, to a man, older. Despite his relative youth, he still had absolute authority. They say that like attracts like but I'm not sure there were too many like Ian.

When we lived on the West Side, he was a protector to me (and my friends,) mostly using only his reputation to keep me from harm. From time to time, however, he would actually step in personally to defend me.

One neighborhood thug, Rodney Jones, several years older than I was, delighted in harassing me whenever we met. He would routinely throw rocks at my friends and me. He would corner us and shake us down for whatever we had on us at the time and generally make my life miserable whenever he could.

Until, in a rather delicious twist of fate, he would come literally face-to-face with Ian.

I had a friend Denise who was, by any measure you cared to use, an 'easy girl.' She was best friends with the Lynn Jackson – the girl who relieved me of my virginity.

One smoky autumn day during northern California's wildfire season, Ian and I were hanging out in front of the corner liquor store, talking to some people we knew, when Lynn pulled up in her car. Denise was with her.

They both jumped out and greeted me enthusiastically, the way that only delightfully trashy girls can. The last time I'd seen both of them together, we were all buzzed and almost found ourselves in a three-way. They were teasing me about it. I introduced them to Ian and Denise immediately took a shine to him.

One thing led to another and we all spent the next couple of days together at Ian's house. During a break from the smoking, drinking and fornicating, we were all sitting in his squalid, little living room watching the news and paying close attention to the updates about a fire raging out of control just above Sacramento.

> *"Speaking of fire burning out of control." said Denise, looking at Ian with a seductive glance.*

> *"I bet my boyfriend, Rodney, would be totally out of control if he knew what I was doing right now."*

Ian just shrugged and smiled.

> *"I bet he would be 'if' he knew how good you were getting it."*

She grinned big at him.

> *"Rodney who?" I asked.*

> *"Rodney Jones." came her reply.*

> *"Rodney Jones? I hate that guy! He and his friends are always fucking with me."*

> *"What do you mean, fucking with you?" asked Ian inquisitively.*

> *"He's thrown rocks at me before, stolen my money, threatened me, pushed me down on the ground, all kinds of shit."*

Lynn came near, hung her arms over my shoulders and kissed me on the ear affectionately. Looking at Ian, she said

> *"It's true. He is kind of an asshole. I know lots of people who don't like him."*

She snuggled beside me and lit a cigarette, exhaling deeply, her breath disturbing the smoke layer around our heads.

> *"Rodney did that?" said Denise, being playful.*

> *"Why would he do that, that's fucked up? Doesn't he know how cute you are?"*

She smiled at me when she said this, then turned to Ian.

> *"Not as cute as you though, baby."*

He grinned at her again and slapped her on the ass.

"I don't know, I've never done anything to him, he just decided he hates me I guess."

Ian looked at Denise.

"Do you have his phone number?" he asked, lighting his own smoke.

"Yeah, baby, do you want me to call him?"

She had a conspiratorial tone in her voice.

"Yeah. Call him and hand me the phone," said Ian grinning through a big puff of smoke.

At this, Denise agreed with a twinkle in her eye that made her look like she might have a small orgasm at any moment. She was responding very favorably to his bravado.

We sat there in Ian's living room, the little ghostly wisps of cigarette smoke floating in the air halfway between the floor and the ceiling, lit up by the afternoon sun. The weatherman was still prattling on about the fires.

"...make sure to keep your distance... homes are being evacuated as close as Auburn... fire burning down everything in its path..."

My heart beat fast with a mixture of fear and excitement as we waited for Rodney to answer.

"Hello, Rodney?" said Denise

Through the receiver, we could just hear Rodney's voice on the other end.

"Yeah. What's up baby?"

"Oh, nothing honey, just wanted to say 'hi.' How are you doing?"

"I'm fine, just chillin' at home, waiting for Teddy to get here. What's up with you?"

"Oh, I'm just kickin' it with some friends."

She said in a singsong voice

"Someone wants to say 'hi' to you, O.K?"

"Who?"

"Just a friend, he says he knows you."

She handed the phone to Ian. He put a little extra bass in his already deep voice.

"Hello, is this Rodney?"

"Yeah. Who's this?"

"I'm the guy who's telling you that you better leave my little brother alone from now on, unless you want me up in your business."

"What? What the fuck are you talking about?"

"My name is Ian and Manny is my little brother, you know Manny right? He says you're always fucking with him."

"I'm gonna fuck with whoever I want. Who the fuck are you?"

"I told you, I'm his big brother and if you fuck with him then you're fucking with me. And you don't want to fuck with me, I promise you that."

"Let me ask you a question, you little bitch, do you have an 'S' on your chest?"

"No, why?"

"Because if you don't, then you're not Superman and you need to be watchin' your tone with me son. I'll whip your ass, punk-ass motherfucker!"

Ian smiled as he calmly said

"Superman huh? We'll see real soon which one of us is Superman, that's funny though... Superman. I'm going to tell you one last time, don't fuck with my little brother anymore."

"Man, fuck you, that bitch Denise knows where I live. Come find me, motherfucker, then we'll see what's what!"

"Yeah, we will. We definitely will."

Ian hung up the phone and asked Denise where Rodney liked to hang out.

"He plays basketball at Victory Park with a bunch of other guys most afternoons. You can usually find him there."

"What does he look like?"

"He'll be the only white guy. He has long, curly hair, like it's trying to be an afro but it's not. Oh, and he's real pale."

"O.K. Cool."

We went back to hanging out, but inwardly I was going crazy. That was some gutsy shit and I'd never seen anyone do anything like that before, especially not on my behalf.

The weatherman was concluding his segment about the wildfire.

"...Very unpredictable... can quickly change with prevailing winds... we all need to be on our toes..."

A couple of days later, Ian called me up.

"Hey! What are you doing?"

"Nothing. Just sitting here. What are you up to?"

"I'm going to go to Victory Park with Moose. You want to come?"

(...'Moose' was the affectionate nickname Ian gave his good friend, Allan. Why moose? He was big as the proverbial moose...)

"Sure. When?"

"I can pick you up in a little while, O.K.?"

"Great, see you then."

I'd no idea what he was up to, but I knew when I hung out with Ian, I was treated with respect by all his crazy, redneck friends and I liked that feeling. I waited impatiently until he knocked at my door. I opened it wide.

"Hey! You ready to go?" he asked.

"Yup. Let's do this."

We loaded ourselves into his van and took off down the road.

The sky was slightly bronze-yellow from the many days of smoke blowing in from the Northeast. You could smell it in the air. There were fallen leaves skittering across the sidewalk as we drove away. It gave a prematurely Octoberish feeling to the afternoon.

I was positioned between the two front captain's seats, squat kneeling so that I could converse with Ian and Moose as we drove on.

> *"I've gotta do something real quick and I thought you'd like to check it out."*
>
> *"O.K. What is it?"*
>
> *"You'll see."*
>
> *"Do you think he'll be there?" asked Moose.*
>
> *"Well we're gonna find out."*

We drove on until we came to Victory Park. Ian circled the van around until we were approaching the basketball courts.

> *"Who are you trying to find?" I asked.*

There was a bunch of guys playing basketball at the courts. I recognized some of them – twins Rick and David Weston, both well over six-feet tall. Freddy Dawd was there with his unintelligent but malicious eyes and Joey Cortez known all over town as a 'playboy' and scrapper because he liked fighting and girls equally. Then there was Gino Gonzales. He lived down the street from me. He was all thug and always being arrested. These guys were legends in my neighborhood – the top of the local food chain. These were the guys you averted your gaze from when you saw them on the street.

> *"What are we doing here?" I asked.*

I didn't really like any of these guys and for good reason. Many of them had fucked with, harassed, or generally made life miserable for me and my friends at one time or another.

Then I noticed him – Rodney Jones – encircled by his friends.

> *"Today's the day Rodney meets Superman." grinned Ian.*

"This should be 'interesting.'" Moose replied, smiling.

My heart started pounding as I realized what was happening,

"Uh... O.K..." I said.

I was counting how outnumbered we were. There were seven of them and only three of us – two if you didn't count me.

"We don't have to do this if you don't want to" I said feebly.

I become very aware of how pathetic I sounded right as I said it.

Ignoring me, Ian pulled the van up alongside their court. Moose opened the side door.

"Wait here." Ian said.

"Roger that." confirmed Moose.

Moose positioned himself at the side door, crouching down with his arms folded on his knees. He stared intently at the crowd of guys. A deep shadow crossed his body at a forty-five degree angle from the opening of the van door, the upper part of his body shrouded in darkness. I was completely in the shadows.

Ian got out and walked through the middle of the group straight up to Rodney. The six other guys stopped what they were doing and locked their gaze on Ian. Never taking his eyes off Rodney, he came face-to-face with him, seemingly oblivious to the others watching him.

"Are you Rodney?"

A gust of wind ripped through the trees overhead.

*"Yeah, who the fuck are you?" said Rodney, dribbling a
basketball as he spoke.*

"I'm Superman, motherfucker. You got anything to say to me now?"

It's one thing to be willing to fight when needed. I knew how to do that. You push through the fear, let the first punch land and from there it's downhill. Once the first connection is made all the rules change. Of course, to do this, you have to have the balls to willfully walk through a crowd of guys, all of them your age or older, all your size or bigger. To do what Ian did that day is in another league. To bravely go into the unknown for another person with definite risk of bodily harm was something else entirely – that is the stuff that makes you a neighborhood legend.

As Ian asked the question, he snatched the ball from Rodney, mid-bounce. He stood there holding it, face impassive, waiting for a reply. That one gesture decided everything. Rodney lost right then. He stammered and stuttered, looking profoundly flustered.

"I,I,I.. didn't know... Denise didn't..."

I looked over at Moose who was smirking. I could see how impressed he was. All at once, I understood why Ian, at such a young age, could command the respect of so many older, seemingly tougher, men. He was the real deal. If he said it, he was going to do it.

Rodney stood there, shoulders slumped, wind whipping his jersey, trapped by Ian's gaze in that way I knew so well from my experiences of being intimidated by older kids on the South Side. All the other guys on the court, watching this, seemed to decide Rodney wasn't worth sticking up for if he was this easily cow-towed by one guy with only one more guy for back up. I was glad none of them could see me while this was happening. I stayed out of sight. This was all above my pay grade.

Finally, Rodney spoke again.

"What do you want?" He said meekly.

"Two things." said Ian.

"First, you don't ever fuck with my little brother, Manny again. He's of limits. If you see him, you go the other way. Understand?"

"Yeah."

"Second, your girlfriend. She's mine now, got it?"

"Yeah."

"If you follow these two rules, then you and me won't have any problems, cool?"

"Yeah."

*"O.K. then, as long as we are on the same page, you can have
your ball back. You want your ball back?"*

"Yeah."

Ian faked throwing the ball at Rodney's face, forcing him instinctively to
flinch. All of his friends exploded into laughter like the cackling of a
thousand crows. Ian was in the zone though. He never broke eye contact
even for a second. He let Rodney recover from the fake throw, then he really
threw the ball and it bounced off Rodney's chest. Ian dominance was now
complete.

He turned and walked slowly back to the van.

I watched, feeling an odd mixture of triumph and pity as all of Rodney's
friends stood laughing and harassing him for submitting so sheepishly to the
will of my protector.

On one hand, I was certain Ian had just remedied one of my bigger social
problems. On the other, it was difficult to watch even an asshole like Rodney
being totally humiliated like that despite him doing similar things to me.
This was one of my first conscious inklings that Moral Man was watching.

Ian started up the van, turned on the radio and we drove off.

The weatherman was on again, still talking about those wildfires.

*"...wind has changed direction... the fires are receding... the
Californian forestry department reports the danger is past... people
are going back to their houses..."*

III

After Lynn Jackson had graciously deflowered me, I discovered that I was
like catnip to the local neighborhood girls. As it turned out, they thought I
was funny, cute and just dangerous enough to draw their attention. They
threw themselves at me to such a degree I never learned the fine art of how
to actually 'woo' a woman (or a girl as the case was.) All I did was show up,

act a fool and take their clothes off. I got to the point where I just arrogantly 'expected it.'

My friends and I would skip school all day, hiding out in the park, getting high. When the school day ended, we would wait at the bus stop for the other neighborhood kids to get home. Usually from there, we'd all go to someone's house and hang out. Those days, it was normal for me to take a new girl into someone's bedroom at least once a week. My indiscretions left not only bedsheets but girl's reputations equally crumpled and dirtied.

Once, we were all at Michelle's house (she of the damaged bedroom door and the incredibly gracious fellatio.) A Portuguese exchange student, Andrea, who spoke no English whatsoever, simply walked over to me, took me by the hand and led me into Michelle's room – the very one I'd dived out the window of some weeks earlier. As soon as she closed the door, she reached behind her head, unfastened her top, pulled it down over her large breasts and then right down past her waist. She shimmied out of her skirt and stood there before me, nude. She was fully developed and aroused. I was broomstick thin with a raging hard-on and a gleam in my eye. We had barely even acknowledged each other before this. She pulled me down onto Michelle's already familiar bed all the same.

A few minutes later, I came out of Michelle's room, grinning. Rob and Chris looked at me.

"Again?" said Rob. "What the hell is it about you?"

"I don't know but when we do work it out, we should definitely bottle and sell it." said Chris with more than a hint of jealousy in his voice.

As a teenager, I capitalized on every opportunity like this. Between all the attention from girls and the totally blasé, nonchalant attitudes to sex and love I saw growing up in the commune, I was like a wrecking ball. I plowed through any girl that would sleep with me, regardless of more-or-less anything except looks. I fucked anything that moved as long as I found it cute.

I inadvertently hurt many of my friends with this and would have hurt many more, if not for the discretion of the females involved. Although everyone else spoke in terms of 'commitment,' 'love,' 'being taken' by another, the examples I learned from my upbringing on the commune were stronger. I simply didn't get 'going steady.' Like speaking a different language, I just couldn't understand why you wouldn't have sex with any girl if she'd let you. Period.

To this very day, those tendencies toward womanizing are still running wild in my head. The only difference now is that I can recognize the thought patterns when they appear and choose to act differently than I did in my youth. I count myself very fortunate not to have a sex addiction in addition to the other demons with which I contend.

In those days, of course, I had no idea there was even a problem. I was just 'lucky.' It was a common occurrence for me to have multiple girlfriends at the same time, sometimes secretively, other times out in the open.

At sixteen, I can remember having seven concurrent girlfriends. They all knew about each other. None of them seemed to care. I spent my time that summer making my daily daytime rounds, having sex with multiple partners, jumping out of bedroom windows, hiding in closets to avoid parents. At night, I'd be going out with my friends, getting totally smashed on whatever combination of intoxicants we could get our hands on.

It was the most irresponsible, consequence-free time of my life. I was living exactly as I was raised to live, rebelling against the structures and the social covenant of the world beyond the communal walls.

At this time, the teachings and philosophies I was exposed to during my childhood began to form a crudely defined ethos inside me. Clumsily, they made their way to the surface. I would brandish Plato, Buddha, Jesus and others recklessly, the way a child who knows nothing of being cut might brandish a kitchen knife. I could 'talk the talk,' but I utterly lacked the requisite character or maturity to back it up. I could not 'walk the walk.'

IV

I could impress and dazzle others with my seeming understanding of spirituality but I was never able to resist manipulating the trust given to me as a result. There was a compulsive, self-serving aspect to my personality that would always step in and take charge after I won others over or gained confidences. I was powerless against this although I knew on some vague, abstract level what I was choosing to do was wrong.

During this time of copious drug use, prolific sexual activity and Herculean binge drinking, rampaging around with my friends, there were more subconscious inklings stirring within me about the gravity of my trespasses but I ignored them. I'd start out with the best of intentions but somewhere in my efforts to help others and lend counsel, I'd stumble upon an opportunity to steer their feelings toward some outcome that served my agenda better. I lacked the strength of character to resist serving my own interests.

I did this time and again until I began to sense a disconnect between what I considered my real self, the inner 'self' who knew better and the person that I habitually was in the world. It was as though I could only act in these shallow, self-serving ways, even though I knew they were disingenuous to my real self. Gradually the gap between the two parts of me increased like two bits of driftwood floating away from shore on a slow, steady tide.

CHAPTER 7

LOSSES AND GAINS

I

Anyone who has done a variety of drugs will tell you they're not all created equal. They can take you to very different places in your consciousness and in your life. Prior to discovering psychedelics, all my drug use had been selfish and utterly recreational, a bit like my life. By the time I was sixteen, I'd drunk a river of booze, smoked an acre of pot, snorted a metric fuck-ton of cocaine and gobbled up Cross-Tops amphetamines and Black Widow ephedrine pills like a chicken pecking at corn.

W.C. Fields, Snoop Dogg, The Fabulous Furry Freak Brothers and Scarface would have been proud

That said, none of my previous drug experiences prepared me for L.S.D. Acid was a spiritual, deeply metaphysical drug – at least to me and my friends – and it stood apart from all of the others.

The first time I took it, I was with Eddie. He'd taken it a few times before and gave me an idea of what to expect beforehand. That didn't really matter, as it turned out, I was a natural. I rode smoothly through the deeply pleasurable body sensations, an elevated mood accompanied by laughter and a powerful sense of wonder and awe, and of course, vigorous hallucinations that could take you to some pretty strange places, if you let them.

I remember that after we put the acid tabs on our tongues, we began to feel a sense of chemically induced anticipation, like a tingling through our entire bodies. Then, after about twenty minutes, I looked up at the sky and saw it turn vivid purple as if some giant hand was slowly pulling a translucent fuchsia-colored gel lens over the entire thing. I looked at Eddie and we both started laughing so hard that we cried. Wiping the tears away, I looked straight into Eddie's eyes and felt such a deep and profound love for my friend it took my breath away. Eddie seemed to feel that depth of connection too. After a short while he came to me and said

"Let's see if we can lose these guys, they're no fun."

We slipped their notice as if it was nothing and spent the next ten hours rediscovering our little corner of the city from a completely new perspective. We went to one secret landmark after another, barely speaking any words between us yet both of us knowing what the other was thinking.

We climbed the walls of the Hall of Evasion and sat on the roof, watching as the sky began pulsing slowly in and out, while the clouds formed kaleidoscopic patterns that expanded colorfully outward and fell back in on themselves again.

We would try to articulate what we were seeing, words failing us halfway through a thought. We turned to look at each other and knew we both 'understood.' We were like two sides of the same person that whole day. When I came down enough to form sentences again, the first thing I said was

"We have GOT to show the other guys this stuff."

It was only a matter of time before all of us were taking acid on a weekly basis. The five of us experienced such a profound sense of togetherness and belonging during that time. The effects of it are still with me today, though life has separated me from my friends. Where alcohol and cocaine merely sped us up or slowed us down, with L.S.D. we were gaining access to the unknowable, the unchanging. We were shown truths too subtle to articulate.

I came to understand how patterns in nature repeated everywhere, in water, air, fire and earth. Late one night on one of our group acid trips, we went to the foggy and isolated Port of Stockton. It felt like we were given the keys to a mystical amusement park during the off-season. Whilst there, we made a fire right at the water's edge. We sat there next to the fire, watching the water move silently past. We noticed the reflections rippling through the water were making the same shapes as the shapes made by the rising smoke, which in turn, blended into the surrounding fog. Looking down at the fire, we noticed the flames were a dancing, changing version of the same exact shapes. It was all one continuous but changing pattern.

From there we began to search for these patterns all around us, finding them wherever we looked. Flame was the shape of smoke, which was the shape of bark on a tree, which was the shape of ripples in the water, which was the shape of tire treads, in the dirt at our feet. Gradually as the night wore on, we began to turn the lens of inquiry inward, and when we did, we really got our minds blown. We began to perceive repetitive patterns of thought and behavior and even patterns of perception.

As the drugs kicked in to high gear, we were all having revelations one after the other until, all at once I had the sensation of being lifted out of my body and brought to a place where I could look down on myself as if from space. I saw all of my senses as shelves that were set right above me. Then I looked up and realized there were dozens more right above those. As I floated there in space, I was staring at the realization there was so much more that I, that all of us could harness and put to use in our lives. Suddenly, presumably at the peak of the acid's influence, an absurd sense of scale overwhelmed me. I was infinitely huge and infinitely small at the same time. I'd no idea how much time had passed.

This experience signaled the beginning of the decline of that night's trip but even the next day – and still to this day – the idea of being able to know and discover those internal patterns has stuck with me. It was as though I was given a gift that night that would not bear fruit for many years to come. Slowly, over time, I would harness the ability to recognize patterns within myself and through that, to change the ones that don't serve me.

L.S.D. began to put me in touch with that inner self, Moral Man, the one that was floating gently away even as I discovered his existence. If not for the drugs influence, I might never have been able to reconnect with that part of myself.

Chris used to joke that L.S.D. is the only drug that quits you when it's good and ready. That's just what happened to my friends and me. Somehow, it just stopped being a good choice for our partying. When we were did it though, we shared such an unbelievable camaraderie, bond and spiritual education. I have never known its equal since.

Before my psychedelic period, I didn't recognize the rift that was forming between my moral self and the self that I was showing the world. Even after that period, it would take almost twenty years before I was able to put the lessons to use and do anything about it. In that state of inner conflict and disconnect, I'd come to find and ultimately squander, the first great love of my life.

II

If it was confusing for me to watch helplessly as I manipulated my friends and lovers up to that point. Watching as I did it to Suzie was a bizarre kind of torture. She was breathtakingly beautiful, sweet, kind, tender and insecure. We loved each other almost instantly.

We met one hot August afternoon. My friends and I were running wild as usual when another friend of ours, Kevin suggested that we walk over to the Taco Bell.

> *"My best friend's ex-girlfriend, Suzie works there and I bet we can get free grub."*

Not the kind of guys to refuse free food, we all agreed to go. I remember the moment I first laid eyes on her like it happened yesterday. We were walking up to the front doors of the restaurant, all of us dressed like extras in a Whitesnake rock music video – ripped jeans and blousy shirts, sport coats with rolled up sleeves, a profusion of strategically tied bandannas and hip belts, long hair billowing fabulously in the breeze.

I saw Suzie behind the counter even before we opened the doors. From the moment I arrived, we never took our eyes off each other.

Kevin was first in the door making introductions but I barely heard him. I swept past everyone else and gently pushed him aside. My eyes never broke contact with hers. I walked right up to her and said

> *"Hi, I'm Manny."*

She blushed furiously as she looked back at me and said simply, perfectly,

> *"Suzie. Nice to meet you."*

I took her hand in mine, lifting it gently then kissed the back of it. It tasted like fake Mexican food but I couldn't have cared less. I can't tell you what it was that happened that day. It certainly wasn't her looks. She'd almost no make-up on. Her hair was pulled back in a small ponytail that peeked out of the opening on the back of her 'too-big' Taco Bell baseball cap. She was wearing a polyester work shirt that tented indiscriminately over the (impressive) curves underneath.

But her eyes were huge and impossibly blue and they never, not once broke my gaze until I left the counter. As we were leaving, Rob addressed the group blithely, saying

"I think I've got a shot at that girl, I'm gonna go ask her for her number."

I just looked at him sympathetically and said

"Sorry, buddy. This one's mine."

"How can you be so sure?" He said, apparently oblivious to what had just happened inside.

"I don't know, but I promise you, she's mine."

Kevin looked at Rob and said

"Fuckin' Manny!" as he shrugged his shoulders.

A couple of days later, we were at Kevin's house, standing around in his front yard when his dad came outside.

"Kev, you got a phone call."

Kevin went inside for a couple of minutes and then he came back out, looking at me, a mixture of envy, admiration and confusion on his face.

"What?" I demanded.

"That was Suzie. She called wanting to know if you were here. She wants us to come over. Her parents aren't home. Why would she call here looking for you?"

"Just lucky I guess." I smiled.

Suzie lived only a few blocks from Kevin's house so we all decided to walk over. It was a cool afternoon and we were all dressed to the nines. Chris and Rob were each wearing sport coats over their mostly unbuttoned blousy shirts. I had parachute pants on underneath my strategically ripped and frayed jeans, black Reebok high-tops and a cream-colored sweater. Around my neck, I sported a long knit scarf that made my now mid-back length hair even more flowing-looking than usual. I was sporting a crystal goblet with red wine in it for good measure.

We made our way to her front door where she was waiting for us. I walked up, smiled broadly and said, 'Hi Suzie, offer me a drink?' extending my almost-empty glass. She smiled ear-to-ear, blushed ardently and looked at me as if I was some kind of strange, exotic show bird – not an unfair assessment. Within moments of entering her house, she and I were sitting in her father's recliner kissing and holding each other tight, completely losing track of the other people present. We didn't stop for almost three years.

I swear Elton John wrote Crocodile Rock song for me. His 'Suzie' was my 'Suzie' too. She turned my world upside-down. To say that she was beautiful or gorgeous would be crass and tawdry. I'd had dozens of beautiful girls before her. Suzie was something different, something else. Yes, she was a beauty but in my heart and mind, there was something more inexplicable, intangible and completely irresistible about her. Perhaps we were like a chemical reaction, a reaction where the final result is more than the sum of its initial constituent parts.

I'd never known attraction like this before and yet, when we were apart, I found myself unable to remain faithful. I knew she wanted fidelity. I wanted with all my heart to make her happy. But there was a fundamental disconnect still. It was like trying to solve a jigsaw puzzle with some of the border pieces missing, or trying to build something from instructions written in two different languages. Some parts of being a good boyfriend I totally 'got' but others, I just couldn't.

And so, with an insufficient understanding of the task ahead and a set of tools unfit for the labor at hand, I bargained off and sold piecemeal the first great love of my life. I took it for granted. I took her for granted, right up to the day she left me. In so doing, she left me in pieces. Thomas Payne once wrote, 'that which we obtain too easily, we esteem too lightly.'

He was right.

III

I think of these years as my 'psychedelics and Suzie' phase. My friends and I – who were already learning to be very decadent and excessive – took our partying to more and more indulgent levels.

Most people who parked their cars on the strip on weekends to see and be seen would furtively stash twelve packs of beer in the trunks of their cars, or duck down to smoke a little pot out of view of any potential cops driving by.

In contrast, we favored parking in our VW bus – sideways – pulling the door wide so we could see all the action. We sipped champagne from crystal flutes and did our cocaine right out in the open with hundred dollar bills for straws. I didn't matter to us we were usually one small step from being flat broke. It was all about looking good – and we did.

From roughly sixteen to nineteen years of age, we seldom missed an L.S.D.-fueled weekend. We would elaborately plan our acid trips to start on Friday and not come back down until Sunday.

One of the unexpected lessons we learned from doing so much L.S.D. was that you looked less obvious if you were more open about it. We brought a level of style and brashness to our proceedings that earned us a reputation all over town. Everywhere we went, people we had never seen before knew our names and wanted to be part of whatever we were getting into.

Many times, while posting up on Pacific Avenue on a Saturday night, or sitting out at Ladd's Marina, we would watch amused as the cops came down on the people right next to us. They did sweeps of the entire area, only to somehow overlook us. All of this only encouraged us, of course, to keep pushing the envelope. There is a Latin phrase, 'esse quam videri.' It means, 'to be, rather than to seem.' North Carolina liked it so much, that they used it on their state seal. We were moving in the opposite direction of that motto as fast as we could, far more concerned with style than substance.

With my life was barely staying on the rails, Suzie called me up one day out of the blue. She informed me that she would be moving to Sacramento with her new boyfriend to go to college. Her parents had decided to pay for it on the condition she break up with me. She said 'she was glad for the time we spent together.' She politely wished me well, just like a Hallmark card, hung up the phone and was out of my life forever. I felt like a storefront window that someone had thrown a rock through.

IV

Well that was it. My life stopped completely. I cried on my floor, right below where the phone hung well into the evening and on-and-off for the next three days. I could not wrap my head around the reality of the situation. From the time I was eleven, until I got sober, those were the only three days that I didn't get high and that was because I couldn't get up or out of the house to get it together enough to do it. When I did finally get out of the house my substance intake from that day on, made my former habit look like 'amateur hour.'

Now armed with the convenient justification of a broken heart, unhinged, I ripped full-blast through every bottle, every thrill, every girl or woman, every high and low that I could find. Often times my binges made even my friends, my brothers-in-arms cautious of my stability. Truth be told, I was clearly unstable.

I have often suspected some angel or another must have taken a liking to me though I could never understand why. How else to explain the fact that I am not dead? After Suzie's departure, I pushed my friends and myself to what I thought was the limit. We robbed street-corner drug dealers back on the South Side. I tried to start drunken fights with a rogues' gallery of the wrong people. I drove far too fast while far too drunk, began to favor methamphetamine over every other drug and generally attempted to self-destruct. I felt like a Molotov cocktail of self-loathing, rage, self-pity and righteous indignation.

I became unable to hold a job for any length of time. I would find reasons why I didn't fit in which actually led to not fitting in. This usually led to me storming out in a blaze of glory or simply not showing up. Seeing this behavior getting worse, mom and members of the commune began to encourage me to 'drop out of society.' Back then, their advice seemed like a slam-dunk. Fool a psychiatrist, get awarded those government S.S.I. payments for the rest of my life, and party on!

CHAPTER 8

PRECIPICE

I

I couldn't know it then but I was simply being brought back into the fold. That's what cults do. That's what the brainwashing is all about. It was our own little rite of passage.

> "...sure, you can go out and see what the outside world has got to offer... but you'll be back."

I took this idea to heart and started the application process right away. Eight months from the day it was first suggested, I was on S.S.I. and didn't have to worry about working any more. Things became a blur. I have only vague memories of the period from when I turned nineteen to the time I was twenty-two.

I do remember living with four other bachelors in a one-room apartment. That summer, my room was the balcony. I had a mattress out there. I was hot to trot. We lived maybe fifty feet from the freeway and I fell asleep on the nights that I slept, listening to the rumbling rhythm the drivers made. Every day was a continuation of the night before. We filled fifty-five gallon trash bags with crushed beer cans weekly, sometimes twice a week. Once a month we recycled all of them and bought enough beer for the next two days with the proceeds. We were living the dream!

I made many new friends in those years. Everyone would always tell me how talented I was, how I should be doing something more, something 'bigger' with my life. I didn't realize it then but most of those people were just tourists. They were only visiting in the place I lived. How dare they tell me to strive for more, this was it, this was me doing what I was born to do, self-destruct.

Though I always felt like I could have done great things if only the circumstances were different – the fact is they never were. No matter how much I did the same things, nothing ever seemed to change. The voice of my Moral Man alter ego, 'he who would do good,' grew almost entirely quiet during these days.

One lunchtime, while my roommates were all at work, one of our friends, Matt, stopped by. He poked his head round the front door of the apartment.

"Hey, pally! Whatcha doing?"

"Just sitting around," I answered.

"Where is everybody?"

"No idea" I replied, "What are you up to?"

"I got these girls up in Modesto that want me to come up there and fuck around with them. Does Manny Wolfe want to come get some pussy with me?" He giggled conspiratorially.

"Shit! Yeah, he does!" I said, "But I'm broke though."

"Quit ya bitching, fool. I got beer in the van and gas in the tank. Let's go get laid!"

"Hell yeah" I shouted.

I jumped up, grabbed some condoms and other incidentals and we headed out to Matt's van.

We did about eighty-five miles an hour all the way there and made great time, laughing and telling tall tales all the way. We arrived about two hours before dark. As we pulled to a stop across the street from the park, Matt spotted a group of guys standing by a telephone booth. With the mischief in his eyes that defined him as a person, he looked at me and said

"Watch this"

He pulled up to an abrupt stop right in the middle of the small group and jumped out the driver-side door.

"I swear to God, if I don't get to fuck these girls then I'm gonna need to find someone to box with" he said.

He looked towards the knot of guys whose loitering we had just interrupted then asked

"You guys know anyone I can whip on if I don't get lucky today?"

The group remained silent. As I exited the vehicle, I surveyed them.

"None of these guys want any shit bro!" I said grinning.

Looking at the phone booth where they were congregating, I noticed it was loose in the ground and leaning over to one side. For some reason, the thought that crossed my mind was, 'I wonder if I can tip this over?' So, I began pushing it back and forth, building up momentum as I did. The floor bolts began to creak and around them, the concrete began to turn into powder. Then, with one final heave, I toppled it in a primal gesture to warn off lesser males. It came crashing down on the ground in a glorious symphony of shattering glass and twisted aluminum. As if this were somehow a testimony to how much of a bad ass I was, I looked over the guys and said

"What, bitch?"

Then I looked back at Matt added

"Yeah, that's what I thought, these pussies don't want none!"

Matt and I strolled calmly across the street through the park. We met the girls and began passing the time in the usual way, drinking, flirting, telling more tall tales. By the time the sun began to set, we were in full swing, fairly drunk and having a good time. I remember the lights in the park coming on one by one, little sheltering pools of light against an encroaching purple-black dusk. The smell of the grass and the sound of bugs flying began to lock in the feeling of sunset and approaching night. We were feeling great.

As we were sitting together, now in two groups of two with our girls, we heard a voice in the pitch blackness between the park light glow.

"Fuck you, bitch!"

Matt turned his head towards the sound.

"Blow me!" He shouted back to no one.

---

*"Go fuck yourself, motherfucker" came sailing out of the dark a
moment later.*

"Who is that?" asked one of our girls.

"I don't know," I said, shrugging my shoulders as I looked at Matt.

*"I don't know either, but I know I'll fuck him up if he wants any
shit" he responded.*

"I fucked your mom last night, bitch!" came the voice.

"Fuck that! Let's go, Manny Wolfe!" said Matt.

He jumped up, guzzled his beer, tossed the empty can aside, grabbed another
full can in each hand and began marching into the darkness.

"Well, here we go!" I announced to the girls as I followed suit.

I remember looking back at the girl I was with saying

"Wish me luck..."

As I went to leave, I moved in quickly and kissed her for the first time.

Drawing my face back from hers, I winked and ran off to catch up with 'Matt
the Fearless.' The park was utterly dark apart from those occasional pools
of light from the lampposts. It wasn't until we actually came to the picnic
bench where the sound originated from that I saw them – all seven of them.
It was the same guys from when we first arrived. I looked on, somewhat
horrified, when Matt shouted into the group

"Which one of you pussies has the mouth?"

No one answered. Instead, they silently got up and began surrounding us. I
noticed baseball bats, a couple of chains and even a croquet mallet. These
fuckers were not fucking around. I looked at Matt.

"Maybe we should go now?" I suggested.

He looked back at me, beaming like a lunatic.

"Just a second..."

He scanned them, found the biggest one and without hesitating, threw a full bodyweight, knockout punch at the guy's chin.

It was amazing. The powerful punch knocked the would-be attacker's head back by a good two feet. His feet up lifted up into the air. He fell backwards and by the time he hit the ground, he was out cold. One down, six to go. Matt turned to me looking pleased with himself.

"O.K. Run!"

By this time, the others had surrounded us. I cut through the guy closest to me like a hot knife through butter. He never knew what was coming. The rest of them however, snapped right into action.

"Go-go-go-go-go-GO-GO!" I shouted as Matt and I ran for our lives.

I don't think I've ever run so fast ever. I was like pure adrenaline in linen pants and sandals running at full speed. I just kept repeating 'go-go-GO' to myself in my head. As I was doing my best impression of one of those desert lizards who never keep all their feet on the ground together – you know which ones I mean – I felt the occasionally swing of a bat graze my hair or blow a gentle breeze on an ear as the person wielding it tried valiantly to remove my head from my neck. Twice I felt something make contact with my shoulder but, thankfully, I was moving too fast for it to make a meaningful connection.

When a situation is developing like that, reality becomes utterly different from its normal mode. Time, as they say, slows down. A lot. I could hear each beat of my heart distinctly. I could sense the coursing of my blood through my veins. I felt no pain whatsoever in my body from the running nor from the glancing blows from the Louisville slugger so desperate to attack me.

I was so hyper focused I still remember a kids play area looming ahead of me and deliberately making the choice to run straight across it. I had time to weigh the pros and cons of running full speed across soft sand with sandals on. I found the only straight-line route through the obstacle course of play equipment. I even formulated a plan for if I should trip while in the sandbox. This last bit of deliberating proved to be invaluable because I did, in fact trip in the sand. According to the plan I'd just outlined in my head, nanoseconds earlier, I rolled with the momentum of the fall, bowing and tucking gracefully and never losing a stride.

I regained my feet and continued my four hundred yard flat-out sprint to safety. I can only imagine what my would-be assailant must have thought. One moment I was upright, running at full speed, the next I was toppling, then I was back in a fully upright position, moving at the same speed as before the spill. Must've been frustrating for him – fuck him.

I don't know how long I ran. It seemed like a second and a lifetime at the same time. Wind zipped by my head, heart fit to burst, hands swishing like blades, eyes wide open and senses sharps as razors. I could see the edge of the park nearing. Freedom! I bolted faster somehow, determined to outrun this cocksucker behind me – I was going to do this. Soon tonight's events would be an awesome story we could tell our friends in Stockton later. Perhaps we would come back in numbers and look for these park dudes. They wouldn't be hard to find, seven guys who liked jumping innocent guys who were just trying to have al fresco sex with someone's daughter.

Right smack in the middle of this narrative, I was wondering about what things would be like once I crossed the finish line, once I reached the safety of the lights, left the dangerous dark behind me, complete with the things that went bump in it, when I went down. The black asphalt of the six-lane road that outlined the park came rushing up to meet me. What the fuck was happening? I thrust my hands out and tucked my knees as you do when reacting to an unexpected fall. The asphalt bit hungrily into all the skidding flesh. Bright yellow-white pain shot up from my palms and knees, snapping me out of any kind of trance state I was in. All at once, I realized I was on the road and by that, I mean ON THE FUCKING MAIN ROAD! Traffic on this road zoomed by at sixty miles an hour.

I looked to my left just in time to see a black Ford Bronco screeching to a halt, bumper at eye level to my head. I could smell the tires burning with the friction of the sudden, unanticipated stop. (Remember just a few minutes ago when I was talking about how time slowed while I was being chased? Well, as it turns out that level of clarity does not compare to the level of clarity you experience when you're sure, I mean positive that you're going to die. How could anyone survive being hit by an American-made sport-utility vehicle doing sixty – while they were kneeling?)

I noticed everything around me all at once. Talk about a Gestalt moment! I could hear the birds in the trees, the slowing and retreating footsteps of my pursuers. I heard people in the 7-Eleven parking lot across the street remarking as they noticed the scene unfolding before them. I heard the driver of the Bronco as he whispered sharply

"Oh shit! Oh my God..."

I noticed the reflections in the chrome on the bumper, most notably my reflection, warped and distorted by the shape of the metal but reflecting a serene expression nonetheless. Looking back, I was clearly convinced of my imminent demise. There was no purpose in fear anymore. I'd die. Now, in the strangest way I can imagine, it was a perfect moment. It would just simply end. On to what's next. This has been Walter Cronkite reporting for CBS evening news. Thank you and have a good night.

Now as you may have figured out, I didn't die that day. The Bronco ground to a shuddering halt less than three inches from my kneeling body, stopping so abruptly that it rocked back and forth so close to my face that the wafts of air it made actually moved my hair. Suddenly, the perfect moment was unleashed like a terrorist bomb. The world came flooding in on me. All at once, I felt the excruciating pain of the flesh that had been ripped from my body as it skidded along the asphalt. My senses were in overload – the blinding headlights, the smell of burning tires, the grit on pavement, the taste of blood, bile and copper in my mouth. All around me, were the sounds of car horns and skidding as other drivers swerved to avoid the now stationery vehicle that had unexpectedly slammed on his brakes right before the intersection – an intersection with enormous green traffic lights urging you to keep on going – hell even speed up a little if you want.

I slowly began to move my body. Now the effects of sprinting for what was actually closer to five hundred yards (I went back and paced off the actual distance a few weeks later) began to show themselves. Every part of me hurt. Badly. My muscles were bright orange-red with pain. Everywhere a muscle connected to a bone, it felt like a dull, serrated knife had sliced part way through. My heart wouldn't slow down. I was probably hyperventilating but didn't know it – I just couldn't catch my breath. My joints all felt like they had been hit with a 'ball-pein' hammer. The real pain was my left knee because it had been the first part of me to contact the pavement.

There was a pool of blood on the ground and my pants, well, what was left of them, were soaked red-black. As I looked at the damage, I saw a chunk of flesh about the size of a quarter stuck to the ground. Gingerly, I tried to get up and let out a scream as my knee exploded in pain, sending shockwaves rippling through my body.

The Bronco driver got out of the car, looked at me and shouted

"Are you alright?"

"I can't move..." I said

As I spoke, I began to weep uncontrollably.

Just then, Matt ran up. I have no sense of how much time had passed or where Matt was before then but he scooped me up effortlessly and ran me across the street to his van.

"Wait here!" he shouted.

"Are you hurt man?"

"Badly." I said.

"Fuck this! I'm going to kill those motherfuckers!"

What I saw next I didn't fully understand until later.

'Bronco man' and Matt, without saying a word to each other turned toward the park. Bronco man got back into his car, cranked the wheel and drove at high speed straight into the park, cutting directly across the grass. He disappeared into the darkness. Matt took off his fanny pack (yup, it was the nineties and fanny packs were cool,) folded it into what was supposed to be a 'gun shape' and ran back into the park shouting

"I'll blow your fucking heads off you fucking pussies. You didn't know you were fucking with a crazy motherfucker did you?"

I sat in the van for about half an hour before Matt and Bronco man returned. As it turned out, the guys who jumped us were not very nice, as a rule, and had beaten and hospitalized Bronco man's teenaged son a week before. Matt was unable to find them and so, also unable to 'shoot them' with his fanny pack – which was probably not loaded anyway. (I did tell you Matt was crazy.)

As a parting gift, the park-jumpers left us a switchblade, which they carefully placed in Matt's rear, right tire. We didn't discover this until we made to leave. If you've ever ridden in a VW van, you know the handling is 'dicey' under the best of conditions. When you only have three tires to help you along things definitely get weird. Why did we only have three tires you ask? Well, the park-jumpers didn't just pop our tire. No. They took some time and sliced the sidewall too. There was a gash about eight inches long when we discovered it. Matt thought it would be smart to just see how far we could get with a gouged tire. As we began to drive, the tire simply removed itself from the rim as it shredded. And of course, it had to give out on the freeway as we were going seventy-five miles an hour towards the hospital to get my knee looked at.

Should you ever decide to drive a VW van at seventy-five with a ripped tire, here's the lowdown on what to expect. The steering wheel itself will become much more a 'suggestion' and less of an 'authority' on which direction you will go. This means you'll need to do a great deal of on-the-fly course correction as you shoot forward. For example, the front of your van will be facing west but the vehicle may move in a north by northwest direction or south by southwest, depending on how you position the steering wheel. Another one of the joys of a rear-wheel drive vehicle with a tireless rear-wheel is enjoying a profusion of sparks the rim makes as it comes into prolonged contact with the asphalt. These sparks will shoot out gloriously from behind your vehicle, like a magnificent rooster tail, drawing the attention of anyone within, say, a six-block line of sight.

When I hit the asphalt at the end of the chase, I landed with such force that I pulled flesh off of my left kneecap down to the bone. I could see my patella and the tendons and torn muscle that held it in place. The pain was so fantastic, so intense, that all of my skin felt hot and my hair hurt right down at the follicles. All I could do to distract myself was stare out the window. As it happened, my window had a lovely view of the tire that had been switch-bladed. I saw vanish first-hand, just after we got to the freeway, followed by the free 'light show.'

The combined effect of erratic steering and the stream of bright sparks reminded me of the way I used to take my Hot Wheels cars when I was a kid. I'd force them to skid sideways, imagining tails of fire were shooting out from them as they did. Most of us just dream it. I was now living it.

And so, we 'sailed' more than drove, at the top speed that Matt's VW van could bear, heading towards Stockton hospital. I was convinced that my recent S.S.I. medical insurance would only work there. Matt was in too much of a panic to guess otherwise.

So there we were, me screaming, Matt going too fast down the road with only three tires making contact, sparks shooting wildly out the back, making frantic, last second corrections and hoping that nothing went wrong. Somehow, we made it to the hospital and my knee was bandaged up.

For the moment, I was fine, but something was about to go very, very wrong.

II

Three weeks after my fall, I was still limping badly. Every time I breathed, pain would start at my knee and radiate outward to my extremities. I discovered that getting and staying shit-faced drunk really helped a lot and I endeavored to do so as much as possible. No big change there.

One day Charlie (of the outlaw royalty) and I were heading back from the store down the street and back to my balcony home in the bachelor apartment. It was a sunny day and we were making small talk to pass the time and distract me from the pain of my lingering injury. We were slowed by my knee as well as the case and a half of beer in tow. About three hundred yards from the stairs to my front door, I heard someone yell,

"There they are! Right there! Get 'em!"

Upon hearing this, I thought some neighborhood bad guys might treat us to some in-fighting or something. Before I had a chance to process what was happening, two cars had pulled up alongside us. One of them stopped partly on the curb, blocking our path. Seven guys jumped out and quickly surrounded us. Without saying a word, another guy got out. He was shorter than me, with thick arms and a barrel-chest.

He had a look in his eyes I've never seen before or since. The instant I made eye contact with him, everything went into slow motion once more. I saw in his eyes, pure hatred – raw, unchecked rage. All sounds became warped. I could see everything like I was moving at hummingbird speed. I was staring at evil personified. He was shaking with anger. He yelled something that sounded like he was speaking in tongues but I understood it nonetheless. His words said

"What's up white boys? What's up with the beer?"

What he really meant was

"You're going to die today, I'm going to kill you right here, right now!"

Somehow, I had time to look in the eyes of each of the others who blocked our way and saw nothing, just emptiness. They were like stone-faced demons, impassive and unyielding. Before I knew what I was doing or how, I'd grabbed Charlie by his shirt and yanked him hard toward me. I felt a huge, almost overwhelming surge of raw adrenaline, like white-hot fire, summoning every cell in my body to the same task. I pushed me towards the man who stood directly between the apartment staircase and me. I straight-armed him in the chin without skipping a beat. He fell backwards hard. We were so close to home I could see my doorknob from where I stood.

I don't know how but I was on the other side of the circle in a flash. I'd lifted Charlie up off of his feet and was dragging him behind me. He freed one of the beer bottles we were carrying and threw it into the crowd, hitting one guy in the nose. Blood spurted everywhere.

Yanking Charlie towards our door, I looked back to see the angry man reach for him. He grabbed Charlie's shirt with one hand and I felt a slight jerk. Then he punched Charlie in the chest and I heard the air leave him but I just kept pulling. I set my sights on our door and dragged Charlie along with me, never glancing back.

For some reason, none of our assailants followed us up the stairs, perhaps because our friends began spilling out of the apartment. By the time we got to the top of our stairs, I was out of breath and the pain had returned full force to my knee.

"What happened?" demanded one of our friends, Jeff.

"We got jumped just now. I don't know why. We would've given them the beer if they had asked..." I said, slightly incoherent.

Just then, Charlie had finally reached the top of the stairs, said weakly

"Dude, I don't feel so good."

He fell almost flat on his face. Jeff looked at him.

"Oh shit, man! What the hell?"

Charlie lay there, his face going pale right in front of us. Clutching his chest, blood was flowing out from beneath his shirt and pooling thickly under him.

"Call 911 NOWWW!" Jeff yelled. "Do it now! GO!!"

He fell down beside Charlie and began pressing hard on his chest. Blood was gurgling up between his fingers, climbing up his arms. 'How could there be so much blood?' I asked myself = just before I fainted.

A couple of seconds later, I came to. I could hear sirens getting closer. I looked at Charlie again. He was sheet white. He looked so small lying there. His eyes rolling gently off to one side. The worst thing I've ever seen is the life draining from the face of someone I love, leaving only the husk of them behind.

Now anger replaced nausea in me.

"Where the fuck is the ambulance?"

As soon as I said that, they pulled up. Three paramedics ran up the stairs and took over.

"What happened here?"

"He was stabbed I think. He's bleeding badly. Really badly." Jeff explained.

"We'll take it from here. Please move out of the way."

Jeff grabbed one of them by the scruff of the neck and drew him in so close their foreheads were touching.

"Don't you let him die!" he said plainly.

"We'll do everything we can. Now, please sir, move."

Jeff did not let go.

"Do. Not. Let. Him. DIE!!" he repeated then stepped back.

III

Charlie's heart would stop twice on the operating table – for long enough to be considered legally dead too. Twice the surgeon operating on him would resuscitate him, literally bringing him back to life. Charlie would bear the grizzly proof of that day for the rest of his charmed life, in the form of a long crooked scar from stem to sternum. It resembled one side of a macabre railroad track. One more length of the same track ran from the bottom of his ribcage horizontally to meet with the bottom-most end of the first.

The doctor had cut a trap door in the side of Charlie's chest, breaking and pulling back his rib cage to access his heart and lung, both of which had been nicked by the switchblade concealed in the fist of his attacker. The blade had gone in at an angle, just under the nipple and first punctured his lung, then owing to the trajectory of the blow, had turned and sliced the upper ventricle to his heart.

That explained all the blood.

The surgeon speculated the blade must have been no more than three inches long. If it had been three and a half inches, it would have severed his ventricle completely, killing Charlie instantly. Less than a half inch of steel was the difference between life and death.

Something gave way inside me after that. I was done with Stockton. It hit me all at once how crazy that city was. All of the near misses, the brushes with the law, with dangerous people, with death itself, came crashing down around me. I didn't belong here anymore. I didn't want to be here anymore.

One of my good friends, Todd, who I'd met at one of the many jobs I'd tried to hold down prior to getting onto S.S.I., had moved to Chico several years before. Every time we spoke, he would tell me how incredible it was and that I really needed to move up there. He would talk of the girls and of the parties and the general high level of fun a single guy could have there.

Being of a stubborn nature and not having any frame of reference for how things could be different somewhere else, I disregarded everything he said, until Charlie got stabbed. Suddenly, I was open to new places, new experiences. I would have gladly moved to hell's doorstep on the off chance it was slightly better than what Stockton had become in my mind.

I called Todd up and said

"I'm ready. I'm coming up there to Chico."

"Really? That's great, why the change of heart?"

"The other day, Charlie and I got jumped and he was stabbed in the heart."

"Oh shit. O.K. I'm on it. Give me a month to get everything organized."

"O.K."

Twenty-eight days later, I packed up everything I owned into my 1986 Chevelle Super Sport and Todd's Toyota pickup truck and headed up to Chico. At that time, Chico ranked as the 'Number One Party School' in the nation by Playboy Magazine.

When I pulled into town for the first time, the sun was shining brightly, there were college girls lining the streets and people actually waived at us as we drove by. I was really going to like it here. Distracted as I was by the promise of so much debauchery, I think I must have missed the sign at the entrance to the city that read 'abandon all hope, ye who enter here.' To be fair, it was probably hidden behind the wall of beer kegs that reached up to the sky.

I felt like Tom Joad when he and his family first arrived in Monterey. Chico was just girls and beer and parties and drugs and weed and parties and girls and parties and more beer as far as the eye could see. I felt like I'd struck it lucky on some kind of hedonistic lottery. It was as if the universe was saying

"You and your best friend got jumped. He got stabbed. You both survived. Now you're here. Fuck Stockton. Go nuts kid – you made it."

And, of course, I did.

CHAPTER 9

FREEFALL

I

Todd had found us a little apartment right off of The Esplanade, one of the main streets through the town. We set up shop and I began settling into my new home. It was awesome! Everywhere I turned there were people my age, partying and living the dream. Every night there was a great bar to go to for drink specials or a 'multi-beer keg party' at a new person's house.

(...I'd like to take a moment here to address those partygoers reading this book who might have done your hellraising AFTER the age of the keg. Perhaps you and your friends have all chipped in for a little pony-keg or one of those prissy little five-gallon pussy kegs of 'designer beer.' Well that's bullshit. Grow a pair, Sally! I'm talking about the old school, dull silver kegs that two big guys would struggle to carry! We could keep thirty college students drinking all night on one of them and we usually went through three or four in a night! If you're going to self-destruct, do it on concrete, not in a bed of daisies. Anyhow, back to the story...)

Chico was a living, breathing bacchanal drink-a-thon. A pulsing, undulating carnival. An enormous organism with a central nervous system composed primarily of alcohol, methamphetamines and sex. They were everywhere, all the time. Beneath the facade of the khaki-shorts preppies, the sport sandal wearing hacky-sackers, the Bob Marley white boys and the whitewashed black guys. Under the skin of the rockers, artists, rednecks and thugs was a unifying hunger. A singular, wanton urge.

When you pulled back that skin and sifted out the chaff, filtered out the tourists, those who were just dipping their toes, what remained was a licentious 'Orgy of the Damned.' Of course, you couldn't see it right away.

Like everyone else, you started on the first level. Admission to each new layer had to be earned.

Killing time with Chris at the Washout, Chico, California.

The beginning days were filled with bright sun and more beer than I thought possible. Effortlessly, I charmed my way into a big circle of friends and began to know my way around. There were of course, weekends, when Chico could no longer bear the weight of its facade and the underbelly came crashing through. It tripped over its own salivating tongue – all assholes and elbows, spilling into the streets. But for those of us in the know, every day of the week offered something decadent, some way to soak ourselves in excess.

There was 'Bear Hole,' a riverhead surrounded by easily navigated rocks and smooth, flat patches of grass and dirt. It was a meeting place for the sun worshippers among us. We would puff out our chests and the girls would arch their backs as they reclined in preening, waiting for the bold among us to approach.

Then there was the river shore area known as 'Washout,' a long, pebbled stretch of the Sacramento River. It was secluded but popular. It wasn't uncommon to arrive there during the day only to find ninety or so cars, trucks and the like, already parked. You could prop yourself up on your, or a friends tailgate, bring chairs, or simply sit in the shallow water passing the day. This spot was favored because there were only two entrances, each more than two blocks from the other and very easy to watch. When the police did arrive, which they often did, they were easily spotted and warnings could be sent down the line faster than they could travel.

Chico also boasted no less than forty-two bars, pubs and watering holes within a ten-by-ten block radius in the downtown area. In addition, there were another thirty or so, dotting the outskirts of the city. These would do promotions on certain weeknights to bring up their visibility amongst the alcoholic elite, the 'Olympic drinkers' amongst us.

On Tuesdays, there were three bars in walking distance from each other, J.B.'s, Joe's Lounge and the Final Yard, who all teamed up to offer absurd specials, one after the other. Quick to serve, mix drinks were their weapon of choice. The first bar, J.B.'s, started at six p.m., with twenty-five cent drinks until seven-thirty. Joe's fifty-cent 'well offer' ran from seven-thirty until nine. Then, the aptly named Final Yard finished strong with seventy-five cent drinks from nine until ten in the evening. Wednesday mornings were always rough. Often we wouldn't even make the Final Yard, already too wasted and opting instead to seek out a little 'chemical stimulation' instead to keep us from falling over.

But occasionally, we would prep in advance and be ready with mid-game triage, otherwise known as the amphetamine, speed. When the alcohol began to hit you in waves, from the four-ounce glasses that you would suck down as fast as the waitress would bring them, nothing brought you back to life like a nice, strong bump. 'Snort!'

"Ahhh. Ready to go again. Put me in, coach, I'm ready to play!"

If you ever got tired of the bar scene, you could always count on a rousing house party. If you knew someone who was having one, great! If not, all you had to do was walk the streets within a several block radius of the college you would have your choice of events to attend. We spent many a happy, tipsy night roaming the lettered and numbered streets of 'college town,' the informal name given to the neighborhood surrounding the Chico State Campus.

Me and the Chico locals

So, any night of the week was another opportunity – another shot at glory. You only needed to take the downtime you required, never what social limitations set upon you. Even the restrictions imposed by working a day job were offset by the raw torque and sheer virility of our youth. Some of my best friends there would revel into the late hours every night, only to rise early the next morning like some kind of genetically engineered super phoenix, never understanding they were taking from one end to shore up the other.

How could we know? We were 'golden gods' back then. I could drink a big bottle of tequila, have sex five times in a day, (even if it was with the same girl,) snort a bag of methamphetamines and smoke two packs of cigarettes. Then, without skipping a beat, I could get up and do it all over again the next day – my id dipped in testosterone, wrapped in machismo, deep-fried and sent into the world.

There is an old expression that goes something like this, 'time makes fools of us all.' In fact, there are swathes of quotes about living fast and hard while you're young and foolish enough to still think yourself invincible. All of them applied here.

II

As I hurtled at break neck speed through that wonderland, I never slowed down enough to notice the scenery was changing around me. What was once lush became a little bleaker. What was once good became a little more rotten, like wine turning to vinegar and then slowly, imperceptibly to rancid.

With my days and nights blurring as they did, I began to seek something to anchor me. I needed to feel some small sense of purpose – a punctuation in the unrelenting celebration. I began to want a little cheery light in the place of all that bland grey, so I thought to try my hand at college. In addition to the renowned state college there, Chico boasted a very good community college, known as Butte College. It was there I made my stand. I enrolled in some art classes, being somewhat skilled already – some even said gifted.

What I expected to happen was to saunter into my chosen classes and 'wow' fellow students and teachers alike with my creative talents. It did. What I didn't expect to happen was to find an even more dense population of willing girls and fellow scoundrels. At the concentration found on college campuses, the female pheromones emitted by the co-eds was simply more than my system could handle. I'd cut class to chase them, sometimes catch them and occasionally even conquer them, right on campus or in their cars.

I found drugs all over the place. I met whole new circles of friends to corrupt. It was as if someone had taken the entirety of Chico and somehow condensed its already volatile levels of angst and urgency by removing ninety-nine percent of the adults. What remained was a 'distillate.' Like when you make old corn into moonshine, it was almost too potent to be contained.

I attempted to have 'steady' (for me) girlfriends while I lived there. I even found the second great love of my life, a nice, damaged girl named Lacey. She was kind, beautiful and most importantly, she was broken enough to fall for me. We met at one of the huge parties my friends were famous for.

We were all out in a big field somewhere, or possibly some gravel driveway or something, all of us orbiting a Keystone keg that was placed unceremoniously in the center, like a flat, grey sun. The boys, most of us, drifted between the little knots of girls. They were in their slinky dresses clinging to their figures, leaving little to the imagination. They would all be standing together, facing inward, talking quickly to each other, little constellations only the fiercest comets amongst us could breach.

I'd seen Lacey before at other such gatherings. We had made eye contact, exchanged smiles but nothing more. She was pure female, all youthful feminine essence, in her little dress and bangles, high heels and ratted hair. She was all of nineteen and I was just twenty-one.

That night she somehow managed to cantilever an oversized belt, made of leather and hoops, off of one hip and secured by the apex of the other, held in place by her proud, gravity-defying derriere. The effect was very persuasive, promising ripe, juicy delights to anyone who could crack the code. It was so sweet, I could taste it from twenty feet away.

I'd previously inquired about who she was and how to get her, the response unanimous. She was 'unattainable.' Every one of my friends had tried and none had succeeded – all contenders valiantly shot down. She now held the rank of 'honorary sister' to the boys in the group. Since the guys could not gain trespass to her, they all became comically protective of her instead. Many of them warned me off of my goal, no doubt thinking this gawky, chivalrous gesture could potentially ingratiate them to her and thereby earn them another 'chance.' And so it was, with no small amount of upset to the status quo, that I walked boldly up to this 'un-gettable' girl, there in the midst of several of her girlfriends and in the eye of all the other guys said to her

"Hi, I'm Manny. You're Lacey, right?"

Before she could answer, I grabbed her in my best impression of a Hollywood silver screen heartthrob, looked deep at her for a couple of seconds, then, turning her gently, I kissed her. Not lightly, not tentatively, no, I kissed her as though we had just saved the world together. As though I'd been searching for her through lifetimes and galaxies – as though she were mine to kiss. She kissed me back, matching me ounce for ounce in passion and need – and more besides.

Her friends were speechless, standing in a circle around us, gaping like buffoons. They watched as the kind of embrace all young girls dreamed about took place right in front of them. Lacey and I kissed the way they wished they could be kissed – but never thought they would be. It was happening, right there within arm's reach but not for them. I shifted her back to an upright position and she stared at me silently for a moment, then, in a windswept voice said

"Hi."

We were together for six years after that night.

III

Of course, she was destined to be another casualty of my downward spiral, just as I was destined to be a casualty of hers. If there is one great truism about relationships, it's this – 'like really does attract like, like it or not.' We stick with the people whose strengths or weaknesses match with our own.

Lacey and I were no exception to this rule.

We were toxic for each other because we were both highly toxic. I put her through hell with my cheating and drug abuse, as the Moral Man inside me looked on horrified. She, on the other hand, was like a tempestuous character, straight out of a Robert Louis Stevenson novel. Most of the time she was a good girl, even a good wife when the time came. But unlike me, who wore my darkness out in the open like some sort of badge of honor, she kept hers hidden most of the time, until she could contain it no longer.

There were times when it did come bursting to the forefront and when it did, the abused little girl, now in an irresistibly sexy young woman's body transformed into a demented kitten with a bazooka. Her inner demons, unleashed by alcohol, came bounding out on some bizarre, destructive nighttime errand. These nights were called 'girl's nights.'

I quickly learned to dread them.

On one of her girl's nights, she and her friend April got all dolled up to have cocktails together. April was a hard-drinking, quick-to-fuck, type of girl, to whom men flocked. I hated Lacey spending time with her. On this particular night, April called me less than two hours after they left. I was sitting at home with a couple of friends when the phone rang.

"Hello?" I answered.

"Manny?"

"Yeah, who's this?"

"It's April. Manny, you'd better get down here, Lacey is really drunk and she's acting crazy. I'm kinda worried about her."

"Goddamn it, not again! Where are you?" I barked into the phone.

"You know the 7-Eleven downtown?"

"Yeah. Is that where you are?"

"Yeah. We're out front."

"I'll be right there."

I hung up the phone, grabbed the keys and headed down there, explaining

"You guys stay here. I need to go get Lacey..."

I looked back at my friends sitting on my couch. It was understood amongst us I always did this task alone.

I got to the 7-Eleven about fifteen minutes later. I saw a crowd of college boys making a semi-circle around something. I knew just where I'd find my girl. Squaring up my shoulders, I pushed through the press of horny, drunken frat boys to find Lacey there, lying on the ground, her shoulders and head up against the wall. She was giggling and mumbling nonsense, still holding a mostly full 40 oz. bottle of Mickey's Malt Liquor. Her already short skirt was hiked up unceremoniously to her hips. Her panties were slightly lowered. She looked a total mess. Her hair was ruined. Her makeup was smeared. Despite all that, as she lay there, she was grinning.

Sensing the mood of the group of guys surrounding us, I shot April a black look, walked up to Lacey without saying a word and lifted her over my shoulder. She began kicking and flailing her arms wildly as I carried her towards the wall of onlookers. As I approached, some of them called out

"Don't be dick, let the girl stay!"

"Yeah man, she obviously doesn't want to go with you! Fucking let her stay!"

One of them moved to block me as I made my way to the car, girl in hand. I grabbed him by the hair, pulled his face right up to mine and screamed in it as loudly and menacingly as I could – a scream that came from the depths of hell itself. It must've worked, because when I released him, he stumbled backward and fell onto his ass, scrambling away from me.

In a fit of strength and surprising coordination, I reached the car, opened the door, poured her in, slammed the door shut and got in the driver's side. As I started to drive away, somebody's Big Gulp drink cup hit the rear right side of our car and splattered loudly. I stuck my hand out the window and, using the only sign language I knew, I told them to go fuck themselves.

Lacey was incoherent all the way home. She would randomly lash out kicking and hitting me. I wrestled her into a hard wristlock, using her hand to pin her body firm against the passenger-side door and forced her to sit still. After a few minutes, she calmed down, so I relaxed my grip. We were navigating the one-way street area of downtown Chico, when suddenly, she lunged a hand out, grabbed the steering wheel and yanked it hard. Before I knew it, we were aiming the wrong way down a one-way street on a Saturday night, right around midnight.

Having no other choice, I put the high beams on, slowed down and drove down the bike lane, forcing a steady stream of oncoming vehicles to swerve, stop or have an accident – their choice. I was furious beyond comprehension but miraculously we weren't pulled over and I got us home safe.

I never figured out what happened to her that night, what she took or how much she drank. April reported that she 'just slipped' into that state as they were out at a club having drinks. One minute she was fine, the next she just came undone. Sadly, this wasn't uncommon. The fact of the matter was that every time she went out with her girlfriends she came back in a similar condition.

IV

I was far from a victim in this situation even though I played one when it fitted my needs. For every one of Lacey's episodes, there were a slew of indiscretions from me. Quantity and quality of let downs – that was us. I stayed out all night, lied without regard to anything, chased and bedded other women as often as possible and was generally a scoundrel. I somehow managed to keep the infidelities from her, though for the life of me, I don't know how. I could not have been more brazen about it. I think I was only saved by a combination of the 'bro-code' (thou shalt not tell) and a general level of jealousy other girls had for Lacey, based solely on her looks and the fact we were together. Indeed, many of my dirty little conquests were girls right in our group.

One night, I was at a party. Lacey had stayed home. I was in the bathroom with one of the girls from the group, me behind her, my pants at my knees, her skirt up around her hips, undies moved to the side. She supported the weight of my tired, tingling body. As we hung there, breathing heavy, she said, almost inaudibly

"Now, I've had him too, Lacey!"

She smirked at me as I left the bathroom went back downstairs and chugged a beer bong.

Unlike Suzie and me, Lacey and I fought like cats and dogs when we were not fucking. We exploded at each other at parties, she, storming off with girlfriends, me stomping around in full tantrum mode, growling at people or grabbing them by the throat for no good reason, pushing them against walls.

I used our constant rows as convenient justification for my ever-increasing meth consumption and erratic behavior. I'd run to my friends, get exceedingly high and weave bitter, self-pitying monologues about how 'no one could be expected to live like me, suffering these injustices as I did.'

Those crazy days when I didn't even realize I was on the edge of a razor, were the days when the methamphetamines slowly, insidiously, took control. Meth started as such a good friend, always willing to help keep things going smoothly. But like Eddie and his rabble-rousing, it began to whisper things into my ear, little-by-little, infiltrating the very marrow of my being. It swapped out my friends for doppelgangers, macabre shades of those close to me.

Meth did bring me new friends. O.K., perhaps not 'friends,' think of them more like fellow travelers, others I met along the way. We made common cause and confused that for friendship. Alas, there was none of the glue of real friendship, so alliances would change quickly. Trust was scarce, even among those with whom I spent most of my time.

These new 'compatriots,' I suppose they were, had more of a cast to them of where I was going and less of where I'd been. They were made grotesque by it – often seeming more like malevolent demons and imps, than men to me.

Meth swapped the women I'd encounter from those who, at least insisted on beds and music, to urgent, fetid wretches who wanted it anywhere, anyhow. So desperate were we for our equivalent of meaningful human contact, fueled by the sexual primacy created by our shared condition, a dumpster near a road would suffice. Standing up, back pressed against filth, skirt pushed aside. Just get it inside her. Do it now. Condom. No condom. Shut up and suck it. Bend over. I just need to fuck, now! Never mind the risk, the cars driving by honking, the people on the street, any of it.

Meth replaced Lacey. She would not be the last of all I'd lose but she was certainly the most memorable, most bitter, in the losing, even then, only in hindsight. I finally pulled ahead in our race to the bottom with the help of my new friend, 'Speedy.' She simply couldn't compete.

I'd stay out for days at a time and then come home falsely repentant, swearing never to do it again. I'd talk her through her sorrow and her fears gently. After, I would have her dress in whatever lingerie I'd been thinking of her in while I was gone, then fuck her slowly and deeply for what seemed like hours as she wept. When I finished, I'd hold her close until we fell asleep. Within a day or two, I'd start the whole cycle over again until she disintegrated like sand through my fingers.

No one had yet taught me anything of words like 'co-dependence,' or 'dysfunction' and for my part, I loved her dearly. For all of the explosions and bizarre behaviors, we were very close and deep in our own version of love. If it was muddled or warped, it was only because neither of us were given the right tools for the task – not for a lack of sincere desire. For every moment of chaos we shared, there were many of bliss and I count her as a person whose soul I was able to glimpse the truth of.

IV

You really can't know what parts of yourself you are willing to bargain away until the devil makes you the right deal. But contrary to popular belief, he doesn't deal with just any one. No, you must come to him, one compromise at a time, inch-by-inch, until you find yourself far from where you came and what you knew. When your humanity itself is in question is when he makes his entrance. You can't meet him until you pass through all nine circles of Dante's hell, from 'limbo,' to 'il tradimento' – treachery. 'That which we commit to others is nothing compared to that which we commit upon ourselves.'

Chico had become a shadow city for me. The same place that welcomed me with bright sunshine and tree-lined streets, friendly girls and parties every night, had become a strange, nightmare landscape, a bit more 'abandon all hope, ye who enter here.'

Perhaps, I'd brought that sign with me when I arrived?

The last year I spent in Chico was the lowest point of my life, the darkest time I have ever known. Sadly, due to the grip amphetamines can have on you, I didn't even comprehend the position I was in. It was a freefall.

I was homeless most of the time, living out of boxes hidden at friends' houses and out of bags hidden on my person. I was increasingly surrounded by guns and the type of people who liked to carry them. I'd become some sort of string puppet, imitating in gross parody, the rhythms of the life I used to live. Still strutting and boisterous, fed on nothing yet full to bursting with misplaced pride.

In appearance, I resembled something ghoulish. My eyes were wild, yellowing and sunken, with dark bags under them. My long hair, once luxurious, was now coarse and unkempt and resembled an unruly mane. My cheeks were hollow and my skin sallow and uneven. I took on a multitude of nervous ticks, from fingers to tongue to shoulders and head, all moving to their own odd, faltering tempo.

I must have seemed like skin stretched too tight over electricity and bone, somehow animated, moving herky-jerky through space.

This was my normal state that led up to the day that signaled the end of that life. That was day that I was arrested, the day that ultimately lead me to the long car ride back to Stockton, in the company of two strangers and one familiar though long-estranged companion. He who I put behind a glass wall while I made my catabasis, that long, slow descent into my own private hell, ultimately to face off with the devil. I was about to step into the ring knowing only one of us was coming out again.

He, who watched all of this unable to act on his or my behalf, was the Moral Man.

CHAPTER 10

PRODIGAL SON

I

Mom had no idea that I was on my way back to her, spending the dark hours on the freeway from Chico to Stockton. In the backseat, I watched the reflections of the road stripes fly overhead on the rear window, like silent grains of sand counting the seconds until I was home. My brain was stuck in a loop, replaying all that had just happened, plus all that happened in the last year, the last five, the last twenty.

I didn't realize how emotional I was until the girls I was riding with pulled up to mom's house. I tried to thank them for their kindness. Instead, where words were supposed to be, there were only stinging, hot tears. As soon as I tried to speak, I simply broke down. They had no idea I am aware of about why I was even riding with them in the first place. They only knew that they were doing me and my friend Kevin – the one who arranged my transport – a favor.

I can only imagine what they saw in my face as I tried to say goodbye. What I do know is that the driver stopped the engine, they both got out and hugged me hard and long as I wept there, clutching two small cardboard boxes that held all I had to show for the eight years I'd been gone. These two girls, in a redemptive act of human goodness, simply held me without asking questions or saying anything.

They held me until I quietened. I pulled my head gently away and choked out the words

"Thank... you..."

I tried to drag myself back into some semblance of solid human form, then walked up, knocked on mom's front door and waited for her to answer. When she did, when I saw her face, surprised and grasping for what my unannounced arrival meant, I looked at her and simply said

"I'm done."

She moved to embrace me. I dropped my worldly possessions at my feet, hugged into her and cried all over again. I cried for myself, for Lacey, for everyone I'd wronged, for the pain we all must endure, for humanity itself.

I cried like a baby in the arms of mom.

I'd like to say that my early sobriety days were akin to a phoenix, rising magnificent, fresh and renewed from the ashes. In some sense, those days were. I began to gain much needed weight and the color returned to my skin. Slowly, I took on the appearance of a human once again. Yet, the deeper emotional process was never that graceful for me. Many people I knew, many people I saw during those days did have such a beautiful transformation – elegant and streamlined it seemed. I watched with wonder as they simply reintegrated into straight life, finding jobs and partners, making friends and laying down roots.

Perhaps that was just how it looked to me, everyone else motoring along with minimal effort, while I fought for every inch of ground. Maybe it was easy for them, or possibly, they just were good at hiding their personal struggles? In any case, I didn't know it at time. Part of the reason things were so slow for me was because I had much more to reckon with than I originally imagined. I began to suspect I had more to reckon with than most.

In those early days, the rooms where those alcoholics or narcotics anonymous (A.A. / N.A.) meetings took place, the coffee shops where we would congregate, even the simple proximity to others who had accrued more clean time than I had, were little oases to me. They were tiny alcoves against a torrent of submerged emotions that had been wrested free when I cut off the supply of what kept them restrained – namely drink and drugs. I clung to those places and their good Samaritans, for fear of being swept away back into the frenzied life I used to live.

I'd scurry to-and-fro between venues, waiting as it were, for low tide to make my way safely from one to another and back to mom's house, where I could hide. I'd bury my head and shut out everything while the movies in my mind played on an endless repeat. It seems only from this distance, this vantage point, could I let myself feel the insanity of the old life I'd just recently left. While I was in the midst of it, there was no time or opportunity for such musings.

I became addicted to recovery. I got not one but two sponsors. First was mom's boyfriend, Larry. He was a small Mexican man with a big grin and a proud mustache. He and mom had gotten sober together and taken up running as a couple. By the time I came in out of the cold, they were both accomplished runners and because of his skill, Larry always walked with a light springy gate. He had a wry twinkle in his eyes I really loved.

The second sponsor, Teddy, was an ex-gang-banger from Atlanta. He was like a superhero to me during that time. There was nothing I could say about my past that impressed him, so bragging was out of the question. Once, when I was trying to sound important in front of him, he simply looked at me and said

> *"Man, you need to save your stories for the National Enquirer.*
> *When I was your age, I was gorilla pimpin' ho's out da side*
> *door and chump–stampin' punks and stuffin' them in the trunk.*
> *Go find you somebody who gives a fuck!"*

I did all of my recovery step work with gusto and energy usually reserved for the 'born again' I was, not in any religious sense but a new man nonetheless. I'd never felt so good.

II

Most people, when they find themselves in a twelve-step program, assuming they can keep themselves away from whatever brought them there to begin with, struggle with two things. First, the idea of a power greater than themselves and second, completing the infamous Fourth step.

The twelve steps are a system for integrating a new set of spiritual principles, which, when applied rigorously, can free a person from the tyranny of compulsion. Now, if you're reading this and thinking it sounds suspiciously like religious rhetoric, you're not alone. In fact, though the system is patently non-religious many newcomers stumble, even fall, when confronted with the idea of 'a power greater than themselves' – a power, it's suggested, they must 'come to believe' in.

You could view the Fourth step as the first real-life step to securing long-lasting freedom from addiction. This can prove to be a bitter pill for many to swallow. I watched as many of those who I knew from my time in recovery, struggled with this concept. Some of them ultimately rejected the entire program outright on the basis of this single suggestion.

I myself might not have chosen such a direction, were it not for the fact I'd so recently been privy to such darkness. As it was, I was willing and able to grasp at the heart of the intent of this Fourth step. I saw with clarity the words offered access to the essence of what needed to happen but the meaning was not held within the individual words themselves. Besides which, I have always been a mischievous wordsmith and enjoyed pondering what it could mean.

So, I glided smoothly over that first hurdle, past the Second and Third steps and onto the Fourth. I recalled those recovery friends fell at this step. The Fourth step requires us to 'make a searching and fearless moral inventory of ourselves.' In short, we must delve back through time, dredge up every encounter, every interaction with another person where we felt slighted, cheated, or wronged in any way and write them out in detail. A laundry list of the sins committed against us, as it were. My list contained no less than 248 people who I felt were the cause of nearly one thousand 'infractions.' Carrying all this resentment around with me for so long, it's no wonder I had a chip on my shoulder.

Most people find this to be a very disagreeable task. So much so that A.A. is littered with members having multiple years of clean time who have not completed this step. White knuckling it as the saying goes, I could not get to it fast enough. I was promised that there would be a sense of relief and release at the other end of that step and I wanted it. I wanted that peace, just like the others who do the work.

And so I did 'the work.' I dug deep into my memory, searching out everyone I could ever remember holding a grudge against, no matter how obscure, old or random the transgression. I left it all out there on those pieces of yellow legal paper, 10 pages in all, each one covered with the wrongs committed against me.

I slit my wrists on those sheets.

When the bleeding was done, I had trapped a homunculus there in the ink. It was the part of me that was all rage and hurt, the part that vacillated between aggressive and self-destructive. I kept him caged in a manila folder after I finished. I was waiting for Larry to help me with the fifth step, the one where I shared all of it – the entire list – with another human being.

If writing the Fourth step is like slitting your wrists, then sitting down and completing the Fifth step is like asking someone else to clean it up for you. You must confess everything. That's the entire point of it. You put it all out in the open in the hope of forgiveness. You strip down naked and exposed, before another human being, whose only 'qualification' for being there is the fact they have been through a similar trial.

But that's the magic.

Addicts and alcoholics are creatures of secrecy, darkness and deceit. Both from themselves and from others. Defiance is the calling card of the addictive personality. Therefore, admitting the exact nature and amount of our secret grudges, vendettas, resentments and intentions, openly and honestly to another, constitutes in itself a supreme act of contrition. This in itself can be potent enough to free us.

It was certainly this way for me, although I didn't have the revelation I was hoping for that the Fifth step promised, until the very last name on my list was read out loud. When it finally came, it was like the moment of clarity that I'd had Chico. Standing there with a gun in my hand, realizing I wasn't going to kill anyone. It just all became clear. First, it wasn't and then it was.

The big truth, the grand epiphany in all of this, was that I'd had a part in all of it. Everything, every single event I'd written on that list I'd participated in some way. Every person who wronged me was triggered by my need for the feeling of martyrdom.

As Eleanor Roosevelt famously said, 'no one can make you feel inferior without your consent.'

All at once, I saw how I might begin to have a different life if I started making different choices. I understood how reframing my deep identity could help me to step out of the need to play the victim or the aggressor in order to get a feeling of significance. When I gained this understanding, sitting there in the coffee shop, across from the little twinkling-eyed Mexican man with the proud moustache, I lost the fear I'd somehow wind up drunk again, or high on speed, without knowing how it happened.

I lost that fear. That said, contrary to the popular feeling of getting over the 'big hurdle' of recovery experienced by many of my fellows, I had a profound sense the work – the real work – had only just begun.

III

As I dived deeper into the recesses of my own soul through my step work, guided by my sponsors, I'd wrestle free anything dark and menacing I found and dragged it back to the surface for examination in daylight. In my mind, this was a life – or death – process. As a result, I pulled no punches and was disciplined with myself.

I became something of an invisible man, not in the sense that I went unnoticed but in the sense that I hid nothing inside myself. I adopted an attitude of total transparency with those around, asking others to feel free to share any observations about me they thought I might be able to learn from. I became the human equivalent of an open letter, a walking suggestion box. This was a very eye-opening experience and definitely not for the faint of heart!

I learned lots about myself through that process. Also, I learned more about other people. You can tell a lot about someone by how they treat others when they think there are no consequences. I took everything, the good, the bad, the ugly, the oddly personal and vindictive, the totally inappropriate or irrelevant – all of it. I took it and found a way to extract value from it. I'd not trade that painful protracted experience for the world, but I'd never, ever volunteer to do again either!

The reason I entered into this self-inflicted, agonizing experiment was because as I integrated myself into the recovery community around me, I began to notice certain unsettling behaviors from my fellows. They developed tendencies towards a certain level of apathy in their spiritual growth and I feared that for myself. I feared that was the reason why people who seemed to be doing just fine for years on end, suddenly found themselves drunk or high again out of the blue.

Somehow, I just knew, if I should find myself out in the grips of my addiction again, I'd not survive. I was not going to let that happen. I'd much sooner open myself completely to the judgment of others, whether they were fit to the task or not, than ever, under any circumstances, let myself use drink or drugs again.

IV

There is a period in early recovery known as the 'pink cloud.' It refers to the state of euphoria experienced by newly sober people. It's something that most newbies experience and it feels great. It's a time when a newcomer can get a lot done and set the tone for their recovery. Oddly though, when those with lots of clean time under their belts see someone in the midst of the pink cloud, they are frequently dismissive and even smug about it.

'Oh, she's happy now but that's just the pink cloud. Give her some time. It'll wear off' and other comments like that regularly followed newcomers around, though too quietly to be heard.

Much to my good fortune, when I hit this phase, someone was thoughtful enough to say to me, 'kid, what you're feeling is the pink cloud, it doesn't last forever but while it's there it's great, so make the most of it!'

Being the willing pupil I was, I took that advice to heart. My own pink cloud lasted about two years, during which time I was immensely productive. In addition to doing all of the twelve steps with my sponsors, going to multiple meetings a day and reading the two main A.A. texts cover to cover many times over, I went to the gym five times a week, took up the bass guitar, produced many high-quality art pieces, found work at the grocery store. I even got a girlfriend for a while.

I felt like a warrior. I had never known such an empowered, energized feeling in my life. A whole new side of myself was emerging. I felt unstoppable. I remember one day in the midst of this sustained surge of optimistic productivity, thinking back to the dream I'd had when I was a

Setting the mood with my glittery shirt

boy, where I was finally able to fight back against all the white-outlined assailants that had me surrounded against the red mist. I smiled and chuckled to myself for the recollection, because I realized I was living that dream in real life.

V

Perhaps it is just human nature that most of us cease to explore when our discomfort stops. We find a comfortable nook somewhere in the machinery of modern life and begin settling, often by degrees. We no longer seek whatever might lay just over the next rise. Perhaps it is also human nature that the ones who do not stop seeking become strange looking – unrecognizable – to those for whom mollification of desire has been confused with happiness, like two divergent species from the same genus.

As it turned out, I was of the exploring species, especially when the dream to be explored was that of human nature. I'd always been prone to philosophical tangents, even as a boy. And I found the spiritual component of the A.A. lifestyle served as a catalyst for my natural curiosity. I'd take one idea, one suggestion at a time and slaver over them, like a dog with a particularly tasty bone. I'd turn something over-and-over in my mind, finding where it sat most comfortably in my heart, my soul. I'd closely examine the way it interrelated with the one before it and the one after it.

I read the basic text of the recovery community repeatedly, going through first one then the other, starting again as soon as I finished. In this way, I read both the 'Big Book' and the '12 x 12' more than one hundred times each three-year period. Long after I completed all of the twelve steps, I continued to dig into the concepts. I was in what the great writer Douglas Adams refers to as the 'long, dark teatime of the soul,' a time when my focus was turned profoundly inward.

VI

I spent a great deal of time back then with my family, reuniting and getting to know each other after our long hiatus. By the time I left for Chico, it seemed to me that my role within the family had been firmly established. I was the lost boy and the oldest child. I lived my life in a way that was mythic, doing things that must've seemed like they were out of a teen-party movie, like my life was a beer commercial.

When I came back from taking this lifestyle as far as I could, broken and hollow from my absurd, child-like under-estimation of the destructive power of the forces I was playing with – addiction, demoralization, self-loathing – what I wanted and needed was to be brought back into the fold. More than anything, I needed to be met where I was, seen for the veteran I was of the ravages I faced and the work I was putting in to fix the damage done.

I had high hopes and expectations of the way I would be treated by the family I had so often put on pedestal while in the depths of my addiction, secretly using them as a tether to reality during the most 'untethered' times of my life.

I think I built them up in my mind to be 'more than human.'

There was mom, the phenomenal chef, famous in her own right, with the published cookbook to her credit - a rockstar chef before they were the rage. My brother Greg, away on the other side of the country finishing his master's degree in theater arts, undoubtedly on the cusp of being discovered and made famous. My sister Annabel, the musical prodigy who was training at the prestigious University of the Pacific Music Conservatory. James, my youngest brother would, without question, outshine them all in whatever it was he decided to do.

Dad was the closest, in fact, to being actually famous or world-class. He was a brilliant musician who had recorded and released albums. He'd worked with some of the greatest names in jazz. His debut album, 'First Date' became a top ten hit.

Then, there was me, the sad martyr.

Somehow, all the talent in my family seemed to miss me, so I lived the way I did, content to be the shiniest among pennies, sad and forlorn even while happy. There were of course my illustration abilities. In my mind though, these were no contest to the gifts of the others, barely a skill set at all and certainly not worthy of praise.

This was the backstory I had in my head when I reunited with my family.

I'd been telling it so long I'd begun to believe it myself. There was little chance of them ever living up to the legend I'd created of them, especially when they had no idea of it to begin with. I, likewise, began to sense they had created a 'myth' around me. I began to realize I'd been cast, in my absence, into the role of the 'black sheep of the family' – the prodigal son and brother.

VII

Upon my return home, mom would take me around to the places she liked to go, flitting and fluttering whenever a young shop girl or barista she knew would help us. Grinning and twinkling, she'd quip 'This is my son. He's with me.' putting me on display. Amongst the flattery and preening, I could feel a small, curdling sensation I could not place at the time but I now recognize. It was just like I was seven again, earning points from mom with my face.

My sister, who only ever knew me as the over-protective big brother – the one who pushed Mark Jackson off of the monkey bars and broke his arm after he made her cry at school – would introduce me to all of her friends, then gently guide the conversation towards details of the crazy life I'd just left behind. She seem to bask in the reflected glory of my exploits of the 'crash and burn' years or take strange comfort in making a show of magnanimous empathy for all I'd endured.

My youngest brother, James, had turned from a child into a young man during my absence, so he didn't really know what to expect of me, or for that matter, I of him.

My middle brother, Greg, as I mentioned, had been away at school.

After a short while, I came to understand a lot had occurred on the 'home front' while I'd gone roaming far and wide. I was not the only one who had developed some self-destructive habits. It was mom after all who introduced me to A.A. When I returned to Stockton, to my family, I learned some reasons why mom had entered in the program the first place. I sort of knew the reasons already and yet, had managed to ignore and normalize them.

While she was still in the commune, mom had met the great love of her life. It was not my dad but the father of my siblings. A small, bright, hippy-intellectual type named Phil. They were sort of an 'it' couple within the group and the closest with Stephan, the founder, of the commune and his wife, Iris. While in the commune, Phil also met the great love of his life, not mom, mind you, but Iris.

I don't know how long she and Phil we're seeing each other before they came out in the open with it but when they did it shattered mom. I do not believe she's ever fully gotten over it – even to this day. The reality of the man she thought was her 'soulmate' and best friend leaving her for her other best friend after she'd had three of his children was more than she could bear. She went into a tailspin lasting for several years.

Every night during those years, she would take a bath while we were going to bed. In the bath, she would have a big can of beer with her. What I didn't know until many years later was after we kids fell asleep, she'd get dressed and go out to some bars with a couple of her girlfriends, leaving us sleeping alone in the house. I do not know the full extent of what went on while she was out or how much she drank but I do know that my relationship with her during that time went from bad to impossible.

I believe she was trying to drink away the profound grief and anger that she felt about what had happened. Consequently, she and I found ourselves on opposite sides of every conceivable issue. She was drinking and distracted, not really there, which in turn made me rebel by drinking and distracting myself, in an attempt to deal with my own incomprehensible grief and anger. It was a vicious circle with a sharp downward tilt to it.

She was brokenhearted and dazed. In truth, she was barely functioning at all, left there with four children, forced to watch as her husband shifted his focus and his life over to another woman who happened to be her best friend. Better women than her have turned to the bottle for much, much less.

Many years later, I'd watch Phil die, that's to say I'd speak to him only hours before his death, as he lay there wasting away with a rare form of bone marrow cancer, looking like blotchy, translucent paper. For the only time I can recall, he told me that he loved me and I said the same to him. To the best of my knowledge, he never expressed an apology to mom for what he'd done to her.

Within the communal group, mom was perceived in many ways, thanks to her husband's choices. She was an object for sympathy and pity. She became a martyr, a newly available potential sex object, even the recipient of some judgment and scorn. It isn't possible, perhaps, to overstate the damage done to her and her children by this one act. Though it was 'done' to her, we all suffered. For my part, I was denied any opportunity to know the real, authentic version of mom, free from the effects of Phil's affair.

I think though, I had an easier ride compared to what my sister and youngest brother went through. Not only did they get the same as me, a disconnection from a real mom, they witnessed all of her falling down disgraces and humiliating displays from front row seats. Once when I was home from Chico for the holidays and having not yet announced my arrival, I happened to see mom coming out of a pizza parlor near her house. I was sitting in the passenger seat of a car of a local girl I liked spending time with when I was in town.

I was sitting there waiting for my friend to come out of liquor store next to the pizza place, when mom came teetering out of the door with the pizza in a box, held up with one hand. It was dusk, more dark than light. She was wearing dark glasses. I watched silently and she weaved her way to her car, pizza box threatening to fall. She misstepped, one foot going off of the curb. The box tipped and fell, spilling some of the pizza out onto the ground. Seeing this, she simply wobbled her way to the ground, picked up the liberated slices off the gritty floor, put them back into the box and kept walking.

My heartbreak at that moment was exquisite. When my friend reappeared, I had tears running down my cheeks. She, seeing this, put her arm around me and asked me

"What's wrong baby?"

"It's nothing." I said." I'm fine. Let's go."

As we pulled out of the parking lot, I was discreetly watching in the rear-view mirror as a little car swerved its way toward the street.

During the time I lived in Chico, things got to the point with mom's drinking that my sister felt obligated to care for James, essentially raising him for a time. Whether or not the reality of the situation matched the impression in the hearts and minds of my little sister and brother is unknown. As far as they were concerned, mom had turned her back on them. Only able to focus on the devastation she felt, she left them in the woods to fend for themselves – to survive or to perish.

It was Annabel, not really, a woman yet herself who taught James about things like sex, looked after his food and chores and played mom to him.

Not surprisingly, she built up a huge resentment for this, as did my brother. To this day, my sister is hypervigilant about anything she perceives as another person putting her into a position where she is obligated to them. So deeply has she been affected by this, it has touched every relationship in her life. She has not found forgiveness strong enough to release her from the pain she felt.

Since I did not know then how to see past my own nose, how could I understand what I was coming home to? My only focus was my own catastrophic spectacle. For my part, I was too blind to see that mom, several years into her sobriety, was a slave to her grief. First for the wounds inflicted upon sister and brother, compiled with the wounds inflicted on herself and those of her husband. All of this stemming from the one jugular act, his selfish and reckless decision to abandon his family to blindly follow his heart.

A thing of this size, of these mammoth proportions, can't long go unnoticed in something as small as a family. And so, after a time, what was a happy reunion returned to its dismal equilibrium point, only now with me in the equation as well. It came to pass the contrast between our group dynamics, festering and resentful and the tools and concepts I was learning in my recovery practice, took on too strong an oil and water quality for me. I began to argue with mom regularly, though I could not identify the underlying reasons why. I began to simply spend less time in the company of mom and my siblings.

Though I clearly sensed something unhealthy, something toxic in the air, I could not say then what it was. This inability to articulate, to give a name to the situation, became like a room with no doors for me. A claustrophobic prison and I found myself plunging deeper into the spiritual teachings of A.A. as a shelter from it. I was looking for a way to understand what I was seeing in my family.

CHAPTER 11

A FANTASTICAL REPRIEVE

I

During my first few months of recovery, I'd also been meeting with my new P.D. about my drug charges and pending court date. When I went to meet him the first time, only a few days after coming back to Stockton, I was still terrified about almost having gone to prison. I walked into his office and began immediately babbling about how hard I was working trying to make changes in my life. I told him all about going to meetings, being sober and anything else my sizzling little mind could spit out in my defense.

He sat there looking at me amused. After a minute or two of my rambling, he raised his hand, as if to signal me to stop. Once we had regained sweet silence in his office, he asked me simply

"What are A.A.'s first three steps?"

I rattled off

"We admit we were powerless over alcohol... our lives have become unmanageable... we believe a power greater than ourselves could..."

By the time he raised his hand again for me to stop, I'd nervously gotten to around step eight or nine.

He smiled at me.

"How do you know about the twelve steps?" I asked.

In response, he reached into the collar of his shirt, pulled out a fine chain until it revealed a medallion. The medallion had number '15' stamped conspicuously into the center of a square. I'd recognize that coin anywhere – it was a 15-year sobriety chip. He mentioned an A.A. 'insider secret.'

"I'm a friend of Bill W. too" he said and smiled at me yet again.

Then, he told me he would make a deal with me. If I'd agree to go to meetings, collect signatures at the end of each meeting on the sheet of paper he provided and come to see him every month, all the way in Chico, he would, in turn, work as hard as he could between then and my court date to make sure that I'd be O.K. I agreed gladly.

I left our meeting feeling lightheaded and excited. I'd never expected to like a lawyer, unless of course they were buying drugs from me.

I did all he asked of me and more. In addition to everything he stipulated, I called him every couple of weeks, just to check in. I was determined not to waste the chance he was giving. I'd do everything in my power to prove to him that I was serious about turning my life around.

Those trips to Chico to check in with my P.D. were punctuations of solitude to the run on sentence my life had become. While I was in Stockton, my days and nights were filled with meetings, coffee shop visits with other members and some old friends – the ones who I felt safe visiting – reading and doing step work. There were meeting with sponsors and family time. I was almost never alone. When my meetings with the lawyer did come, I drove solo the four-and-a-half hours from Stockton to Chico, had my meetings, then turned around and headed straight back.

I had to borrow other people's cars. Often there would be no tape player, only radio. I'd wind up talking to my Higher Power or praying out loud for miles at a time.

When the day of my court hearing arrived, I was feeling very confident. It was a beautiful, sunny late-spring day, the kind other places dream about and California takes for granted. I got up early, made some coffee, packed up the snacks I'd prepared the night before, put on my best suit and tie then hit the road.

The sky was blue with big, puffy cotton ball clouds. The birds were singing. It never occurred to me that things might 'go wrong' on such a beautiful day. I got to the courthouse and checked in at the window. I was told my case would not be heard until after lunch, so I decided to hang out in front of the building for a while. Once the lunch recess came and went, I filed in to the courtroom with everyone else and took a seat. I watched with wonder as the parade of the unrepentant shuffled up to the judge's bench, one by one.

I don't know the reason, but defendant after defendant stood before the judge that day, inappropriately dressed, with bad posture and terrible manners, making the judge more and more irritable as the long afternoon wore on. At one point the bailiff reprimanded one defendant who actually and answered with a loud 'YO!'

The judge was not lenient on him.

The sunlight that was filtering in through the dirty courtroom windows was dropping slowly as I sat and waited my turn. I'd seen my lawyer in the lobby just before we entered for the afternoon session. He was in high spirits about our chances. My own mood, alas, began to sink as the sun did. It just didn't seem like it should have taken this long to get to me. All the waiting was working its way under my skin.

At some point, I begin to notice the room was emptying out. One person after another was leaving, some out of the front doors, others in handcuffs off start their sentences. Four-thirty rolled around and still my name had not been called. Four forty-five and five o'clock came and went.

The room was almost empty now. There was another defendant, me, my P.D., the judge, plus two members of support staff, the bailiff and the stenographer.

The setting sun was turning the room a golden color. I was aching from sitting so long on the hard wooden seats. I looked at the clock on the wall. Five twenty – court was supposed to be over 20 minutes ago. The judge was sounding very testy as he spoke to the person before me. Losing patience, he admonish him for his tenuous grasp of the English language.

At last, my name was called. I walked to the spot where so many before me had recently had bad news delivered to them. Stopping in the correct spot, several feet back from the bench, in the middle of the aisle that divided the two sides of the room, I noticed the empty space made the shape of a cross. It was my own personal crossroads, right there, although, oddly, I'd not noticed that before.

The judge spoke

"Counsel, your client, Mr. Emmanuel Wolf has been charged by the State of California with felony possession of methamphetamines, intent to distribute methamphetamines and being under the influence of methamphetamines. Additionally, he is charged with misdemeanor possession of marijuana and possession of narcotics paraphernalia. How does your client lead to these charges?"

My lawyer responded

"Your Honor, my client pleads not guilty to the felony possession charges, but guilty to the misdemeanor paraphernalia charges. Also, your Honor, my client has been attending Alcoholics Anonymous meetings regularly since his last court date and we have the signature papers to prove it. I am requesting leniency for my client, as I genuinely believe that he is making a change in his life."

"Request denied, counsel. Defendant is hereby ordered to serve a sentence of no longer than two years in San Quentin State Penitentiary."

The judges' gavel making contact was the loudest sound I have ever heard.

The sun that had been making its way sluggishly through the room, filling it with the dirty golden light and setting the dust motes to motion, was directly on me now, as I stood there in disbelief. Did I just hear him right? Two years in prison? How can this be happening again? What about all the meetings? I was quaking inside. I began to tremble.

My lawyer did something then that I still can't believe. He kept his word and would do all he could for me. He spoke back to the judge.

"Your Honor, this young man has consistently been attending meetings of Alcoholics Anonymous without anyone telling him to, of his own choosing. He has been driving from Stockton to Chico every month to check in with me and calling me every two weeks of his own free will. I must insist that you show some leniency in his sentencing."

The judge replied with that familiar testy tone I'd heard earlier.

"Counsel, I am not in the habit of arguing with the Public Defenders who come before this bench and I don't intend to start today. My verdict is final."

Down went the gavel again. 'Thwack!'

I was absolutely freaking inside – and probably outside as well. There was no way I was going to dodge the same bullet twice. My mind started racing about what my life would be like after serving two years in the state penitentiary. I imagined horrible rape scenarios, fighting as hard as I could, living in abject terror. Then a truly frightening thing happened. It was as if something inside me sank. I resolved myself to the thought of killing someone there for that one moment. I stood at the crossroads in the courtroom, making peace with the thought of killing another human being!

The very same thing, the very same act that was so reprehensible to me that I vanished from Chico and my old life rather than do it.

I decided I'd rather bear that burden then be utterly broken by the men in a prison, which in my mind, I surely would be. This feeling overtook me then that I'd cross that last final line and become irredeemable. Better that than the other option. I stood there, absorbing that sickening feeling, letting the darkness close in on me, accepting it, even in some perverse way, welcoming it. It was decided. I'd become a murderer rather than someone's bitch.

Then another incredible thing happened, I began to recoil from that sensation. I began to tremble but it was different from when I heard the judge sentence me. I was trembling from the part of me that could not reconcile the thought of what I was convinced that I would need to do in prison. It was the Moral Man inside me, raging for how things could come to this, refusing to give into the fear and the darkness.

The next thing I knew, I was kneeling down in the courtroom, right there in the center of that cross and I was praying out loud. I was praying to God that I would not have to endure this test of character. I'd not be made to walk any further down this road. I made promises upon promises I'd be a better man. I would be an example of what kind of things men can accomplish with strong hearts. My voice got louder and louder.

I didn't realize it but minutes had passed, minutes during which my P.D. had continued to argue on my behalf. Actually getting into a full-blown argument with the judge in his own courtroom, at five forty in the afternoon. Everyone else had gone home. There was just me, the judge, my P.D, the bailiff and the stenographer.

When I snapped back into what was happening around me, the lawyer, my defender, both in title and in truth was actually shouting at the judge,

"YOUR HONOR! I must insist you show simple, human decency to this man!"

He pointed to me.

"I have never seen someone take so much initiative to change their own life as he has. He is deserving of a second chance!"

Somehow, against all odds, the judge was silent. He sat there for a full two minutes. I know that because it was so quiet that I could hear the tick-tock of the clock on the wall. Finally, the judge exhaled heavily and said

"Very well, I will grant him drug diversion."

He looked me and continued

"Son, someone up there must like you a lot. I have never known this man to ever take a stand like that for a defendant. If you know what's good for you, you will not let him down."

I looked at my P.D. savior and weakly confirmed

"I won't, I definitely won't."

"Now get the hell out of my courtroom and never come back! Do you understand me?"

"Yes, your Honor."

It was shortly after that day in court dad called.

CHAPTER 12

PATERFAMILIAS

I

I'd not heard from or spoken to dad in years. The last time we had spent any time together, I was still a teenager. He'd shown up in Stockton, blown in with the wind and hung out for a few days. He found me, proceeded to out-party all my friends and me then, simply disappear again, just like that.

This time he was sober, a good thing too, during his last visit, we robbed a liquor store, he shortchanged a half dozen clerks, we trashed an apartment and blew up my car and then he was gone. I was not in a position to one-up that performance.

He'd found me through the commune. As it turned out, he'd gotten sober around the same time mom did. He'd been living in a place called Sonoma County where some members of the commune had moved many years before. After he'd been sober for a while, he reconnected with them. That's how he discovered I was clean and living with mom in Stockton.

The truth is even though he was never there for me, had never been a dad to me, I absolutely idolized him, I romanticized him and the life he'd led and built him up to an impossible height. When he called and offered to have me come and live with him, I couldn't say no. I took his offer as nothing less than a sign from on high it was time for me to go forth and seek my destiny and so off I went.

There is much to be said about my dad, not so much as a man but as a living, breathing legend – more myth than reality. His name was Steve Wolfe and he was a truly brilliant musician, as I mentioned. He was also a truly brilliant hustler, addict, thief and raconteur. The story goes mom kicked him out when I was still an infant. He came home late and loaded on heroin. She pushed him down a flight of stairs and told him to leave.

In my lifetime, he reportedly toured the entire world twice, playing in jazz clubs from Amsterdam to Zanzibar and all stops in between. He recorded that top ten jazz album, 'First Date.' He shared the stage with musicians such as Frank Zappa, Robert Cray, Dizzie Gillespie, Wayne Shorter, Miles Davis, Ray Brown (who also played bass on First Date) and too many more to list – according to him.

In addition to this resume, he was known, admired, respected and simultaneously resented by virtually every man in our commune. His exploits and chicanery cast a huge shadow, in which I spent most of my childhood. He was reported to have stolen from, conned, or slept with the girlfriends of all of them. There was not a person in the commune who ever let me forget that I was his son and he was dad, thus the legacy passed along.

So potent is the Wolfe D.N.A, even though I spent less than three months with him throughout the entirety of my young life, I resembled him almost completely in looks, mannerisms and lifestyle. Nature definitely overpowered nurture. I believe even mom was affected by my resemblance to him, often letting the man he was influence the way she treated me.

The old saying, 'the apple doesn't fall far from the tree' means, of course, to reflect similarity but in my case it applies in sheer terms of scope as well. Dad was larger than life in a way I have never even come close to, a way only found through profound pain and heartbreak – and dad was no stranger to either.

He once told me that the Steely Dan song, "Deacon Blues" was written about him after he met and played with singer, Donald Fagan. The song tells the story of a man whose life is an exercise in mythic failure, a reaction to the vagaries of his father and his circumstances. A man who becomes something else, the epitome of suffering and creativity, driven by his demons to become the best in the world at his craft. Once his excellence is achieved, he collapses, crushed under the weight of his own burgeoning self-pride, only inches from any meaningful finish line.

What I can prove is dad reached the level of mastery at his craft anyone would consider 'great.' There have been more than a few times where, upon discovering someone I was talking with was a jazz fan, I'd tell them who dad was and they would stop, agog and say to me

"Steve Wolfe is your father? THE Steve Wolfe?"

The day came when dad picked me up in Stockton at mom's house. By that time, my two little boxes of belongings had grown to a 'few boxes' and some clothes on hangars as well – still not much to show for a life but slowly getting respectable. Besides, I really didn't need much stuff. My whole life was internal at that time so we packed up my few belongings and headed to sunny Sonoma County.

When we got there, contrary to the way he'd made it sound, it turned out dad was renting two rooms in the house of a Brazilian lady. 'My room' was a sleeping bag on the floor of his music studio. I slept amongst a plethora of wires and musical equipment. When I'd turn out the lights at night, there were dozens of small L.E.D.s still burning brightly on the various pieces of recording and performing gear that I shared the room with – so much so, it never really got dark in there.

I can't speak about what kind of man dad was while he was using drugs, beyond what I'd been told and what little I'd seen. When sober, he was hell on wheels. I have never seen anyone who worked harder than he did. He still made his living as a musician but by the time I got there, he'd become an entire one-man industry, spending twelve hours a day on his marketing system. He was a job-getting machine.

I helped him with all facets of his business. Envelope stuffing, writing copy for his little flyers, drawing logos and graphics, packing, setting up, tearing down and unpacking his gear. I watched in amazement as he played an average of ten gigs a week. Most weekdays, he did one gig – two a day on weekends. Above all else, what impressed me about dad was his utter confidence in himself and what he was worth. He didn't flinch at charging two hundred dollars for ninety minutes of his time. In 1998, that was a lot of money.

Dad also introduced me to the world of 'personal improvement.' He'd let me listen to the audio programs of people like Dale Carnegie, Earl Nightingale, Tony Robbins and others. We would do exercises like writing out our five-year goals, our perfect days, making lists of our strengths and weaknesses and on and on. Everything suggested in those programs, we eagerly implemented. It seems foolish to me now but back then I'd never considered there was such a proactive way to approach your life. I was amazed at the ideas I was being exposed to.

These were people who had literally turned their own lives from despair and wreckage to unbelievable levels of success and fulfillment – exactly what I wanted to do – and there they were they were laying out step-by-step programs for how to do it!

Dad's work ethic, his unfailing optimism and confidence, the self-help mentors, all of it, was a completely different way of thinking, being and living life than anything I'd ever even dreamed of before. Working alongside dad meant total immersion in these ideas. It was all he talked about – that and recovery.

II

We attended at least one meeting a day, every day, usually more. He liked Narcotics Anonymous (N.A.) so we that's where we went. We sat and listened as person after person shared their horror stories about when they were using. All anyone seemed to talk about was the difficulties, the obstacles they were dealing with. I found myself needing a more positive environment. I wanted to talk about the good things that were happening in my life. I began to feel the support and acceptance of my A.A. / N.A. brethren was contingent upon my willingness to accept their way of going about things.

Over time, the rift I was beginning to feel between me and the 'sobriety crowd' began to widen. I found I could not bring myself to spend any more time with them than I needed to for my daily meetings. By my fourth year of sobriety, I'd even stopped attending meetings, though I deeply internalized the twelve steps and the spirituality of recovery. My mantra became one of keeping my connection to my Higher Power strong and clear. I began to live by the principle I needed to have that connection first, in order to sustain anything else of meaning in my life.

I found the more I dived into the spiritual principles of A.A. / N.A. and the teachings of the self-help mentors dad had introduced me to, the less I could accept the stagnation and complacency that, to me, plagued the recovery community. I found myself gradually moving away from that scene towards what would prove to be a fifteen-year journey in search of my real, authentic self.

What I would only realize in hindsight was that I was starting from absolute scratch. I had to rebuild my identity, my ego, my 'self' from the ground up. This was part of the reason things seemed to take me so long, compared to others in recovery.

I remember one day, many years into this process, a friend offered to do a tarot card reading on me. When the cards had been dealt, she surveyed them, took a deep breath and gave me her analysis.

> *"Wow, you are really shaking your tower to its foundation, it'll be interesting to see what's left standing."*
>
> *"What do you mean?" I probed.*
>
> *"You have called down the thunder on yourself. You're on a quest to see what parts of you are real and what needs to go. This is heavy shit you're dealing with."*
>
> *"You got all that from those cards?" I thought out loud.*
>
> *"It's all right here, the tower, the fool, the devil and the dead man. You are not fucking around are you!?"*
>
> *"No, I'm not, actually." I replied.*

What really struck me about this incident was the fact that, in a dark moment, a moment of surpassing frustration and confusion a few weeks earlier, I'd actually fallen to my knees alone in my living room and shouted up to the sky

> *"O.K. God, I can't do this anymore! Give me everything you've got! Hit me with your best shot. Don't pull your punches! Let's get this done!"*

I was doing this because I'd hit yet another dead end in my spiritual development (or so I thought,) another place where I was stuck – stopped dead in my tracks. Nothing I was doing seemed to be paying off. I was broke, alone, angry and depressed. The Moral Man had no words to soothe this moment. This shit was hard and I was pissed off. Turns out, there would be a lot of that as I did 'the work.'

One of the things I'd learn about dad was his optimism was not always helpful. For him, the positive outlook was intended as a self-fulfilling prophecy most of the time, a good way to get through the day. But some of the time, it was as though he believed looking on the bright side was some sort of 'gypsy cure-all.' Whatever ails you, it would fix it if only you trusted that it would. Even snake oil.

III

During my own 'rebuild,' sometimes – many times – it was a painful and extraordinarily difficult process. I understand now struggle was a sign the strongest bonds were being formed. Still, it was no place for blind optimism. No, the only way to really do it right is to accept pain and sculpt your soul with it. There is no real avoidance of pain, only the choice not to stay in suffering but we don't like the sound of that. We all want quick fix solutions. The problem is quick fixes tend not to work.

This runs contrary to the Western notion of spirituality. In our cobbled together ideas of Zen, Buddhism, Taoism and certainly with Christianity, we have enlarged the aspects we like and glossed over the rest. What we are left with is a very easily marketable and enticing pseudo-system for 'premature enlightenment.' It's important to note certain things can't be circumvented. There are no shortcuts to character development. There certainly are shortcuts to the 'appearance' of character but it is only through the gauntlet of adversity that true character is forged. We learn and grow in proportion to our challenges.

Anyone can look benevolent, steadfast, kind, charitable and thoughtful when everything is going well for them but very few can bring those attributes forward when the chips are down and they are struggling desperately. My goal had become to be the kind of person who personified those traits at all times – come hell or high water. I wanted to prove to myself and to the world, I could be more than what my past suggested I would become. If those 'audio program mentors' of dad's could do it, then so could I.

This was the mindset I was developing while I was working and living with him. I could sense the inherent worthiness of it but I was like a child with a cut throat razor, flailing it around like a toy. I had the information at my disposal, ready to quote, pontificate, even judge others without really understanding the ways which made me simply too reckless to be holding it. And like a runaway razor, I cut myself many times while learning to wield it correctly.

I think of this as the 'pompous ass' period of my development.

In fairness to myself, I was trying very hard to embody these new teachings. However, in the beginning, most of the time I failed. I was merely applying lip service to these things, these core teachings for humanity. Like the rest of life, here was an arena where it was crucial a person 'walk the walk' before they 'talk the talk.' It's fair to say 'the fool runs his mouth while the wise man listens.'

I was still moving around. I lived with dad for about a year, then mom and the rest of my family decided to move from Stockton to up to Santa Rosa. I joined them in a big house we all rented together. After a couple of years, I'd move back in with dad and my sister, Guinevere from his side of the family, whom I'd never had a chance to know.

But I do not wish to relate my time in a pure chronological sequence. It does those days a disservice to merely line them up, one after the other, like suspects. If the time before then was characterized mostly by feeling the effects of – and learning to deal with addiction – then these days were about feeling the effects of and ultimately learning to deal with the effects of 'family.' One can be as debilitating to a sense of wellbeing as the other.

What I didn't know then was just how much I'd built my family up in my mind. I made them, forced them really, into an idealized version of what I needed a family to be. Each of them had been assigned roles in my head. The constructs I'd built had been a key part of my emotional survival while I was out in the depths of my addiction. I depended on my mental images of them to justify my life and my behaviors. If they weren't so damned perfect, how could I get away with being so flawed?

It was a bit different with dad since he was actively participating in my daily life while we lived together. It was easier to relate to him. Besides, he was still living a version of his mythic life in my eyes. Waking up every day like

Sisyphus from Greek mythology, a quick cup of coffee, a snack and he was off to push that big boulder up a hill again. Sometimes the boulder stayed up there. Sometimes it came rolling back down again crushing everything in its path. When it did roll back, he would not be daunted.

He believed in the idea of stringing together a series of small victories, one after the other – like beads on a necklace – in the pursuit of your bigger goals. Every day, without exception, he did this. He had failures – many of them – but he never stopped pushing. I suppose that, at least, was worthy of remembrance.

During our time together, we lived according to his vision, his ideas of how 'things ought to be.' We steeped ourselves in recovery, self-help and long hours of work. These sessions I punctuated with frequent and vigorous exercise, which, much to my joy, dad also began to engage in.

Things moved along smoothly with dad until, as is often the case, I began to see through the mystique. We fell in to a routine together. A good level of comfort was established between us, a level that made dad think it was O.K. for him to play the role of 'father' to me again, offering unsolicited advice on my comings and goings and generally trying to 'parent me.' This most unwelcome – I was a man now. I felt I'd grown past the need for it.

He saw it differently of course and though he never expressed it in words, his actions did. In time, I began to feel those old rebellious stirrings inside of me, the part of me that loved to defy authority, especially when it was coming from someone who was not there or present with 'moral authority' when they were supposed to be. I can't say how I would have reacted to the influence of a 'father figure' in my youth – positively I think – but in my mid-adult years having been through so much a good dad is supposed to shield you from, I was in no mood.

Things between us gradually became strained and I began to do other things for work than simply apprentice to him. Just like my teenage years, I held down many jobs for short periods, always struggling for enough money to make ends meet. When mom's side of the family, the side I had known better all my life, went to Santa Rosa, it seemed like a perfect opportunity for me to wriggle out of living with dad and return back to the rest of my family. I had clearly glossed over the issues I had with them – the very issues that led me to accept dad's offer in the first place.

I might have stopped being 'dad's apprentice' but I was still the apprentice to my own spiritual growth. I was not a master of my own awareness by any measure. Had I been more masterful, I'd never have chosen to return to the fold but as I say, I wasn't and therefore I did. We all found a nice big house in a decent part of town, signed the lease and moved in. This would become a time of crushing insecurity for me. I was trying desperately to adapt to the 'family dynamic' in such tight, close quarters. Yet, once more, I found myself banging my head repeatedly against a proverbial brick wall.

IV

Packed in on top of each other, our dysfunctional dynamics played out like a caricature with each of us falling back into specific roles. Mom's guilt was focused primarily on my sister and brother. She allowed them to verbally attack her at will while she cowered and scurried. This in turn would make me sick to my stomach, prompting me back into the unwelcome 'protector' position that had caused me so much trouble as a child. It reminded me of all those times I came to mom's defense – only to be told not to.

My sister's then boyfriend and smug future husband, Paulo was living with us too. It seemed to me his primary contribution to the household was as a catalyst to bring forth the most arrogant parts of my sister and brother's personalities. Paulo and Annabel had both recently left the music conservatory at the prestigious University of Pacific College in Stockton. They both came out of the school very skilled – and very pompous! I found them insufferable. My young brother James had also undergone an intense musical education in a high school marching band, allowing him to fit seamlessly in with the two of them.

I found I had little in common with the lot of them. Furthermore, it seemed the things I was interested in, they found to be 'disdainful' or 'beneath them.' I was interested in working out, getting my body healthy, for which I was categorized as a 'lunk' or a 'meathead.' I loved rock music and eighties new wave bands. They felt those things too far beneath them to even bother with. Even mom, herself an avid runner, seemed unable to comprehend my passion for working out.

It felt like there was a secret understanding between them as to what was 'acceptable' and what was not and they were not going to share the information with me, not when I provided so much fodder for their cannons. To be honest, I'd say I have never – and I measure my words when I say this – ever seen people behave more arrogantly, more pretentiously than my own family did while we shared that house. Inside a bitter struggle was underway. The part of me that was insecure and desperate for their approval, trying anything to feel welcome, railed against the other part of me that knew better, disgusted my own family, my flesh and blood, could all think this type cruel of behavior was somehow 'O.K.'

Looking back, it is a source of shame to me that I tried to mimic them, if only temporarily, in an effort to be accepted.

V

Another divisive issue in our house was playing music. We had all known going into it, we needed a music-friendly household (in the sense of people playing instruments) and there would be band practices and rehearsals taking place there.

What I could not have predicted, was how much I'd want mom's approval as a budding musician and how utterly I'd not get it. She would fawn all over my siblings and Paulo too, happily, eagerly, engaging them in discussions about musical topics.

I'd watch from only feet away as she did this, smiling, eyes sparkling as they bantered back and forth about jazz greats or what band was currently cool enough to hold their sacred interest. When I tried to engage her in similar discussions, she would be flat and non-committal with me. My temper would flare and I'd hurl accusations of favoritism and a big conspiracy, my feelings deeply wounded. She'd blatantly deny any of it, arguing love and approval was being distributed evenly amongst her children.

I will respond here as I did when she made these ridiculous claims. If there is a debate between a self-aware child, that is to say, one who can recognize and articulate the feelings that are going on inside themselves and a parent about whether or not love and approval are being transmitted from parent to child. Barring any sort of narcissism or psychopathy on the part of the child, the child is always right. It is not a matter of opinion.

What might be casual to the parent, a simple touch or kiss on the head, a clear, attentive exchange of only a few words, or a loving boundary setting, an affirmation or acknowledgement of a thing done well, are not at all 'casual' to the heart or soul of the child. They are manna. They are life-sustaining nourishment. Excluding immediate threats to survival, these are the most important things in a child's life. All of their senses are precisely attuned to the frequencies of these messages as if their very lives depend on them – because they do.

To suggest that a parent is more attuned to this than their child, especially in defense of the parent's indifference is laughable, bordering on obscene. I did not understand it then, but this was at the very core of the discord between mom and myself. What I did know was this was the same dance that we had been dancing together for many years and I hated it with every ounce of my being.

I was likely more insecure during the time I lived back in the fold of my family than even the first months of my sobriety. The rough sea I was navigating at home, I have outlined. But internally, I was also struggling greatly with the deep issues of identity and self-acceptance. I was aware of a connection between the two battles but the lack of self-esteem I was grappling with was so overwhelming, an awareness of it did little to remedy its damaging effects.

I went through a long period of adopting 'personas.' The way a child might try on different costumes, hoping in some way, to stumble across the real me, by slipping into identities one after another. I suppose by eliminating those that were obviously not me, this process did serve a function. However, the feeling of trying desperately to make something work that plainly didn't and the awkwardness that caused, was a far better teacher.

I tried to be a hipster, a hippie, a player, a grunge guy and a gym rat. I did the whacky artist and street urchin looks. I pretended to be punk. I sported sport coats and slacks and even donned skater garb trying to fit in and figure out who I was at the same time.

I felt like a tourist, a fraud, a charlatan, a huckster and a chancer, masquerading as this and yet with no identity of my own. There was an upshot to all of this though. All of the strutting and mummery, all of the flailing superficiality on the surface was actually having an opposite effect deep inside me. On the inside, I was reducing, carving away little-by-little, the detritus and the filler.

I was becoming solid. Every false start, every misstep was a learning opportunity I seized upon. In terms of my rate of progress, there was no wasted motion. Although there was a great distance between me and where I was going, at least I was 'going.'

I began, partly as a protest aimed squarely my family, partly from genuine desire, to form a band, looking for like-minded musicians to collaborate with. This was a childhood dream I didn't even realize I could achieve until the possibility of it happening became real. I got myself into a habit of asking everyone and anyone I'd come across if they played music. If the answer was 'yes,' I'd ask them to play with me, to jam together in search of some kind of creative connection. Slowly, I found members for what would be my first band, 'One Eyed Jack.'

A committee formed of equal parts hindsight and nostalgia inform me this was my first benchmark accomplishment in sobriety. I agree with them of course. Objectively, the band and its music were reasonable. If there were a 'band exam,' we would get a good pass.

What was important for me at least, was I that proved to myself I could do something real, something concrete, through sheer force of will. I had chalked up quite a list of achievements. I learned to play my instrument, searched for and found band mates, secured a practice space, (the drummer's garage,) collaborated to write original songs, found places that would let us perform what we had created and biggest of all, got up on stage and performed them.

Me playing bass in Groove Juicy

VI

To some this will seem an accomplishment, to others a trifle but to me it was monumental because I'd been quietly convincing myself for most of my life I couldn't do anything like this. I was the lost child, not the 'other-side-of-the-tracks' royalty that my family was. I was no musician... or was I? If I could do this, I mused, what else could I do that I'd previously thought 'impossible?'

Though seemingly insignificant in a town where everyone seemed to be playing in a band, this was a huge and profound turning point for me. As odd as it sounds, having done this 'thing,' made real this 'dream,' affected not only the obvious things, like my confidence, but it actually found its way into my weightlifting. I began to ask myself challenging questions like

> *"If I can do that, if I can actually put together a band and play music for people and have them like it, then who's to say that I can't bench press two hundred and fifty pounds?"*

I began to use the evidence of these little victories to help me push myself further in other things, weightlifting at that time, being chief amongst them. I began to experience huge improvements in all measurable strength tests. In a period of only a few months, I'd reached my goal of two hundred and fifty pounds on the bench press, starting at the very modest one hundred and twenty pounds. My pulling strength increased by over two hundred percent as well. My leg strength, well, that increased by a factor of almost five, going from struggling to press three hundred pounds, to being able to press over thirteen hundred pounds.

I developed a method for going deep within myself between each set I would do, clearing my mind and focusing as intently as I could manage. I'd envision myself with perfect form, strong skeleton and muscles, executing a massive push or pull, bringing all of my body into the task. I'd harness my breath, mental energy, even tap into my family-induced rage inside and then unleash it all in the direction of the weight to be moved. The results were amazing and they all stemmed from the confidence I'd found through the achievement of creating my first little rock band.

Somehow, that small but not insignificant thing freed something else inside. It was my first proof on a real, tangible level, of all of the work I'd been doing on an intangible plane. This would prove to be the first step for me in rebuilding my self-esteem, in learning how to assess the feedback I was getting from the outside world about how I was showing up and not living and dying by the judgements of my family.

Dad was, of course, thrilled and 'not at all surprised' I'd crossed the bridge into full-fledged musicianship. He was so excited he proposed him, me and my sister Guinevere get a house together where we could all play music and continue to rebuild the bonds we should have forged many years ago.

For my part, I thought this to be a very good idea, perhaps for circumstantial reasons as much as for any other kind. I'd become very much ready to again extricate myself from the complexities and disappointments I struggled with at mom's house. There have been moments during my post-sobriety relationship with my family where I have been able to see with uncanny clarity and precision, the ways our power dynamics flowed, as if, I managed somehow, to ascend high enough to see the lay of the land.

In those moments, I saw a matriarchy. A transfer of both prerogative and emotional damage that flowed from mom to daughter, was filtered through the unique issues that my sister was burdened with and out to my youngest brother. He, in his own way, a recipient of the same issues that my sister bore, interacted with both of them in the only way you might expect him to act – petulant, needy, angry and verbally aggressive.

Paulo, being an outsider and put on a pedestal by both mom and my sister, possibly even my brothers, was both exempt from any overt judgement (except from my sister, of course,) and given a kind of 'carte blanche' with his own behaviors. Generally, I found Paulo to be snide and condescending. In the way you can see a completed electrical circuit, so could I see these dysfunctions as they made their way around and around the loop, that was my family.

The curious and utterly baffling thing for me was I had these moments of clarity where I saw all plainly and could explain it to anyone easily. When the event triggering my clarity passed, when the emotional charge receded, it was as if an aperture closed, drawing a hazy, dirty lens back over the issue. I was not able to bring it back to conscious understanding at will.

This kind of thing happened when dad asked me to move back in with him and Guinevere. After I said 'yes,' we were talking and he asked me how things were going with mom. I answered him with the most lucid, clear explanation of how things were that can be imagined, only to lose my grasp on it, utterly, a few days later when he brought it back up again. The problem with this is it's impossible to address a problem you can't articulate.

If I'd been able to hold on to that clarity, how much easier might the next years of my life have been? But the fact of the matter is the things a family provides for an individual are profoundly important. They are hardwired into our psyches, our very D.N.A. We don't quickly learn to draw our hand back from that particular coil when it glows red and hot.

I moved back in with dad who, after much discussion and agreement, conceded not to try to make up for lost time as a parent and instead, to accept me as the fledgling adult I was so desperate to become.

Once back with dad, things were good again, perhaps even better than before. He did an honest trade in just being a friend and mentor, seldom overstepping his bounds, which, for a 'Wolfe man' is no small feat.

By this time, my band, One Eyed Jack had split up due to 'creative differences' amongst the members. I take little pride in my role of our demise. The 'differences' were that I thought things should be done my way. The two other musicians wished also to have 'a say' which I did not see the need for.

We went our separate ways, each free to pursue whatever interests we wanted. For me, this meant a return to school to study music. I wished to learn more theory and perhaps network with other musicians there. Once immersed, it wasn't long before I connected with other like-minded individuals and a new vision had begun within me – I'd start a seventies style funk band. It would be complete with horn section, female backup singers, stage costumes – the full works – and would be called 'Groove Juicy!'

CHAPTER 13

FINDING A MUSE

I

The idea suddenly came to me while I was sitting in a beginner's musicianship class. I can't find any witnesses to this, but I swear a beam of light came in through the high window above the teacher's podium and shot into my soul, causing my entire body to light up and vibrate. Where upon I turned to a classmate sitting next to me, grinning as if I was part devil, part idiot. He sat there obviously transfixed by the 'spectacle' that was me. When he finally asked me why I was looking so strange, I said to him

> *"I'm going to start a twelve-person funk band and call it Groove Juicy!"*

I set to this task in earnest, asking everyone I passed in the halls if they liked funk music. Some said 'yes,' some said 'no,' even more said, 'funk... what's that?'

The truly strange thing about all of this is (and I'm not making this up, I promise) I'd never listened to funk music a single day in my life before this happened. I was strictly a rock and roll guy up until that point, always had been and thought I always would be. Even the music I'd written with One Eyed Jack was all in a rock vein. This was utterly new to me but I knew that this thing had to happen. Groove Juicy would live, breathe, jump and boogie (on down.)

There were many twists and turns on the road to making this dream a reality. I went through thirty-plus musicians before we even had one song learned. In all, I estimated close to ninety people called themselves members of Groove Juicy at one point or another. As I was living at dad's, along with his years of experience on tap, I persevered, found an initial line-up, learned four hours' worth of songs and got our first gigs.

Many of our performances were noteworthy in their own right. We were, it seemed, about fifty percent music and talent and fifty percent raw sex appeal. But the first 'gigs' will forever hold a special place in my heart. As time went on, I confess I did indulge in the trappings of local celebrity, namely the women it brought me. In the very beginning though, in that college room with the holy light hitting me square and filling my soul, I was truly on a mission. In my mind, I was an 'Ambassador of the Funk', an emissary from the mothership, chosen to bring everlasting funk to my sleepy little town.

Our first chance to do this came at a time just before we, the band, felt ready to do it. My saxophone player, Blane, a square headed, juicy mouthed, phallic symbol of a guy came to band practice and announced that his cousin, an intrepid musician named 'Root Dawg' had offered us the opening spot at a show he was playing in a little town called Nicasio.

We were informed the location was a good-sized social club and teen center and we would be given half of the proceeds for the show that came from ticket sales. With some debate and a little bit of wrangling, the band as a whole agreed to it. We all practiced extra hard leading up to the day of the show, went out together and bought stage clothes and even perfected some smooth dance moves for effect.

The day arrived and we all packed our gear into our cars and headed out to the venue. When we arrived, we discovered it a mere block and a half from the 'exact middle of nowhere.' The fact we drove through hills and fields for the last hour of the journey should have been a clue, I suppose. We remained steadfast feeling, at least, we'd get to get our first show out of the way.

There were three people at the venue when we arrived, four when we were halfway through set up. When Root Dawg's band showed up there was an 'impressive' total of twenty-four people – which was really a meagre twelve if you didn't count band members! For those of you who are unaware, let me tell you it is not a galvanizing feeling when you suspect you are going to be performing for less than or equal to the number of people in your own band!

Root Dawg kept saying

"Should be a good show. Should have a good turn out."

Perhaps having a five-person band gave him a very different sense of what constitutes a good 'turn out,' than say, a twelve-person band. Whatever the case, I did not share his optimism. We finished our set up and began to mingle. At one point, I overheard Root and Blane talking.

"Did you get to do much advertising?" asked Root.

"No, we really didn't do any..." Blane replied, not incorrectly.

"How about you?"

"The usual, some flyers downtown (...downtown where..?) called all the peeps. You know the deal." was Root's response.

Blane opted then for his trademark phrase

"Cool."

He then stood in repose.

A few more people did trickle in as we waited for our start time to arrive. There were a couple of cute girls who were friends with Root's band, then some parents. At ten minutes before our scheduled start time, there were possibly thirty (count them!) people in the building.

"Oh well, it's better than nothing." I said to the Steve, our drummer.

Old and veteran, he smiled and shook his head, not being a fan of 'small talk.'

A funny, wondrous and utterly unexpected thing happened next.

We decided to take the stage at nine o' clock. When we left the small crowd and took up our instruments, the number of people in that cavernous room looked sad and pathetic. Undeterred, we started with a song by Earth, Wind and Fire, 'Let's Groove.' At the first note, the floor was empty but by the time we finished that one song, the entire place had filled to capacity. I was in awe, as were my bandmates. We exchanged looks of disbelief as an audience rapidly materialized before our very eyes. Suddenly, the place was filled to the corners and out of the doors.

Knockin' em dead in orange camouflage

By the time we struck the last lingering notes of our final song, the whole place erupted in cheers! It was amazing, unbelievable and overwhelming.

Spurred on by this flood of approval, we ripped through our entire set with an energy that in turn, set the floor to a bounce. I could feel the vibrations of the dancers, moving to the music we were making. I was truly and honestly, an ambassador of the funk.

The dance floor never thinned out during our entire set, it was a (tiny) ocean of swaying bodies with smiling faces and stomping feet. It reached from wall to wall and right up to the stage line. The musicians and the audience were putting each other into a kind of mutual trance. They fed off of us, we in turn, fed off of them. Root whooped with pleasure as we played hit after hit from the playlist of 1976 dance smashes. Everybody loved us.

Then, when we were finished with our set list and we had no more songs to play, we thanked the audience profusely for their love and approval and began to tear down our equipment. Then another strange thing happened. As inexplicably, as the venue filled at the last possible minute, the dance hall began to empty out again. We as a band, stayed to watch Root Dawg. It seemed like the only decent thing to do. Plus, none of us was ready to go home just yet.

By the time they were three songs into their set, the place had emptied out to well under half-capacity. This was very strange considering no one in this new town could possibly have come to see us – we were unknown, never having played anywhere before then. Root's band was established with several albums to their credit already and a large following. Why had the place filled up for us, only to empty out again as soon as we were done? It was truly a mystery only the gods of funk knew the answer to.

When dad heard of our victory in our soft debut, he was so proud he offered to become our manager, taking over the responsibility of finding and booking shows for us. Since every person in the band looked up to him, we accepted his offer unanimously. While we were busy making a four-song demo with him in his studio, mom decided to have a Halloween party at her small apartment. (She moved there when I went back to dad's.) She asked if our band could be the feature event of the engagement. We accepted this show and the date was set.

She went to the city authorities and secured a temporary noise permit for the agreed upon night. We were to play our show on the large sun deck that was the top of the covered parking right in front of her apartment. Since it was Halloween, we all bought or made special costumes for the occasion. I think collectively we assumed our first performance was some kind of fluke. After all, no one even knew who we were, so, realistically, why would people come out to see us?

With this show, the consensus was that it would be a few friends and family, gathered to have a good time and nothing more. Once again, the gods of funk surprised us. I can only assume they thought we were doing good works in their name because once again, they blessed us with a crowd beyond all reasonable expectation. It was not long into our set that the entire sun patio was filled with reveling partygoers. Beyond the normal group everyone expected to be there, there were actually people from Stockton, many folk I knew from other social circles in town and plenty of new faces.

By the time we were well underway, the parking area below us was crowded too. People were spilling out into the street. I looked around and wondered if I'd really stumbled onto something with the style and format of this band.

But the biggest surprise was yet to come.

Santa Rosa at that time was a city with a vibrant local music and art scene. There were many great places for bands to play but perhaps the crown jewel of all of them was a place called the 'Inn of the Beginning.' An aptly named place for us because it would prove to be the beginning of our reputation as a full-tilt, good time, party band everyone wanted to see.

We were in the middle of rehearsal one afternoon at dad's house when he walked in, motioned for us to stop playing and said

"Do you guys want to play a show this Saturday?"

"Saturday night?" I asked. "Where?"

"At the 'Inn of the Beginning.'" He said.

"Really? How did you get that spot? Who do we open for?"

Dad looked at me, looked at all of us, smiled and said

*"Open for? You ain't opening for nobody, son. You're Groove Juicy
and other bands will be opening for you. But not on Saturday,
you've got the whole night to yourselves. Are you up for it?"*

We were stunned. This was the kind of thing a band would usually have to
work up to through months of reputation building and perseverance.
Excitement sizzled through our ranks,

"Hell yes we're up for it!"

*"Good, the pay is a thousand bucks, minus my ten percent, of
course."*

*"A thousand bucks! You're... you're!?" I blurted "How the hell
did you do that?"*

*"I told them who the fuck you were and they were getting you
cheap at that price."*

He smiled again.

When the night of the gig came, we were all very nervous. This was a real,
professional gig. We arrived at the place and it seemed huge to me. In reality,
the registered capacity was somewhere around three hundred and fifty but
that night it seemed like it could've held a thousand easily. We set up our
equipment and were told we could spend the time between then and the
sound check in the green room if we wanted. This we were very excited to
do, the green room at the Inn of the Beginning was a 'legendary place.'

It had been used by such personalities as Buddy Guy, Tommy Castro, Buddy
Rich, Joan Baez, Neil Young, Jefferson Airplane, Carlos Santana and more.
We felt honored to be counted amongst such lofty talent. We did our sound
check at about eight o'clock then went back backstage to await show time.
We were all very excited and nervous, to the point where we couldn't talk
without stuttering. I, myself, couldn't stop the little trembling sensations that
were coursing through me. All I could do was wait until it was time to go
on.

When the moment finally arrived, someone from the venue stuck their head
in the door and said

*"O.K. Time to go. It looks like good crowd out there. Break a leg
guys."*

He left with a smile.

We made our way to the back entrance, through the courtyard between the green room and the main building. I noticed there were quite a few people mingling and smoking in the outdoor area. I did not know what meant. As we made our way to the door, a bouncer smiled and waved us to the appropriate entrance.

> *"Should be a good night," he said noncommittally as he opened the door for us.*

When the door swung wide, so did my eyelids. The entire place was wall-to-wall twenty-something girls, each of them dolled up and on a mission. It was like walking through a sea of hips, breasts and smiling eyes. Many of them turned and smiled. Some of them reached out to touch us. I had to pinch myself slightly. I floated to the stage feeling no contact with the earth whatsoever. I was being carried gently along by the electrical current of feminine approval.

We took the stage. I could barely feel my fingertips as I passed the strap for my bass guitar over my head. From the vantage point of the stage with its slight elevation from the crowd, I saw there were in fact, some men there also. Who knew? They, too, were making eye contact and cheering us on.

I realized I was too edgy to signal the start the band. We stood there looking out at the crowd, in reality four hundred or so people but feeling as if it was thousands, frozen in that moment. The energy was amazing yet it was like everything was somehow stuck, then I heard the drummer mercifully yell

> *"ONE, TWO, THREE, FOUR!"*

We launched in to our first song and the effect was like in the movies when time starts up again after being stopped. The undulating crowd was screaming. No need to warm them up – they were raring to go. Every note I played, every step I made, eyes followed me, overflowing with desire and approval. To compare our first two shows to this one would be to compare hopping over a puddle to soaring over the ocean, feeling the wind in your face and smelling the salt water in the air.

As I looked around, I saw that the crowd was spilling out the front door and on to the street, where there had to be two hundred more people, all trying to see us, moving to the sounds we were making, utterly captivated by the juggernaut that was Groove Juicy.

As the night went on, girls spontaneously ran up on stage to dance with us. There were people dancing on the bar and tables. Female undergarments landed on my shoulder and on my bass at different times. There was even a group of seven guys who came in, all dressed as seventies disco kings, with polyester suits, huge sunglasses, gold medallions and afro wigs who started a 'soul train' line in the middle of the floor.

As the evening got better and better, the crowd more frenzied, I ran out of new things to do to signal my approval and finally, like a dog who has had too much fun, I simply resigned myself to the foolish grin plastered across my face. When a new girl or guy would look wave, or give me the old thumbs up sign, I'd just shrug at them, grinning like an idiot. If the gods of funk had smiled upon us at our first two shows, they actually touched down for this one, taking the forms of partygoers and secretly blessing the night's festivities. At two-thirty in the morning, long after last call, the club finally got everyone to go home by shutting off the lights.

We were a hit. Just like that. We started getting calls to play shows from Mendocino down to San Francisco. All the local clubs would clamor to be the first to book us when their calendars were being filled. We were busy every weekend and often had bookings Friday and Saturday nights. It was a great time for me and the rest of the group. I began to live and breathe funk. It permeated my wardrobe, the way I walked, the way I talked, the whole deal, baby.

Music and performance consumed me for a long time after that. I thought I'd spend my life as a working musician, performing, teaching and following in dad's footsteps – at least the as far as music was concerned. I felt like I'd discovered my calling. I dived into my music studies, continued playing shows every weekend and spent my free time dreaming on a bigger and bigger scale.

For the time being, my life was fulfilling. I had popularity, girls, (some) money, satisfaction and purpose. The only thing I couldn't seem to get was the approval of my family, especially mom. Apparently, creating the most popular band in an area, playing filled to capacity chock full with raving fans wasn't enough to get the thumbs up I so desperately wanted. Mom was still insincere and dismissive any time I tried to share stories of my success with her.

My band went on to bump the biggest, highest paid local band out of both their coveted Halloween and New Year's Eve spots at The Inn of the Beginning, something no one had done in over five years.

When I told my mom about this accomplishment,

"Wow, that's really great," she said flatly.

She nodded her head as if she was talking to a child who has just shown her their tenth scribble drawing in the last hour.

That Halloween we got paid six thousand dollars and New Year's Eve, we made just under that. Not bad for a night's work but not good enough to impress mom.

II

I'd love to tell you that during my change and development, becoming day-by-day more like the man I have always wanted to be, reaching out to Moral Man lurking within, that I had been able to heal the rift between mom and her side of the family.

I really would like to be able to say these things but I can't.

I can't tell you that through my own personal gauntlet of calling down the thunder upon myself, through my intensely painful process of violently shaking the very foundations of my core to discover what was good and worthy inside of me and what had to be cut away, that I was able to find a way to show up within my family in a way that felt authentic. Or that helped them to see me differently, more for who I am and less for the malignant collection of unexamined assumptions and left over memories of my former self that they seemed to be using as my proxy.

I wish I could say that I have come to understand why mom has so often seemed uncomfortable in my presence, or that I've somehow succeeded in making her or my sister know what an outsider I've felt like for all of my life. Alas, those things have not come to pass.

The deepest fears of the little boy, the fears that manifested themselves in comic-book images of a dark outsider, tentatively allowed a seat at the table, but never trusted, always watched closely, treated with an unusual degree of caution and skepticism, seem now to have been not fears, but portents, an intuition with uncanny accuracy beyond what the little boy should have been able to sense, but did, nonetheless.

So strong is the pull back to family for me, even as I sit here now, writing these words, as the man I am now, not the man I am describing for you, my mind attempts to betray me, to tell me there is some other explanation.

If only there was some other reason that can be blamed for the schism but the moral man knows that this thinking is nothing more than emotional widdershins, an unnatural, but very normal reflex to accept blame in the name of the preservation of the ignus fatuus – the false dream that kept me alive until it turned on me and tried to tear me apart.

Perhaps, this is the legacy of drug addiction, universal but unexpressed. Perhaps, the boy who cries wolf too many times can't be seen differently as a man. Perhaps, I am not alone in this. Maybe there are others, many of us, who feel a similar disconnect from our families, from the shelter that is our birthright.

Whatever the truth, whatever else can be said about this, there is one deep lesson to be taken from all of it and it is deep like a laceration. No matter what the poisonous person or influence in your life is, once you ascertain that it is toxic, you must separate yourself from it, make a clean break, or it will drag you down.

CHAPTER 14

GLASS SLIPPER BLUES

I

Dad had created a very effective marketing system for himself as well as finding great gigs for Groove Juicy. In addition to the local clubs and restaurants that were low hanging fruit for him, he learned how to get himself booked into wineries. Once he cracked that code and started playing those venues regularly, he was making on average, five thousand dollars a week, driving all over four counties to accommodate all the bookings he got. He began to bring home cases of wine, which he was also taking as partial payment for his gigs.

Being a house full of sober people, I was naturally a bit concerned about this choice but he assured me it was only so he could sell the wine later and make a better profit from it. I didn't think anything of it when he began to wear his sunglasses in the house during the evenings and spend all of his time in his bedroom. I even managed to normalize it when my friends would come up to me during band practice and say things like

"I thought you said your dad didn't drink?"

"He doesn't." I'd answer. "He just works around people who are drinking at the wineries... that's probably why he smells like it."

I didn't notice how he began to avoid getting to close to me, even though in the past he was always a hugger and back slapper. I only noticed it one day when he came home drunk and started an argument with me about some trivial thing, trying to be a 'parent' in spite of our explicit agreement. I smelled the booze seeping from his pores and I just exploded on him. I guess the thought of him drinking again had been on my mind, even though I'd not been aware of it because when he began badgering me about this and that, I just opened the gates of hell on him.

I turned on him so fast and screamed at him so loud that he actually fell down and began to back away while still on the ground. I followed him all the back to his room shouting

"Don't you ever fucking tell me what the fuck to do, you fucking asshole. You don't get to tell me anything, motherfucker! Do you understand?"

When I did it, when I let the bottom fall out like that, he simply shrank. He reverted. I'd never understood how broken he really was before that moment and when I saw the terror in his eyes, saw that I was making him relive some bloodletting of his past, I stopped, as suddenly as I'd started and I embraced him. That was when I knew for sure. I smelled the old and already processed alcohol on his skin. Not the smell of new alcohol, laced with a hint of seduction, but the smell of liver-processed booze that has had to pass through an old man's body before you smell it, mixed with sweat, failing testosterone and spiked with fear.

Once again, but not for the last time, my life cracked and fell to pieces.

Things moved quickly for me after that and I did what I always did. Without thinking, I went directly back to the dubious shelter of my mom's family, moving into an apartment that was literally below the one my mom had moved into and kitty-corner from my brother's and only a couple of blocks from my sister's.

After I moved out of the big house we had shared, they could not afford to keep it. Everyone got their own places within two blocks of each other. As I said, the aperture had closed and the lens was very dirty. In spite of what I knew was best for me, I went back into the fold.

II

While I was studying music in school, I met Chett. He was creative, brilliant and zany. We hit it off immediately. Chett was one of the few people I'd ever met who had as many big ideas as me. We would do homework together or be out at lunch and the creativity between us would just be flying back and forth. It was effortless. During one of those meetings, we began riffing on the idea of a musical. As the idea grew and took shape over the course of several weeks, we both began to realize that we were on to something very cool. We didn't know it at the time, but we were in the early stages of creating a modern re-telling of Cinderella from scratch.

We gave it a host of offbeat characters. Our protagonist, Rella, had an imaginary friend who went by the name, Paco del Taco. He was an amorous matador with a hopeless crush on Rella. There was the big bad wolf from Little Red Riding Hood who found Rella so irresistible that he came over from the other fairy tale just to try to seduce her. There were a host of others as well, including but not limited to, a perverted sidewalk who hit on her as she walked to the ball. It was all in good fun, of course, until one day, Chett and I looked at each other and realized we had to do this for real.

We named our play 'Glass Slipper Blues' and it took us almost two years from inception to completion. It would prove to be both the hardest and the most rewarding thing I'd ever done up until that point. I sold Groove Juicy on the project, wrote most of the songs for the play, painted the sets and pitched in on the writing. Chett financed it, wrote the lion's share of the script, made all the deals we needed in order to make it work and contributed to the song writing as well. We hired, seduced and cajoled local talent, until at last we found ourselves with a cast.

It was an all-consuming project for me, to the point where I even quit my job and virtually lived in our rehearsal space for the last three months until it debuted. Everyone who participated gave so much to the project, but Chett and I, we gave everything, including our friendship and even at times, our sanity.

In the beginning, we would meet at Chett's house and dream up the characters and the story line, the ideas coming fast and furious, the creativity at almost a fever pitch. I'd take the ideas home and come up with rough sketches for the music to guide the action along. With those ideas in hand, I'd come to the band and we would fill them out together into complete songs. When a song was complete, we would bring it to our fans at one of our shows and test it out live. It says much about the level of creativity we were swimming in – not a single song was met with anything less than total approval.

At a point, it became obvious to Chett and I we needed help on the production end of this project. We needed a director, costumers, lights, sound and make-up, as well as stagehands and other minions to be where we couldn't when we couldn't. The first person we hired was a young director named Nena.

Nena would prove to be the next big love of my life. She bowled me over with her face, her vivacious energy, her creativity and her talent. I never stood a chance. Just as Suzie and Lacey were the perfect women for the level of development I was at during those times in my life, so was Nena perfect for that time in my life. I think it fair to say that we were as much in love situationally as we were from real compatibility. She brought a fire to my work, as I did to hers.

Nena and I together traced an almost identical arc to that of the play itself, starting hot, then reaching higher and higher, until gravity seemed itself seemed to fail us and we tumbled down again. Like the play, she and I made some very good music together, struggled greatly at the end and would wind up brokenhearted but wiser – but not before we made something amazing.

III

There were so many times, as we neared the end of making of Glass Slipper Blues that I wanted to quit, just throw in the towel. Tension between Chett and I ran so high towards the end of production I actually pulled a knife on him at one point but thought better of it and used it to peel a mango instead.

To Chett's way of thinking, the actors should have an open door policy for their suggestions and input, to the point of almost completely rewriting their characters to suit their egos. This approach led to every actor in the production angling and scheming to get as many lines and as much stage time for themselves as they could wring out of Chett, often with wanton disregard for the storyline.

To my way of thinking, especially when the end was in sight, the actors could go fuck themselves. Either they could do the play the way we had written it, or we would find actors who would. This attitude led to the actors, for the most part, avoiding me and feeling uncomfortable in my presence, often becoming difficult and non-communicative about issues, or even suggestions.

Resentment began to linger heavy in the air at rehearsals.

Looking back, I can say something in between those two points of view would have been best. But the problem was Chett and I were both so overwhelmed so completely out of our depth, we both reverted to our core personalities. We had been stripped of our entire social pretense by the intensity of the creative process. Chett became a 'pushover.' I became 'pigheaded.'

Nena, Chett and I worked tirelessly on Glass Slipper Blues, doing everything in our power to make it real and to make it the best we possibly could. In the end, we had a complete musical production. We scraped together everything that we needed, from the front of the house to the back of the house, from the actors to the stagehands. We plotted it out step-by-step, joke-by-joke, song-by-song. And just when we thought we couldn't possibly work any harder, Chett showed up to rehearsal one night and announced that he'd secured us a location and dates for the show – we were actually going to perform Glass Slipper Blues!

Somehow, Chett had managed to get us complete access to a local landmark called the Phoenix Theater. For sixteen consecutive days, we overran that old show house, doing all of our rehearsals there, building last minute props and everything else, including performances on a Thursday, Friday, Saturday and two on Sunday. The Phoenix Theater was, in 'performer speak,' a barn. It was big. All told, it could hold close a thousand people, including the balcony. Mercifully, for us, most of the balcony would need to be cordoned off for technical reasons. Still, there was room for over seven hundred people on the floor alone.

Chett and I became many things to each other during the creation and performance of Glass Slipper Blues and most of those things were not good. For me, Chett became a rival, he became the 'Money Man.' and he became, most regrettably, an enemy to me. We started on this adventure together, yet become adversarial to the point of not being able to speak to each other directly anymore – but whatever else I might say about him – he got shit done. In addition to securing us the theater, in itself an unbelievable achievement, he also got us press coverage from the local papers and a San Francisco paper as well. In fact, most of our advertising for the opening night came from a segment on the local news he made happen.

Just as surely as Glass Slipper Blues would not have happened without me, there is no way it would have come together without Chett. He undoubtedly handled more details than I am even aware of. He enlisted his entire family at one time or another in the service of the minutia that goes into a full-on production. Looking back, he must have been everywhere, dashing to and fro between the little emergencies and huge catastrophes. While I made sure the band was tight and the actors were ready, he saw to everything else.

In the movie, 'Shakespeare in Love,' the theater owner, Philip Henslowe, played by Geoffrey Rush, at one point describes the process of creating a play as a series of 'insurmountable obstacles on the road to an imminent disaster.' This had certainly been my experience of the process and without Chett there to do battle with each and every one of those obstacles, we surely would have failed – but we had him and so we made our way to opening night.

I had done opening nights before and since then, in theater productions, with bands, in the restaurant business but nothing else in my life was quite the same as our opening night for Glass Slipper Blues. This was mine in a way that can scarcely be communicated. It was a living, breathing manifestation of my blood, sweat, tears and willpower. I'd sacrificed everything to make this a reality. Me, plus the rest of the actors and musicians were living and breathing the play at that point. I'd come to know the Phoenix Theater like the back of my hand.

For opening night, I'd concocted a novelty of sitting myself out in front of the theater, dressed so as to be unrecognizable and playing the main theme from the title song on my harmonica while people waited in line for tickets. I'd sit on the ground, wearing the same thing I was going to wear on stage, hat, jacket, sunglasses, the whole thing and I'd play Glass Slipper Blues as the people filed by buying their tickets.

As I did this, I could not believe how many people there were waiting in line. The show was scheduled to start at eight thirty and so I came in from sitting and playing harmonica at about eight ten to take my place behind the curtain. When I came back through the theater, there was what I considered a good crowd. About half of the floor area was full as the audience sat in the little chairs that we had cobbled together from out of nowhere. When I peeked out at two minutes before the curtain rose, the entire house was full. There were not only people covering the entire front, between the closest chairs and the stage, but there were also people in both sides of the balcony. As I realized that we had somehow managed, on our opening night, to fill the house, the strangest thing happened. I saw my life flash before my eyes.

Backstage before Glass Slipper Blues

IV

I was back in Berkeley as the little boy in the commune, coming down the stairs to Sunday breakfast in my three-piece leisure suit, complete with the coordinating turtle neck and high-heel shoes. I was the savage child, smashing another boy's head open with a rock at recess. I was the young man, only a teenager, dressed like a ninja, scampering across the underside of the freeway to discover the local hoodlums, all congregating together with their ornate low riders and their jet black hair, watching as one of them shot another because of the fight that we had started. I was the boy losing his virginity to the older woman, the thrower of legendary toga parties and the young man who had cared for his friend when stabbed thought the heart.

I saw the boy who was increasingly trapped in a man's body. A man who had never had a reliable dad, or a mom for that matter, who had been to the gates of his own personal hell more than one time. The man who had gone to the absolute edge and dangled a foot over the side into the abyss and then, miraculously, found his way back again. That man was standing here now, looking through a slit in a heavy black theater curtain onto a full house of people who were here to see what he'd done, what he'd created out of nothing. I saw myself standing there, waiting for the cue, for the minute when I'd walk out on that stage and look out on that sea of smiling faces – faces that recognized me as the harmonica player in hat and shades, out in front of the theater as they filed in.

The spotlight hit the curtain where I was waiting. I slipped out from between the folds of heavy black felt and satin, playing the same refrain on the harmonica I been playing in front of the theater. The crowd erupted as I crossed to where the band's equipment was set up on the opposite side of the stage. (We chose this configuration to allow for interaction between the musicians and the actors, a choice that worked marvelously.) When the spotlight had led me to my destination, like a cavalier, I took off my hat, hung it on my mic stand and strapped on my bass guitar.

As I began to play the intro to the first song, the drummer walked out on stage. We greeted each other with a hug and he sat down behind the kit, jumping in with the bass line I was playing. With the rhythm section going strong, the guitar player entered, then the horn section, then the keyboards. The band was now complete, all vamping on the intro song for a minute or so, the audience clapping along with us. Then the fairy godmother rushed out on stage, telling us to be quiet, there was someone coming. We all stopped playing and the lights went down.

The stage lights came up partway as the first characters took the stage. It was Rella, her evil stepmom and her wretched stepsisters. This was the scene where we established how bad they were and what a hopeless situation Rella was in. This led perfectly into the first song of the night, a soulful ballad called 'Ain't No Man.' sung by Rella when her sinister sisters and malevolent mom, leave her to her impossible chores. The leading lady, an actress, Sarah Rithgen, sung the song to perfection, causing a wave of applause from the audience when she finished.

From my vantage point, stage right, I could see everything. I watched as Sarah poured her heart out for that ballad and then as the crowd surged their approval back to her. I saw how the stage lighting transformed my painted sets into something new, how it brought the costumes and props to life. I was transfixed by it all. I could not believe production was the same thing I'd done final tweaks on only a few hours before.

It was magic, pure and simple. It seemed to me I could see the energy being volleyed back and forth between the stage and the crowd, a pure communication of approval. We were digging as deep as we could and giving them all we found. In return, they showered us with love, creating a positive feedback loop that elevated the evening to someplace incredible.

And this was only the first song.

After it ended, in an unscripted moment of flawless stage timing, the fairy godmother, who was to make the next entrance, purposely held back on her cue, allowing the unexpected amount of applause to subside first. When she made her entrance, adorned in a costume that was a cross between the funk bassist showman, Bootsy Collins and glittery piano-playing entertainer, Liberace, the crowd went crazy again and she actually had to turn to them and signal them to be quiet so she could say her lines.

After introducing herself to Rella and explaining who she was and why she was there, the fairy godmother launched into her big song 'Baptized in the Nation of the Funk.' A high-energy, very funky, number that got the whole house clapping along and during which, she came over to where the band was playing and drew attention to the guitarist during his solo. When the lights went up, the crowd went wild yet again.

We played a masterstroke. Everything we did, every little nuance and gimmick we contrived during our rehearsals was a success. Every joke got a laugh. Every appeal to emotion got empathetic sighs. It was an amazing feeling, made infinitely better by the choice to have the band on the stage. I'd the opportunity to be in the theater to watch from the ideal viewpoint, as everything just fell into place.

When Rella's imaginary friend, Paco came out, dressed in his gold lamé matador costume and sombrero, the crowd waited silently until he launched into his song, explaining who he was and then burst into laughter yet again. When the same actor who played Paco, came out dressed as the big bad wolf from Little Red Riding Hood, joined by me on the harmonica, to sing 'Wolf in Wolf's Clothing,' he brought the house down.

For the song where the sidewalk that Rella walks on to get herself to the ball, comes to life and tries to look up her skirt, hitting on her the whole time, the lights went out and we used dayglow and neon lighting, along with a skateboard, to create a surreal effect. It went over so well, we could have been hitting on the audience's daughter right in front of them and they would have eaten it up with a spoon.

During the prince's ballad, where he spills his heart about not finding any women who turn him on, as the stage lights were low and moody, the band spontaneously pulled out lighters and began waving them slowly back and forth in the air. This was totally unplanned and the crowd began to copy them, laughing and clapping as they did. The actor, who played the prince, didn't understand why the people in the crowd were laughing and holding up lighters, until he looked over at the band, when he realized what was happening. He laughed and lost his place in the song temporarily. He recovered easily but this just sent the crowd further into their ecstatic approval.

Cues flowed by effortlessly. We launched into one song after another as the audience lifted us up on a wave of their happiness. Before I knew it, we were at the end of the performance. I was elated as the lights went down and the audience began to cheer. Then, according to plan, the fairy godmother came out and began an acapella verse of 'Amazing Grace.' This was my crowning glory and I had to fight for it with Chett.

My idea was to have each of the members of the cast sing a verse about their character arc to the tune of Amazing Grace. I had a strong intuition it would be killer at the end of the musical. Chett disagreed strongly but I would not relent and finally he wrote the lyrics for it. In the cast, there was about a fifty-fifty divide between those that liked it and those that didn't – but I just knew that it had to be there. We then worked out it would be the song for the curtain call.

As the fairy godmother sang through her verse, the room was gripped. The electricity was palpable. Then characters came out one at a time and went through their verses, joining hands when they finished. At last, Rella and the prince came out in wedding clothes, with a bouquet of flowers and did a duet for the final verse, clasping hands with the rest of the cast when they finished. Altogether, the entire cast revisited the original Amazing Grace lyrics one last time and then took a bow as a line.

The crowd went wild! I noticed there were tears streaming down my cheeks as I watched this. Then the actors pointed to the band and clapped and the entire audience leapt onto their feet, kicking the portable chairs aside, screaming, clapping, whistling and cheering as loud as they could. It was a massive standing ovation and it stretched from the front of the stage to the balcony.

The house lights came up and I could see the faces of the crowd that had given us back tenfold for every ounce of love that we had given them. Everywhere were smiles and wide eyes, people shouting and clapping loudly, rushing the stage as best they could to shake hands and pat backs.

Moved by this beyond the ability to reason, I turned to the band and shouted,

   "Brick House, on one!"

We broke into a spontaneous rendition of the Commodores classic and the entire theater started dancing.

It was as if all of us needed to get up and move after so much positivity had been shared between us. So, there we were, band, actors and crowd, all dancing together not wanting that moment to end.

When we met at the theater on Saturday afternoon to get ready for that night's performance, Chett was already there. He was holding a newspaper in his hand. It was the San Francisco Bay Examiner. He had it opened to the entertainment section. As I walked up to him, I could see that he was excited.

   "Hey, what's up?" I asked

He looked at me with the oddest expression on his face – I guess it was his over exhausted version of happiness.

"Look, we made the papers!"

I looked down and saw us, on stage the night before, with a small write up under the heading 'Best Bets.' We were listed as the best entertainment option for the night, the paper even going as far as saying that the drive from San Francisco would be well worth it to catch this show. Chett addressed the small group of us that were standing there.

> *"I've been talking with my dad about making a deal to get us to San Francisco if the play does well here. I'd say by the looks of this article, we're doing well here. We sold every ticket we had last night and after they were all gone, we let people pay cash and walk in. We were actually stamping hands just before show time! There were about seven hundred people here last night and tonight should be even better!"*

I couldn't believe we made the papers. I was blown back. Yesterday, last night, was real. We did it. We pulled all of that together, put in two years of work and made something great, something people really and truly loved. We poured our souls, passion, dreams and desire into this project, even though we could not clearly see the finishing post for ninety-nine percent of the journey. It worked and it had worked better than I'd even dared to hope.

V

That feeling, the sensation of building something from sheer willpower and creativity and having people love it that much, is incomparable. There really is nothing else like it. It has been a true north experience and feeling state for me for every day of my life since then.

Though there have been many things to divert me from that path, I have always known I'd find my way back at some point. That is what I was put here to do – to use all of my talents and skills to bear, in the service of others, in the service of humanity. It is my life's purpose.

That is the profound 'what' and 'why' I learned from Glass Slipper Blues. The part that would take me many more years to understand and connect to was the 'how.'

That night's performance was even better than the first night. Nena and I had to find a dark nook of the theater to have sex in during intermission, just to blow off some of the steam. We just came together without words, found a spot and made love right there. It simply had to happen. When we finished, we kissed tenderly then parted without words, she to her entrance and me to mine.

Every show we did, from the first to the last was sublime in terms of the magic we were creating there in the Phoenix Theater. When we finished the evening performance on Sunday, exhausted beyond anything I'd ever known. Chett came up to the cast as a whole and said to us

> *"I just got done talking to dad. We're going to San Francisco! We're taking the play to the city!"*

We all rippled with the excitement of those words. Tired as we were and with good judgement and prudence depleted along with our energy, we let our minds race at the possibilities. Another engagement, in San Francisco! There would doubtless be an expanded budget to make things look more professional, better costumes, props, equipment, professional photos of the cast and band. I envisioned all sorts of things, new cars and fat paychecks, recognition and acclaim, a springboard to other projects. My mind had truly run away with me.

Chett approached me.

> *"We did it. We are taking her to the city. This is going to be a hit! Why don't you go home and get some rest. We'll talk in a couple of days."*

He handed me a piece of paper.

> *"What's this?" I asked.*

> *"It's twenty more shares of the play. Nice work. I love you buddy."*

He reached in to hug me. I grabbed him and hugged him hard.

> *"I love you too man, I can't believe we did this."*

In that moment, I felt all of my animosity towards him melt away.

VI

During the rehearsal phase of G.S.B., Chett had devised the idea of creating shares of ownership in the project. This proved to be a very useful idea. He used them to incentivize the actors and musicians. He used them to buy out a songwriter we had brought on part way through the project, who proved impossible to work with because of a tendency to completely re-write songs overnight and then springing them on the group the next day. Chett used them to create a sense of value for the whole thing. Now, he used them to reward me for all of my hard work.

What I'd not paid attention to during the creation and rehearsal phase of the project was Chett would also buy people's shares from them whenever the opportunity presented itself – just good business practice I suppose. By the time, we had finished our first run, Chett owned approximately fifty percent of the total number of shares and I owned just over thirty. He'd bought up most of what the other members had been given. Only the drummer, saxophone player and a couple of other people retained their equity.

I went home and slept in my own bed. I slept for the better part of two days. When I woke up, I thought I'd awoken to whole new life, a life where I was the co-creator of a successful musical being brought to San Francisco on its inevitable journey to Broadway. I was so inspired when I got out of bed, I went to the window, drew back the curtains for a face full of morning sunlight. I opened my windows and breathed in deeply. To my mind, the air smelled sweeter today than I'd ever remembered. I made myself a French press of rich, dark-roast coffee, doctored it up just the way I liked it and went to sit on my patio to drink it.

All the time I was drinking my morning coffee, I reflected on what we had done, how hard we had worked to create this thing and now it was real. We were going to get to reap the rewards of our labors. With this level of enthusiasm, I called Chett.

The phone rang a couple of times then he picked up.

"Hello?"

"Hey, Man. How are you doing?" I asked.

He laughed in a slightly manic way, as if the question were somehow so obvious the very act of asking it was comedic.

"I'm exhausted man." He sounded almost defensive.

"Me too, but I'm so excited! I can't believe we did it man, we really did it."

"Yeah, we did it."

"So what's the word? What happens now?" I inquired, not really picking up on the subtext in his voice.

"You mean with the play? What happens with that?"

"Of course, the play, man! When do we get back to work?"

"You'll have to talk to my dad. I sold him all of my shares yesterday, he owns my part now."

CHAPTER 15

WHERE INTEGRITY FAILS

I

If you've ever been sucker punched, I mean really sucker punched, where you are just standing there with no idea what is coming next, then you know – as I do – the worst part is not actually the blow. Oh it hurts, make no mistake about that. It hurts and all the more so because you were utterly unprepared for it. You had no chance to steel yourself against the oncoming blow. But that is not what sticks with you after all is said and done. What sticks with you is the feeling, not the pain, but the feeling. Your mind can't let go of the image of being knocked down while you were defenseless.

I have been blindsided before, by tough kids in school, or in my neighborhood growing up. I have been talking to a girl, minding my own business and had a group of boys sneak up on me and push me over while one of them punched me in the head. It knocked the living daylights out of me. I got back up, confused and disoriented, not understanding what had just happened.

I have also been the one to do something like that to another. Once in the tenth grade, a friend of mine started a fight with another guy no one liked. Once this fight was underway, the other guy began to win. He was making light work of my friend. In a moment I am not proud of, I ran up to the other guy, full speed, in his blind spot. When I was about ten feet away, I launched myself into the air and delivered a flying roundhouse kick to the side of the attacker's head. He fell like a stone – gravity plus momentum. He hit the ground hard.

When he recovered himself enough to get up, he was so confused and disoriented, that he actually tried to shake my hand and congratulate me on such a nice kick. I felt sickened by the whole thing. I was disgusted in myself for my choice to gang up on someone. I was angry at him for not having the sense to move out of the way of my kick. I was mad at my friend for starting a fight and losing, plus spending all of that energy to humiliate another person into fighting in the first place.

More than any of that, I was jolted violently back to moments in my own childhood where I was out of my depth, not knowing what to do, where I tried to smile my way out of a scary situation.

I remembered times being stricken with fear, terrified, hoping that I could stretch a grin over it to hide it. It wasn't my fault I had to face so many difficult situations when I was profoundly unprepared to do so, left so often in the company of savages and monsters who seemed content to feed on my fear, so many times knowing things were not right but being too weak to make a change, to do anything about it. I remember having that fucking response hard wired into me, like a goddamn P.T.S.D. trigger, connected to the time when I was too weak to protect myself. It made the bile in my stomach rise to relive that feeling, to know that I'd been so weak I could not defend myself, to see it in another person, to know I'd caused it in the guy who my friend could not 'best' in a fight.

It made the bile rise in my stomach to watch myself from outside as that same response was triggered when Chett told me he just sold the play to his dad, a hard-nosed real estate developer. To watch myself as I reflexively try, from that place of left over childhood weakness, to find a way to align myself with the person who was sucker punching me. If Chett's dad now owned the rights to a majority of the play then I was fucked. I'd been shafted. All my work had been for nothing, like trying to piss a straight line in a hurricane – totally fucking useless.

And in spite of the obvious, I still tried to sympathize with Chett.

> *"Oh, OK, I see. So what should I do then?" I asked him, like an asshole.*
>
> *"Well, he will buy your shares from you, I'm sure."*

Clearly, Chett had his 'sucker punch response' prepped on deck and ready to go.

II

Having had over a decade to reflect, I can say that I have really and truly forgiven Chett for this. I have come to see my part in all of it. I have reached out to him since then and made tentative steps to rekindle our friendship. The truth of the matter is that he was as overwhelmed as I was and he just handled it very differently to me.

In all probability, any approach I might have taken would just as likely have ended up in disaster too. For all of his ham-fisted glad handing, for caving in to the whims of the cast, I would, in equal measure, with all the warmth and flexibility of a cornered Wolverine who had sat so forcefully on a prickly pine cone, that they can't convince it to become unstuck. We both brought a huge creative thrust to the inception of Glass Slipper Blues and we both contributed to its ultimate failure.

Yet, there was this sense I was deceived, tricked out of what I had created, by a plain and simple con, a bait and switch. I know this is the case because Chett went on to revamp our project, hiring professional musicians, musicians with no personal connection to the music whatsoever, to rewrite and overproduce the score. He gave the story, 'his story,' a complete Disney-fication as well, effectively scrubbing clean and sterile all of the raw and edgy magic of the first iteration of G.S.B.

When the second coming was performed, Chett left VIP tickets for me at the box office. I attended but did not speak to him. I watched, brokenhearted as the beautiful thing I'd brought to life, full of fun, innovation, raunch and attitude was transformed before my eyes into something fit for an after-school special.

I can't say if even now, Chett would ever agree with this but to me, all that was special about what we had done, all that made it the recipient of rowdy standing ovations, where people had kicked their chairs aside to get up on their feet faster, all that had made it a 'Best Bet' after one show, was simply gone – bleached out of existence in an effort to achieve – I don't know what exactly.

What we had created was raw, greasy funk. What it had become was elevator music. Overcooked and bland, devoid of all spice and flavor, it was like a white bread and mayonnaise sandwich. I was crushed.

Ultimately, I'd receive a five thousand dollar check for my efforts and my shares. When I combine in my head with the months of rent Chett had paid on my behalf, I estimate all told, Glass Slipper Blues earned me just under ten thousand dollars. Ten thousand dollars for two years of my life and a hefty amount of blood, sweat and tears to boot. Some would say I came out O.K. for my first full-scale project like, others would say I was totally screwed on that deal.

Doing our best to look like we belong on MTV

CHAPTER 16

AFTERMATH

I

After Glass Slipper Blues, I drifted for a long time. I tried to put on a smile and carry on with the day-to-day but if it looked to anyone as though I'd really moved on, they were no keen judge of character. I couldn't find a convincing reason why I would have to go through all I had gone through, both to get to where I could create something like that and all I went through during its actual creation, only to have it ripped away from me. We manifested something rare and special, a truly beautiful thing and it was taken from me with a common bait and switch. I found the contrast between those things to be crass and vulgar.

It had been suggested to me early on in my recovery looking for something of value in every situation was a worthy task. I'd been disciplining myself for some years to do just that – I'd gotten good at it. But this – this was different. All I could take from this experience was negative. I think I was measuring the perceived injustice of it against some arbitrary but pervasive sense of cosmic, karmic idea of right and wrong – some fallacy I had in my mind about how things 'should be' if we act a certain way. Of course, the unpleasant truth is being 'good' doesn't guarantee 'good' things will happen to you.

'Good' and 'bad' are arbitrary moral constructs with no connection to natural laws whatsoever. In terms of the natural world, there is only 'cause' and 'effect.' Nature does not reward for doing the morally 'right' thing, or a 'good' thing. The only sustainable reason for doing 'good' things must be because you feel it is the right way to live. In essence, you must do them for you and you alone, with no expectation of how life or other people will respond to them. When you lay your head on your pillow at night, do you like the person you were that day?

There were many days during the making of G.S.B. where I didn't like myself. I'll wager Chett felt the same about himself too. We hid behind self-righteousness and the pain of self-imposed torture of the recently wronged but we both acted contrary to our true selves, our core values. Both of us cloaked our own misdeeds in the justifications of what had been done to us. As Viola says in Shakespeare's 'Twelfth Night,' 'conceal me what I am, and be my aide, for such disguise as hap'ly shall become the form of my intent.'

I was ultimately able to forgive Chett and to see my part in the situation. Most importantly, I learned from what happened but that took many years for me to 'process.' I took the check Chett gave me (from his dad) and frittered it away. I don't think I really wanted that money, in truth. I bought myself a nice new bass, a TV, some clothes and blew whatever was left.

It is difficult to describe the way a thing feels when nothing else you've felt bears a resemblance to it. Pulling piecemeal from other areas of my life to attempt some illumination, I'd say losing the rights to the play was a combination of depression, the loss of a loved one, such as a girlfriend and the profound unravelling feeling when you discover others who you thought to be close friends have fucked you over. All of these sensations came together to create a sort of 'spiritual destitution,' as if I'd been plucked from within myself by a skewer.

I did my best to conceal my emptiness with whatever bravado I could muster. I created a passable charade with it, fooling all but those who knew me well. My reality that I was cast adrift, untethered and floating. I was required to find work again, which was something I thought I had remedied with the creation of the play. I held down this job for a while, or that one. Never giving anything my honest effort, because the truth was I didn't care. Even when starting a new job, I viewed it as a 'short-term situation,' often vaguely planning my exit strategy while I was interviewing or even deciding a 'start date.'

Perhaps as some kind of response to all of the angst inside me, I began to push the boundaries of what we could get away with in Groove Juicy, making our performances as rowdy as possible. We began pumping more sexuality, more brazenness into them, with various racy themes, including the ever-popular pajama party where we would host a 'Naughty Nightie' contest in the middle of the show.

I'd become disinterested in Nena of late, probably because most of our time was spent fighting and bickering with each other. Meanwhile, everywhere I turned, there were beautiful girls throwing themselves at me. The temptation was increasingly difficult to resist. My heartbreak and loss with Glass Slipper Blues notwithstanding, I was still the young, dynamic leader of the most popular band in the area.

Nena and I went our separate ways. I can't tell you what she did next but I fell into the warm embrace of my female fans. Lately, there had been several very tempting young women who had been making a point of coming out to our shows and dancing and carrying on right in front of me, making eye contact throughout the night and generally making themselves available to me. Having struggled for so long with an 'over-abundance' of disputes and an 'under-abundance' of intimacy, sexual or otherwise, I resolved I'd pursue all of the available young ladies showing such a keen interest in me.

And so, I had a hot streak for several months that did wonders for my confidence and morale, often finding myself in the company of several women in a given week. This in turn, made me want to push the envelope even further in the band's performances and what we could get away with on stage. It was in this spirit we decided to throw the rowdiest pajama party we'd ever done. It would be on Valentine's Day – and we would pull out all the stops.

The evening of the show arrived. The fliers had all been distributed, the papers notified, the word put out on the street. The Inn of the Beginning had done their advertising as well. It promised to be a big crowd.

As the venue started to fill and the start time approached, we were unusually excited. We had worked out some gimmicks we hoped would be showstoppers, including underwear for every band member with hearts and cupids on them. These we planned to reveal all at once, by ripping off the 'tear-away pants' we all wore, during one of our more popular songs.

It was show time. We took the stage wearing our surprise boxers, tear away sweat pants and Hugh Hefner robes. When the crowd saw this, they went wild with applause. We began tearing through our first set, whipping the audience into a frenzy with pulsing renditions of 'Brick House,' 'Roller Coaster,' 'Let it Whip,' 'That's the Way (I Like It)' and more. We would invite girls up on stage to dance with us, wearing their tiny little nighties and stockings, rubbing happily up against us as we pumped them full of bass, drums, horns and guitars, tickling them with tasty solos and crashing into them with funky breaks.

We worked the big reveal, where we would all tear away our pants in unison, to expose the Valentine-themed boxers beneath, into the song 'Ladies Night' by Kool and the Gang. When the time came, the instruments all stopped except for the drums, who were laying down a heavy beat, then the drummer stopped, clicked his sticks together and yelled

"ONE, TWO, THREE, FOUR!"

As he did this, we all reached down, grabbed our crotches, pulled hard and ripped off our pants, right to the beat. The crowd turned themselves inside out.

Only seconds after that, bras and panties began to fly onto the stage and the girls who had just removed them, began to lift up their shirts to prove where the undergarments had come from. There were dancers who would find their way over to where I was on the stage, get in front of me, turn around, arch their backs and slowly pull down their pajama bottoms to reveal their actual bottoms – only for a second – but that is really all they need to make their particular point.

Sex was heavy in the air, acting as an intoxicant, making me light headed and giddy. I felt like a god that night. The power of feminine approval to a young man should never be underestimated. By the time the Naughty Nightie contest finally rolled around, I was more animal than man, a howling, slavering version of my namesake – I was the Wolfe. I was rock hard and falling all over myself, like a Tex Avery wet dream.

We brought on stage all the girls who wished to enter the contest, lined them up, then had them each step to the front to do a little show for the audience to vote on.

(...To all reading this book who find women attractive, I will offer this small piece of advice. There is a definite upper limit to how much pure dopamine a person can handle and still keep their wits about them. When that dopamine is released because the probability of sex is high, well, we all know how disorienting that feeling can be. So, if you should find yourself in a situation where you are corralling ten or so scantily clad, giggling, bouncing women who are all eager to see you smile, no matter what it takes, proceed with caution.

For even if you don't know it now, your reputation in your community is important. It can be tricky to be taken seriously in other contexts once you become known as the bass player who publicly bit, licked, squeezed, nibbled and / or groped a line of lingerie-wearing, nubile, achingly ripe twenty-somethings, however thrilled they might have been to be receiving your attention.

Furthermore, if you should be badgered into taking your pants completely off while on stage, say, by the same line of women accompanied by a crowd chanting encouragement, do it so quickly no one can really be sure what they saw, or if in fact, they saw anything at all. I'd also advise you, at this point to be sure – not 'somewhat' sure but 'really' sure – you are on very good terms with the owner of the establishment where this is taking place. Wanton public nudity tends to be frowned upon by law enforcement professionals...)

It was in the middle of the contest, while I was quite literally, up to my nose in sexy young women, when she walked in.

II

There have been times in my life when the very sight of a woman had a very specific, visceral effect on me, taking hold of me, compelling me beyond my ability to resist. The moment I first laid eyes on Suzie for instance, also Lacey, I saw them and I just knew. The night of Groove Juicy's rowdiest pajama-jammie-jam ever was destined to be one of those nights.

She walked through the doors of The Inn of the Beginning, wearing nothing but high-heel boots that came up her calves to just under her knees, long, golden braids of hair, one on each side of her neck. On her body was a tiny pink and black, tiger-striped, fuzzy bikini. Without the boots, she was easily five foot nine and with them, she was taller than I was! I was up on stage, kneeling down behind the line of Naughty Nightie contestants, testing their individual butt-cheeks for density and springiness – with my teeth. My head was reeling with the perfume of raw desire that originated only inches from where my teeth were.

I came up for air and there she was. Somehow, the crowd had actually parted, like the Red Sea, like willing legs or succulent lips. It parted and revealed her. She who would be my lover, my friend, my enemy, she who would be one of the great tests of my spirituality and ultimately a profound teacher. She was also the mother to my yet unborn son.

I can't say whether it was because of the already obscene level of revelry going on in that room, or in spite of it but when I saw her, everything else became somehow shallow and trite. I set down my bass without saying anything to the band. The music stopped. I walked over to her and just like I did with Suzie, I never broke eye contact. My saxophone player Blane, seeing what was happening, shouted into the microphone

"Oh no, looks like the bass player needs a time out!"

The audience roared its approval at that comment. I was encouraged by it, but she, I think, was a little put upon by the attention. Every eye in the house was, after all, on her.

I swaggered over to her and said

"I suppose that introductions would be redundant at this point,
but all the same, I'm Manny. What's your name?"

"Julia." she replied.

"Nice to meet you, Julia. I'm a little busy right now but I think I
should probably get your number because I'm going to want to
talk to you later."

I grinned at her as if she was a canary and I was a cat.

"Sorry, I don't give out my number to musicians." she teased.

I put my hand over my heart and mimed being shot by an arrow, buckling my knees and gasped

"Say it ain't so. Anything but that!"

She shrugged her shoulders.

"Sorry, that's just how I roll. Besides, you've got your hands full
anyway."

She beckoned towards the stage where there were still a bevy of young, delicious co-eds standing waiting for the music to begin again. Then she turned and walked away, taking care to make sure that her tiger-striped derrière was wiggled to good effect as she did.

I headed back to the stage, feigning dejection, nodded at the drummer who, along with everyone else in the place, had just watched as I was shot down by this tall, saucy, Amazonian vixen. He counted the band in and the music kicked back into life.

And just like that, the mood had been restored. Everyone was dancing. The girls in the contest were wiggling and lacing the air on the stage with their irresistible pheromones. For my part, I kept my eye on Julia, making eye contact whenever I could. She was doing a bang up job of being coy but connecting with me just often enough to keep me hooked.

And I was hooked. I couldn't take my eyes off the one who was not falling all over me. That was something that I wasn't used to – and I found it very intriguing. I watched from the stage as guys approached her. One-by-one, they got shut down, walking away with heads hung low, whilst she stood there indifferent. Sometimes she'd look to see if I'd watched and made an acknowledgement when I had. I'd shrug my shoulders and roll my eyes at her, then smile my most lascivious smile and go back to being a rockstar.

By the time the night was ending, I figured nothing would come of it with her and resigned myself to another of the bountiful selection laid out before me. As it turned out, I'd actually made an impression on Julia. When I was packing out my equipment at the end of the night, when no one else could see what she was doing, she found me in a discrete corner of the venue and handed me a little piece of paper with her number on it. She then leaned in close to my ear, so close that I could feel her breath and whispered

> *"When you get bored of her, give me a call?" tipping her head*
> *toward the girl who was waiting for me.*

I wound up calling her many times before she would talk with me beyond a quick chat. I found this to be off-putting yet enticing at the same time. And when she did finally consent to speak with me, our talks wound up being long and meaningful, plumbing the depths of many important issues, far from what I'd expected. No matter how I tried to keep things light and frisky, it just never worked out that way. She kept connecting with me and making me crave her company but she would never agree to go out with me. I finally got her to say 'yes' to a date by bribing her with tickets to 'STOMP,' the dance and percussion group.

We went to San Francisco to see them. Before the gig, we spent the day by the bay. She wavered between 'touchy-feely' and 'hard to get.' I just couldn't seem to get my bearings with her. Then, as we were talking on the steps of some building or another, or perhaps in Ghirardelli Square, she informed me 'she wasn't available to date anyone and I should not expect otherwise from her.' At least the pressure was off. I knew where I stood. I decided for the rest of the day I would stay in the 'friend-zone.' I stopped coming on to her all together.

We had a great time in San Francisco. Afterwards, we headed back to Santa Rosa. When the other friend who we rode down with dropped us off at our cars, I asked her if she would like to go for a swim at my house. I shared a bachelor pad with three other guys, so nothing was implied when she agreed. I did think it a bit odd she had a bathing suit at the ready in the trunk of her car. I put the thought out of my mind. When we got back to my house, I showed her where the bathroom was for her to change and I went to my room. As I exited my room, she was coming out of the bathroom, our paths crossed somewhere in the living room and I reached out to hug her and thank her for a nice day. That hug lasted us all night and in to the next day.

It was no time at all before we were seeing each other all the time and though she (and I) shunned the labels of 'boyfriend' or 'girlfriend,' it was obvious us both we felt something for each other. I can't say exactly what she saw in me but in her I saw someone who I could really talk to, really connect with. It was not something I was looking for but it was certainly something I loved when I found it.

In a short time, I came to think I loved her too. Perhaps too short a time for anything more than a hint of genuine emotion but convincing nonetheless. And so I began to afford her the trusts and liberties that are usually bestowed upon the object of your affections. I began to favor her over the other girls in my life at that time, wanting more and more to spend my free time with her.

One evening, during a lull in our passions, she began to open up to me. She told me all about a medical emergency that happened to her when she was only fifteen, an ovarian cyst that had ruptured and left her unable to ever get pregnant, according to the doctor. She went on to explain, with all due vulnerability, if we wanted, we could stop using condoms we had been using up until that point.

When I was informed of all of this, I had no reason to suspect anything but the sharing of naked truth from one lover to another. An offering meant to bring us closer. It would have seemed impossible, had I even bothered to stop and think about it, for her to cloak any deception in that moment. It seemed to me her soul was as naked as her willing body – and wanted to be made whole by me. I trusted her and wasn't expecting her to pull a selfish stunt.

We were eye-to-eye. She lay on her stomach, lithe and smooth, propped up at the elbows. I only had to look past her line of sight to see her back sloping gracefully away to its small, only to rise playfully again at the rear entrance to her hips. This to me was such a distraction the house could have been on fire and I wouldn't have noticed. Inspired by the heat in those hips, I found my way back to them and took her up on her offer.

Anyone of a certain age knows the difference between the false promise made by a condom and the real conjugal connection between two lovers. This was our first experience with the latter and I was enthusiastic beyond reason at the prospect of it. I approached my work with a gusto that can't be taught and must come from pure inspiration. That evening, though walls stood between us, my roommates could all attest to the intensity of my inspiration – much to their inconvenience, I think.

Julia and I fell together in a heap, all sweat and breath. Laughing and cooing together at what we had just done. The room seemed to be lit up afterward, as did she. It was all I'd hoped it would be. We laid together, face-to-face on the same pillow for several more hours after that, exchanging secrets and sending tiny promises back and forth like scouts across the small distance between our lips.

It was less than a month later, closer to three weeks, when she came to me, abashed and told me that I was going to be 'a father.'

She said

> "...I don't understand how this could have happened... it was beyond comprehension... her mom was calling it a miracle..."

I did not know what to think but was sure divinity was not to blame here. In this circumstance, as with most, I tended towards siding with the 'Occam's Razor' point of view, namely, the simplest explanation of a thing is most likely to be the correct one.

And a miracle was certainly not, the simplest explanation here.

CHAPTER 17

AND NOW FOR SOMETHING COMPLETELY DIFFERENT

I

None of this theorizing changed the facts. I was going to be a dad and that was that. As I grappled with this new reality, things began quietly, imperceptibly rearranging themselves inside of me. I was taking stock of what my real priorities were in light of this new situation. The fact I'd not had a dad, nor much of a mom, was weighing heavily on me. The way I was left alone to fight my own battle and fend for myself as a child meant I'd always known I didn't want to be that kind of parent. I entertained many fantasies about how I would do things differently. But those fantasies were only abstractions, daydreams. This was as real as things were ever likely to get.

This child would arrive, barring some tragedy and I needed to figure out what to do. I realized early on that being only somewhat involved in its life was not an option for me. I discovered I had strong feelings about what the right thing to do was. I'd be there, come hell or high water. Mine would be a child who knew its dad loved it – and loved it fiercely. I could definitely be more of a parent to my child than anyone had ever been to me.

Once I got over the initial shock and began to envision myself in the role of 'dad' everything else in my life organized around that. And so it was with this mindset I stayed as close to Julia as humanly possible all through the pregnancy of Tobin Alexander Emmanuel Wolfe, the little boy, who utterly, completely and in every way I can imagine, changed my life for the better.

Though many of my friends are in their ranks, I can't understand how so many men can choose, or live with, not being present in the lives of their children as workable strategy. The fact this approach is looked upon as viable option by men is a scathing indictment of our culture and flatly unforgivable for the damage it does to the innocent. There are massive amounts of statistics to attest to this. I will restrain myself to saying the absence of dads, real, attentive, engaged dads, is the greatest social problem of our time. It destroys more lives than alcoholism, drug addiction and violence combined.

I was not going to let that happen to my son.

CHAPTER 18

METAMORPHOSIS

I

In a life that lasts a hundred years, you might get two or three moments like this, moments that alter you, change you forever. When you have an unshakeable sense everything you have done up until then was merely preparation and that it was not enough, they are moments when you know, with certainty, your place in the cosmos. Those moments when all you thought you were, all your pretense and persona is peeled back and your ego is laid bare.

In these instances, we connect to the reality of life. It's savagery beyond anything we can normally comprehend, ripping itself apart for the primal joy of doing so, constantly destroying itself so it can remake itself stronger than before, in a never-ending cycle.

Its intricacy and complexity, so self-entwined and perfectly balanced, we are simply not worthy of observing it, save for the fact we, at our own cores, are it. Three trillion cells all operating in flawless synchronicity, all balancing and counterbalancing each other effortlessly.

And it's beauty, so profound, so heartbreakingly breathtaking, it moves us to tears. It shakes our foundations until, in a microcosm of the universe itself, we tear ourselves down block by block and nail by nail, until there is nothing left standing and we begin to rebuild ourselves again in an effort to mimic the divine.

In these moments, we can grasp, only for the blink of an eye, we are, in reality, made of stardust. We are the creative force of the universe experiencing itself through the subjective lens of our individual humanity. And when a moment like this occurs, time and space fall away and there is only that truth, so strong, it feels like it will separate us back into the individual elements that bonded to create us in the first place and we will be scattered amongst the stars and lost forever.

The only one of these moments I have had in my life so far, was the first time that I held my newborn son. In that moment, a lifetime went by. A lifetime was changed.

The first time Tobin was handed to me, my head was full of ideas about how I'd raise this little boy, this perfect little human, whose brand new life was in my care. Then, I felt the weight of his body, eight pounds, twelve ounces, the weight of his presence, enough to fill the whole room and more. I felt the weight of the sacred responsibility of not only caring for a new life but also knowing I was charged with guiding it, seeing that it turned out right. I felt the beat of his heart and watched as his tiny chest lifted up and down as he breathed. Everything I thought – everything – I'd told myself about being 'a father' went straight out the window.

It all blew away. It was just gone.

II

The moments leading up to his birth, I was nervous, lightheaded and totally unable to focus on anything. I wandered around the room trying to make small talk and failing miserably, doing whatever I could to distract myself from the activity happening in the big birthing tub a few feet away. As the time drew near, I felt the room get hotter and my head got lighter, until, right as he crowned, my vision went all white and shrank to a pinpoint. My legs got weak and I stumbled. Then I heard it, the midwife slapped his back to clear his throat and he cried out clear as a trumpet.

Suddenly my world swam back in to focus and I saw him, tiny to my eyes, but actually a very big boy. He'd been swaddled and given a little yellow hat to wear on his olive colored head. That hat looked like a dollop of Cheese Whiz sauce. His face was squished and I could see how big his closed eyes were, judging by the size of the lids. He'd stopped crying almost as soon as he started and now Julia was holding him. She looked at me and said, "Look daddy, it's Tobin. It's your little boy."

I swooned. He was, unquestionably the most beautiful thing I'd ever seen. I sat there, glassy eyed and smiling a mouth-open smile like I was on a really good acid trip. I had no words.

"Do you want to hold him?" Julia asked.

I had to nod because my face wasn't working right. She handed Tobin to the midwife, who brought him over to me. At this point, he was less than three minutes old. I took him, my little son, this impossibly tiny little boy whose entire fist was the size of most of my thumb, with his Cheese Whiz hat and his swaddling clothes. I took him and cradled him instinctively in my arms. As the nurse brought him to me, he was crying quietly but as soon as she put him in my arms, he was quiet. He reached out, grabbed my finger with his tiny hand and held it tight – tighter than I would have thought possible. He held it there so that I could feel each individual finger of his hand.

He opened his huge, dark brown eyes and looked right at me. He looked right through me, right into me and right at the truth in my soul. He looked at my divinity and at my primacy. He saw my strengths and my flaws.

I was unable to do anything but look back at him. I tried to speak but only noises came out. I still had no words to give. When he heard the sounds I made, he wiggled my finger, as if to say

"Relax. You're going to do just fine. I've got you."

He didn't break eye contact. We stayed there for a long time. Long enough for the room to dissolve and the people around us to become phantoms – translucent, half-images. It was just he and I, locked in each other's gaze, unmoving, silent, yet saying everything. To me it is laughable to hear people speak of the unaware nature of infants. How they can they not know what is happening around them? To this I say 'balderdash,' 'horse feathers,' 'rubbish,' and 'poppycock.'

My son and I communicated a covenant in silence, a solemn oath, one we have both honored to this day. I promised him I'd do whatever was needed to protect him, to teach him, to give him what I was not given – and if by my life or my death I could help him to become a good man, then it would be done. I promised him that I'd do whatever growing was necessary to avoid passing on to him the damage that I'd had passed on to me.

He promised me that he would be patient with me and help me to know how to teach him. He told me he understood I had a big job ahead of me. After all, he was a Wolfe and therefore not easy child to raise. He promised me he would turn out better than I had and in so doing, make me proud. He explained to me this would be the most challenging thing either of us had ever done but we would get through it together.

All of this was being transmitted between us in the gaze we shared. As we sat there together, having this understanding pass from one to another, I was being laid bare. All the layers of ego and identity I'd shored myself up with for years were blown away like sand. I was stripped bare, hitting rock bottom but without the pain. I knew in that moment none of the things that had gotten me there would be sufficient to guide me from that point on.

I'd need to become a new man to become equal to this task. Fortunately, for me, he would prove to be a very good teacher. The room and the world came back into focus.

You may dismiss this as hyperbole, dear reader, but I have the pictures and I was there to witness the whole room, nine people in all, as they all fell to a hush while my boy reached into me without words and touched the very center of me. So they can say whatever they wish about infants and so can you, but I was there, tears streaming down my cheeks and I know what I know.

Finally able to put words together, I said, with trembling, cracking speech,

> *"Hi little man, I'm your daddy. I'm your daddy and I'm going to take care of you."*

After the moment had passed Julia looked over at me and said

> *"Wow."*

> *"Did you see that?" I asked.*

> *"I saw something, I'm not sure what, but I saw something. He knows who his daddy is, that's for sure."*

There was a truth so obvious in that moment it shut the entire room up and it shut me up too. He was mine, he was 'of' me and I was his. I'd protect him and never let him see the side of life that I'd seen growing up. More than the fighting and drugs, which I had only some control over, what I would keep him sheltered from was the damage born of neglect, of the ineptitudes of distracted, unaware parents. The dysfunctions that get handed down, generation to generation, parent to child, on and on through time.

Fuck that! If the devil wanted to infect my son with that poison, he was going to have to fight me first and I am no stranger to facing off with the devil. I would break Satan's teeth to loosen his grasp. I knew it when my boy looked at me. All that been done to me, all that I'd inherited from mom and dad, wouldn't stop with me. I'd be the one who broke the chains of abuse. I'd be the transformational parent. I'd take myself back through my own childhood and protect myself so that I could protect my progeny.

As it turned out that was going to be one hell of a fight.

III

When Tobin was born, he came out of the womb like Superman, one fist thrust forward as though he was flying, as if to say 'Let's get this show on the road, I haven't got all day!'

Once all of the necessary things were checked, height, weight, color, etc., we were free to go home. That was the longest car ride of my life. We needed to travel a total of twelve miles but to me it seemed like we were trekking through enemy territory hacking through the deepest jungle. Everything was a potential threat – every car that passed us as we made our way home, every cyclist or pedestrian. I even found myself checking the skies as I drove us back to safety. I never pushed the speedometer over twenty-five miles an hour for fear of endangering my son and his mom. I was a raw nerve that entire drive, senses burning as I sought to ensure the safety of my passengers.

Those stupid little yellow window signs that people use to inform us they have a 'baby on board' – those suddenly seemed like the work of genius to me. I imagined filling the side and rear windows of our old Pontiac with them until the very signs intended to create an atmosphere of safety, caused a hazard by their sheer numbers.

I'd not known that there was such a savage protector in me. The primal counterpart to the Moral Man. I knew that when cornered, I could call great aggression to my aid, but this was different than that. The part of me that came to the surface for my child was not a berserker, but a warrior, calculating and strategic.

I began sizing up everything and everyone in a way I'd never done before. I'd catch myself subconsciously placing myself between my son and strangers, or carrying an open knife in my sleeve when we went on walks in case of an aggressive dog. I'd scan everywhere we went together for makeshift weapons or possible threats, all the while being totally happy and calm with my boy. Fatherhood definitely brought out my 'Primal Man.'

There was even an incident when Tobin was about three, when I was expecting a girl to come by to look at a room that I was renting in my condo. When she arrived at the door, there was a massive pit bull standing by her side. As I opened the door, the dog trotted in. Thinking that the dog was with the girl, I looked at her and said

"Oh, I didn't realize that you had a dog?"

"I don't." She replied, "He was just here when I got here. I thought he was yours."

By this time, the dog had come in and was heading towards Tobin, who was watching TV in the front room.

"I'll be right back." I said abruptly.

Then without another word, I went to the kitchen and grabbed a butcher's knife, concealed it behind my forearm then moved swiftly to where the dog was, saying calmly but firmly

"Let's go. Get out."

The dog paused and looked at me, looked back at Tobin, then decided to listen to my command and calmly sauntered out the front door again. I relaxed my grip on the knife. As I did, I felt the tension in the room release like a big exhale. When it was over, I was amazed at how I didn't even pause at the thought of fighting a pit bull with a butcher's knife. That was the new side of me brought out by the presence of my son. That was definitely Primal Man.

IV

It was fortunate I had such a strong protective streak where my son was concerned because no more than four months after his birth, and with no reason of any substance ever provided, Julia simply broke up with me. For a couple of months prior, she'd begun acting distant. A few times, she came home smelling as if she'd been drinking, which had been something she'd always criticized in others and assured me she had 'no interest in doing.'

Then one evening, while we were in the hot tub at her parents' house, she told me she didn't feel she needed to be accountable to me or to anyone else for that matter. We should break up. That was all the explanation I'd ever get from her. I'd come to understand many years later, she was far more wounded from her own childhood than I'd ever suspected. Back then, she was the doing the best she could do in those circumstances. She found herself in over her head simply being with me and couldn't do it any longer. In short, she'd never met anyone before that prepared her for me. I was too much for her and so she just broke up with me.

Just like so many of us, her life was one prolonged reaction to all of the things she was made to deal with. There were all of the things her parents should have protected her from, but didn't. Like me, she got both barrels, point blank, right in the face. She had inadvertently chosen a bullish, aggressively, self-improvement oriented man to father her son. When I told her what it meant to make a 'Wolfe baby,' to have me as a father, she didn't listen. She couldn't have listened, because she had no frame of reference sufficient to grant her the understanding to appreciate the sheer gravity of the task ahead.

CHAPTER 19

A NEW TWIST

I

Six months later, Julia and I were sitting on her parent's front porch, side-by-side on a swing. The sun was out, the weather was mild and birds were singing. She calmly said to me

"I'm getting married, moving to Oregon, taking Tobin – and you're going to have to deal with it."

When she said those words to me, she didn't raise her voice. She didn't use any kind of confrontational tone. It was as if she were ordering breakfast, or passing the time with a friend.

I took off my glasses, so I could look her directly in the eyes and responded.

"You must have no idea who I really am. If you try to take my son from me, my child, I will find you no matter where you go, burn down everything between you and me and show up at your door. And when I do, it will be the worst day of your life. I will destroy you and your husband, take my child and disappear, so help me God."

And that was how the legal battle for my son began. After I threatened Julia and her mysterious, soon-to-be husband, I left her house and drove straight down to the family law court to find out what my options were.

When I walked in the courthouse, I was greeted by a room full of women who had spent their careers defending other women from the despicable 'dead beat dads' that California is famous for. I was treated to such a profound level of disrespect and disdain in the beginning, I almost gave up – but of course, that wasn't really an option.

My first trip to the courthouse, I filed a 'party in motion' form and with it, a temporary restraining order. This assured Julia could not legally take Tobin across state lines. Her response was to decide to move to a Californian town as close to the Oregon border as possible but still almost five hours away from me. I could understand why she would try to do this to me. All I wanted was to be a real dad, present and accounted for – to show up for my son. Why disrupt that?

As I always seemed to do in times of stress, I turned again to my family for support. What stands out the most in my memory from that period, was my mom, who would constantly play devil's advocate to Julia. I'd come to her with the latest tale of the things Julia had done, only to be met with,

"I'm sure that this must be hard for her too. She's a young, single mom. This must be overwhelming for her..."

I can remember looking at mom in utter disbelief, unable to find the words to express the level of disappointment and outright betrayal I felt at her response. Even my sister, on occasion would look at her and shout

"How can you possibly take her side in this? We're talking about your son and your grandson here!"

Mom would insist we didn't understand what Julia was 'going through' and we should try to see her point of view. From 'my' point of view, mom's response showed she was blinkered to the pain, confusion and anguish I was dealing with. She was missing the fact her son was grappling with the hardest thing he'd ever had to face – and that, right now, he felt totally overwhelmed and helpless.

It was as if I was ten years old and being kicked out of school for fighting to defend her honor, all over again.

Julia and I went back and forth, contentiously, as parents in a custody battle will do. There were moves and countermoves, threats and retorts, until one day, she and her fiancée, Philippe, had me served with papers informing me they were going to sue me for full custody of Tobin. They planned to gain custody, cut me legally out of the picture entirely, take my son and move to Oregon. We had come full circle but now with lawyers. Tobin was only ten months old.

The day after I got the papers from the lawyer, I was driving with my then boss, Joey Winters, down to the Bay Area to work. Up until that morning, I couldn't stand Joey. He was – in my mind – everything that I thought that I hated about people.

He was on the far right politically and had no problem making racial jokes and expressing racist views at work. He was a born-again Christian. He was aggressive, loud and antagonistic. He also happened to be fantastic at his job. This was the only reason I continued to work for him. Under his supervision, I saw myself improving as a house painter more rapidly than with anyone else.

I think it was a simple matter of my liking the feeling of actually being taught something of value by another man. Whether or not he knew it, he was probably the only real-life mentor I ever had.

We were in his truck, heading down to Marin, when Julia called me to confirm she was definitely going to sue and take my son from me. She informed me I needed to sign the papers she'd sent or things would get 'ugly and expensive.' She knew I didn't have the money to get myself a lawyer.

When I hung up the phone, I was in a full-blown panic. Joey had heard the conversation and could see the emotion running high on my face. He looked at me and said calmly,

"I'll let you borrow the money, you just call a lawyer."

Was this man the same man who had tried to start a fight with me while we were working? The guy who drove me crazy? Yes. Now, it seemed, he was also the man who came through for me. I was floored, rendered speechless by that profound act of kindness, coming from the most unlikely of places. To this day, I count that a miracle – God looking out for me – again.

But that was only the beginning of the day's miracles. After Joey offered to lend me the money for a lawyer, I called the information helpline and randomly asked for 'the first family law office in the book'. After convincing the lady on the other end of the phone I was serious, she connected me. The phone rang a few times. Finally, someone answered. Before I realized what I was doing, I'd prattled on into the heart of my story. I was nervous and on the edge of tears, trying to compel whoever was on the other side of the phone with the sheer force of my testimony.

In the middle of my near-hysterical rant, the voice on the other end of the phone interrupted me and said

"Is this Manny?"

Everything stopped. I went silent for what felt like an age.

"What?" I said.

"Is this Manny? Manny Wolfe? Is this Manny?" the voice demanded.

"Who is this, how do you know my name?"

I was now in a confused state of disbelief, in addition to being agitated and scared about Julia.

"Manny, this is Laura...Laura Nelson." came the voice.

Laura was one of the kids I'd grown up with in the commune, now like myself, an adult and making her way in the world. She was the oldest daughter of the very same woman, Iris, who along with my stepdad had shattered my mom's world so many years ago. Laura and I'd not spoken in over fifteen years. I didn't even know she lived in Sonoma County. And yet, here she was, as improbable a person as was possible to have answered the phone at that time, on that day – and yet there she was.

My head reeled. I felt dizzy, as if someone was playing a bizarre practical joke on me, meant to test my sanity. I could see Joey in the driver's seat, striving to comprehend what was happening on the phone, trying to infer from my baffled expression what the deal was

"Laura!" I stammered. "What the hell... I don't understand... How can you be... Laura Nelson?"

I was not doing a good job of keeping it together.

"It's me, Manny, me Laura. Oh my God, this is so weird! How have you been? Never mind... obviously not great... O.K., let's find out what you situation is? What's going on?"

I told her everything, the whole story. I even went back to how Julia and I met, telling the tale of the wild night at the Inn of the Beginning, not really knowing why I did it, but Laura actually said

"No, that's good, it's good to be able to paint a picture of the kind of person she is."

I continued until the tale had been told, all of it, right up until the phone call we were having. Laura listened, only interrupting to ask pertinent, clarifying questions. When I finished she said

"Let me get your number and call you back. I think I can help you."

As it turned out, she was a paralegal at that law firm and had been working there for many years. She had become a trusted team member there, so when she asked someone for a 'mates rates' favor, one of the lawyers offered to help me.

What happened was incredible. Joey looked at me for a long second and then blurted

"Well! What the hell was that? What just happened there? Don't just leave me in suspense!"

When I explained to him what transpired, how the girl who had answered the phone at the 'first family law firm in the book,' the one I had a stranger pick at random over the phone, was someone I grew up with, someone who knew me from childhood. He let out a shout .

"Whhoooaaaahhhhh!! Don't you tell me that God isn't in your life! DAMN! That is a miracle, plain and simple! Are you sure, you're not a Christian?"

I looked at him and answered quietly

"I am today."

II

Because of Laura's influence, a top counselor for the firm agreed to take my case, with no retainer and at a sliding scale rate. That particular firm usually billed hourly at two hundred and seventy-five dollars but I was charged just fifty. I was guided step-by-step through the entire process, assisted with all the legal papers and forms and anything else that usually intimidates people. I wound up paying six hundred and fifty dollars, start to finish, while Phillipe the fiancée, paid almost nineteen thousand dollars – only to end up being laughed out of the courtroom for his money.

At one point during the process, it was recommended that Julia, Phillipe and I attend mediation, to see if we could arrive at an agreement without further legal costs being incurred. At this mediation appointment, Julia suggested I have Tobin every other weekend, Friday to Sunday. She thoughtfully offered to drive half of the way from the Californian border town where she planned on moving, to meet me in the middle and exchange our son. When the mediator asked her why she proposed so little time with me, the biological father, she answered,

> *"Because Tobin needs to have a chance to spend time with his stepdad."*

Even the mediator, whose very job is to stay impartial, calmly said to Julia

> *"So you propose to keep your son from his obviously loving and involved biological father, who is requesting half time visitation – who wants to be involved in his son's life, so he can develop a new relationship with his soon-to-be stepfather? I can tell you right now, that's going to be a tough sell."*

It was during this meeting with the mediators, when Julia played what she clearly thought (and hoped) would be her 'trump card.' Seeing the meeting was not going as she'd hoped it would, and faced with the prospect of needing to stay in or near Santa Rosa to be close to Tobin, she announced with an air of annoyance

> *"I'm pregnant and Phillipe is going to be stationed in Oregon. I can't be expected to live almost five hours from the father of my newborn son!"*

The mediators (and me) looked at her with a certain disbelief that I don't think any of us concealed very well. My mouth hung open, not at the surprise of her second pregnancy, I was unphased by that but I was astounded at the raw cheek of her comment. The chief mediator quickly composed herself and asked simply

"What about the child you've already got?"

On the way in to meeting with the mediator, I would up having to wait at a cross walk, right next to Julia and Philippe. Each of us was quiet and awkward, no one saying anything. The air felt tense and uncomfortable.

When we left the mediators office after the 'dog and pony show' that was Julia's argument for custody, there was clearly a very different feeling in the air. For me, one of victory, for them, total defeat. My heart was pounding and my steps were light as we left the session. We had agreed to a fifty-fifty time arrangement and that Tobin would be in my legal custody. What's more, he would be required to stay within forty miles of Santa Rosa, so there would not be any question of him crossing state lines with his mom. In short, she could go wherever she wanted, but my son must stay close to me.

After that, we had one more meeting with the mediators scheduled and Julia didn't show. I sat there with the chief mediator and made small talk as we waited. After about half an hour he said to me

"I don't think she's going to turn up, not that there is much left to discuss. It's clear to us she is not a responsible parent. Your son is far better off with you being the primary influence in his life, at least until she can get it together."

In the end, I spent a fraction of what Phillipe had spent in an attempt to sue me for custody of my son. Although the process was terrifying, I came out smelling like roses, with a better claim on my child than I had at the start of the ordeal.

It would turn out that my establishing a better legal claim to Tobin was not enough to keep him from some of the blowback of Julia's irrational behavior. Nor was it enough to shield me. I was able to keep Tobin close to me and therefore, Julia stayed close too. Being swatted in the legal proceedings like that, had caused her to act out in even more unnerving ways. She began doing things like taking Tobin with her and staying out all night, then refusing to say where she'd been or what she'd been doing. Many times, we would arrange for me to meet her at her house at seven in the morning to pick him up, only to find that she wasn't home yet.

She would come pulling up ten or fifteen minutes later, all carefree and nonchalant. When I asked her where she'd been, she would dismiss my questions with a quick, 'out with friends,' or something similar.

She became indignant when I pressed her for more details. As she was handing Tobin to me, she would often drop some kind of bomb on me.

> *"Oh, by the way, I know it's your time with him, but I need Tobin this weekend, Phillipe is getting the weekend off and I want them to be able to spend some time together."*

She was expert at saying things like this with an easy air of entitlement. It always sent me over the red line. Whether or not the request was granted, I'd leave with Tobin, furious at her, often taking half the day to calm back down again. I didn't even know Phillipe. I'd met him only once, but thanks, in large part to her relayed tales, I was developing a hatred for him that I could barely contain.

During that period of my life, the time when Tobin was a little boy, the Moral Man and the Primal Man were at war with each other. The moral one want to take the high ground, believing this was all a test and a growing experience – something to gain a spiritual value from, if only I could persevere. The primal one wanted to rage, to destroy – it wanted vengeance.

I had such intensely savage fantasies about finding Julia and Phillipe alone. I'd grab her by the face, digging my fingernails into her flesh as I pulled her violently down on the ground. As Phillipe moved to defend her, I would reach forward and gouge out his throat with my other hand. When he stopped and recoiled, realizing he was out of his depth, he would see he had inadvertently brought the proverbial stick to the gunfight. I let go of Julia's face, now ruined and brought my other hand, my good hand, fist-closed, onto the ridge of his nose, causing his neck to go limp and blood to spurt everywhere. It washed all over me, dousing me, turning me into an bloodied abomination – something made of rage, here to cause damage, maim and kill.

I'd watch them both on the ground, scrambling for safety, searching for protection. These fantasies were so visceral, so tangible in my mind, they often left me shaking and sweating, with my pulse racing and my head delirious. More than once, I found myself needing to pull my car over until I calmed down, Tobin in his cradle on the back seat. I even began to dream this event. Sometimes waking up, convinced I'd done this thing, I would desperately plan my next move in intense, feverish detail, before I returned to full consciousness.

Always the Moral Man would interject at times like these and he would win. Sometimes, only the thought of Tobin seeing me in prison kept me from acting out this dark fantasy. Meanwhile, mom continued to offer platitudes as consolation when I'd come to her with the most recent stunt Julia had pulled, still telling me 'it must be difficult for her.'

III

I don't know which I struggled with more. Was it the indifference and inability of mom to sympathize with me, her son, as he went through the most difficult ordeal of his life? Was it the fact another man I didn't know could be so arrogant as to try take my own son from me?

I spent a good two years in such a heightened state from all of this. I can't tell you now, how I made it through. The Moral Man was my only compass and I held fast to the belief if only I could endure, if only I could hold out, somehow (even though I didn't know how,) I'd be all right. 'This too shall pass.'

It was an endurance test of my very soul. The only light I had during that time was Tobin himself. He was proving to be an extraordinary child. He was walking and talking by nine months old. He was strong beyond belief. He shone a light that made strangers stop and stare. He was simply amazing. By the time he was eighteen months old, he knew the Latin names of every flower in our neighborhood. While other kids were counting their vocabulary words, Tobin was creating complex, multi-dimensional arguments where he would ask me questions designed to create a limited range of specific responses, to which he'd already prepared follow-up questions.

One day, well before his second birthday, he said to me

"Daddy, if you had to choose between vanilla and mint-chocolate chip ice cream and you had to choose between Baskin Robbins and Screaming Mimi's (...a local ice cream shop...), which flavor and place would you choose?"

I looked at him, smiled and said

"I guess that I'd choose vanilla at Mimi's. Why?"

Without answering my question, he inquired

"Which is your favorite time of day for ice cream, afternoon, or night?"

"Nighttime, why?"

Then Tobin said to me, with the innocence of a cherub

"So it sounds like we should go to Screaming Mimi's, tonight, for vanilla ice cream."

When people ask me what it's like to raise a child as a single dad, I tell them that I have no idea. I do know what it's like to raise a little Superman but not a child. He was mine. He was a little version of me through and through. There was no one else on this planet more qualified than I was to raise him. On the day he was born, I promised him I'd look after him and that's just what I was going to do.

III

After a time, it became clear I was going to have to settle in for a long, drawn out struggle with Julia. She was unwilling to budge even an inch on her unpredictable behavior and refusal to communicate with me. The latter of the two was becoming the more difficult to cope with on an ongoing basis. Phillipe was stationed in Oregon, she was here and she was not happy about it. She was quick to make sure her actions toward me reflected that.

And so my life became a slogging journey as I focused on putting one foot in front of the other, over and over again, as I cared for Tobin. All I did for those years was, work, keep my head down, deal with Julia and deal with mom's family. I'd left the band, dropped out of school and stripped away everything else I had.

All I focused on was being a good dad and showing up, no matter what Julia threw at me. Even if I had to miss work now and then, no matter what it took, my only goal was to make sure my son knew – without question – I loved him and I was there for him. During the mediation process, on the last day, when Julia didn't show, I had the opportunity to ask the mediator candidly, what the best strategy I could take was. The response I got was

"Just show up for your child, no matter what, just show up."

I made that my mantra.

Sometimes being the hero doesn't have any fanfare attached to it. There are no trumpets to sound your arriving. Often, no one even gives you a pat on the back. Sometimes you get no notice at all. The only way I knew I was doing the 'right thing' was by the reaction of my son. I don't know how much he really understood of the struggle I was going through on his behalf, but I could see the love in his eyes every time we were together. It was just otherworldly the way he would look at me, the things he would say and do. After he reached two years old, he never even had a tantrum around me until he was six.

Once when I was having a rough day, he was in the living room with me, playing with his toys. He looked over and noticed I was stressing, so he put his toy down, walked over to me, put his little hand on my knee and looked right into me in that way he would and his little voice said, 'It's O.K. daddy, I picked you. And I know it will be alright.'

Sometimes, only one person needs to know you are the hero and you are trying your hardest.

IV

Julia was 8 months pregnant when she married. By the time this event rolled around, I'd been put through the mincing machine by both of them. I found the wedding a total affront. I no longer wanted Julia for myself. I lost all attraction to her when I was made to experience the depth of her inconsistency and irrational hostility. That said, the thought of it made me furious.

It was in this enraged state, also fueled by how difficult my life in general had become since I met her, I decided I'd target Phillipe with my rage – and I would do it in front of Julia. I concocted a plan to drive to their wedding and throttle Phillipe right in front of her as they left the church. Initially, my angst blinded me to the fact I'd be the prime suspect. Accordingly, I headed over to where they were having their ceremony, heavy metal blasting in my car until it rattled my speakers, black gloves and ski mask on my front seat next to me. Under that seat was a hard wooden stick about the length of a man's forearm. Eddie had taught me well.

I was reconciled to doing this thing, no alibi or anything, heading down the road, too fast when my son's face popped into my mind. I was forced to imagine my child watching this act, horrifying unfolding in front of him and the inevitable consequences – like having to explain why I attacked them to my boy when I had promised to create better life for him. Lots of unpleasant ripples would be created, unless against all odds, I got away with it.

This is my confession here on paper. I genuinely intended to commit this crime when I simply couldn't take it anymore. I was convinced I had to lash out at those who had turned my life into an agonizing test of my will. Those who, with blunt disregard for anything but their own selfish desires, sought to take my child from me using slander, crude legal stunts and flat out lies.

It was also when I realized I preferred to put my son's wellbeing before the need to indulge myself in this gothic display of violence. I had another moment of clarity. I was capable of the kind of growth and self-awareness to break the chains of my habitual, unhelpful thought patterns. I could offer Tobin a better life than mine. If I ignored these selfish impulses, I could see to it Tobin would not have to inherit the same shitty start to life I'd had passed down to me.

Four blocks from the church, I turned my car around in the middle of the street, threw the gloves, ski mask and wooden stick out the window and went home.

If you asked me at any time in my life prior to that moment whether I could endure all of that without retaliation, I'd have laughed at you. I couldn't have imagined letting all that go for someone else – but for my boy – I did it.

Three weeks after their wedding night, Phillipe moved to Oregon alone. Within a year, he divorced Julia.

V

Shortly after Phillipe left for Oregon, Julia began acting erratically, more so than usual, making my life and Tobin's, very difficult. Mine on purpose perhaps, Tobin's, inadvertently. Even now, it's difficult for me to really have a sense of what was going on inside her mind during those years. It was definitely was not the mind of a happy, balanced woman, or a woman who truly had her child (soon to be children's) best interests at heart. She continued to do all the things, to which I was unfortunately growing accustomed. What's more, she suddenly had a whole new circle of friends I'd never met or heard of. This new 'clique' had many single men in it, who Julia brought around freely.

Oftentimes, I'd come to pick Tobin up at our agreed upon time, only to find another new, unintroduced man playing casually with my son. When I'd enter her house, Tobin would come running over to me, greeting me enthusiastically while Julia (and whoever the latest man was,) would sit off to the side, Julia never even offering introductions. In a couple of instances, the new men even had the audacity to act mildly aggressive towards me! They took on an air of disdain or contempt in what I can only assume was an attempt to 'impress her.'

I had the distinct sense these new men, presumably suitors, were being fed a diet of false information about me. Perhaps it was simply Julia's ability to captivate the males of the species and make them feel like they had to thump their chests around me. Either way, I was not shown the respect due to a newly single dad who was trying to figure out how to make the best of a difficult situation, be a good parent and keep things 'civil' with everyone else involved.

Very close to Tobin's second birthday, Julia gave birth to Aiden. Tobin was now a sibling, which he, like many first-born children, didn't care for. Although he took it as well as could be expected, he did grow closer to me. More often, he preferred to stay with me and would become slightly difficult when the time came to go back to Julia's.

Phillipe was virtually out of the picture now. He would come to visit every few weeks, for a few days at a time in the beginning. After a while, he stopped coming back at all. He left Julia all alone with their newborn son. The same man who spent nineteen thousand dollars trying to take my son from me had hastily turned his back on his own son when things didn't go his way. He wanted a 'family-to-go.' When he realized he wasn't going to get one, he chose to jump ship.

Julia was forcing me to get over her fast. She acted with such incredible disregard for me or my feelings. I began to feel I'd actually done something to her that I was not aware of. I felt like she was taking something out on me. How else to explain the behavior? It was definitely beyond being inconsiderate, it had moved into being decidedly hostile.

My sister's husband, Paulo lost his job about then. After looking for ages, he finally found work with a big software company in Sacramento. It was decided he would take the job and they would move. In a snap decision, the rest of the family in Santa Rosa would move with them. At the risk of sounding petty, I am certain no one in my family would have ever shown a similar solidarity to any big life decisions I had to make – since they never had.

It occurs to me it was just another example of how I've been left to my own devices for all of my life, while the rest of them stuck together. I left as soon as I could when I was a teenager. They all stayed together. Greg went off to Pennsylvania to college. They all stayed together. James moved down to Santa Rosa, the others followed. Annabel and Paulo moved to Sacramento, the others followed.

I do not know what caused this dysfunctional bond between them unless it was when mom was drinking to mourn the departure of her husband. Plus there was the other things she exposed them to during that time. What I do know is that, for some reason, I never got a family, not a real one. Not the kind all of us want, need and crave. So, they got each other, yes – but not in a healthy way, in an enmeshed, entangled and convoluted way, where boundaries were blurred, one where each person is emotionally fused to the others.

Another thing I know is the damage a dynamic like that wreaks upon a soul. In such an incredibly real and tangible way, I was stuck in the role of an adolescent boy, desperately needing his family but also trying to break away because his very life depended on it. Here was a man who wanted to create his own identity – an identity his family would never fully accept. This bind, this 'Catch 22,' is the spiritual equivalent of being stuck in tar. It cut short any significant forward momentum through life, stymied me and kept me rooted in place for years.

And so it was, I was caught between Julia, who herself embodied many of the characteristics I struggled with in mom and my family and being a good dad. I was pinned and I didn't even know it. Oh, I knew something was wrong but I couldn't figure out what. And so my family choosing to move to Sacramento as a whole, would actually being a small blessing in the sense it bought me some breathing space. The space I got meant I could focus on Julia and Tobin. That was it.

Life had different plans. I had set myself on a trajectory when I began the process of self-improvement. The next phase of that journey was about to begin. Understand when the 'universe,' or 'God,' or whatever you choose to 'call' the connection between things, sets out to teach you something, it does it by putting the problem you need to address right in your face. And the more times it has to do it before you get the lesson, the higher it raises the stakes.

Sometimes, it even puts it in your face in the form of the most beautiful woman you've ever seen.

CHAPTER 20

THE NEXT GREAT LOVE OF MY LIFE

I

After mom moved to Sacramento, she enrolled in school again. During her time there, she wound up having class after class with the same girl, a blonde bombshell named Lila. Mom would tell me about her all the time, saying she just had a feeling if ever Lila and I could meet, we would really hit it off.

After about a year of this, Lila and I had an opportunity to meet. Mom was right – we hit it off. Lila was alarmingly beautiful. I couldn't maintain my composure very well the first time we met – which was fine as it turned out – mom and my sister were there and they monopolized the conversation. Somehow, I managed to get Lila's number and after a few days of waiting – to look cool – I invited her to come and visit me in Santa Rosa.

She accepted and stayed for three days.

Lila and I were bonded instantly. We spent every spare minute together. Any time I wasn't with Tobin, I was with her. The beginning of our relationship was like nothing I'd ever known with a woman. She was smart, beautiful, incredibly talented and active in her community. A musician and a martial artist, I was so crazy, goofy stupid in love with her I don't think I stopped grinning for three months.

For about a year, all I did was raise my boy, work and wait to see her. When I spent time with her, it was a delirious blur of sex, deep and wide conversations, eating at great restaurants, more sex and sharing our dreams. I was so intoxicated by her I even started to sacrifice my time with Tobin in order to see her. A little at a time at first but I was doing it all the same. I thought nothing of this in the beginning but that's because once again, I didn't see it coming.

Lila was not (merely) a woman, she was a profound teacher for me. She was a life lesson incarnate that, through all the trials I'd previously overcome, had earned the right to face off with. It was Lila who got me to crux of my family issues – mom in particular. I took her through the deepest, most painful things she'd earned the right to hear. I returned the favor and we explored her issues too.

What I know now, but did not know then, is we as humans come together for growth. Everyone, in each of our lives, serves the role of potential teacher. Everything is an opportunity for us to become more than what we are. We are charged in this life with learning how to take something positive, something of value from every experience we have. In the beginning, it is usually at the admission price of pain and discomfort. As time goes on and we develop, we can begin to learn without as much discomfort. But in the beginning, the discomfort is our guide.

For Lila and me, we both lacked sufficient impetus to delve into the murkiest depths of our psyches ourselves until we met each other. Only after we both experienced the profound level of connection, acceptance, love and belonging, did we become ready to make that journey. And it's a good thing we felt as deeply for each other as we did, because our relationship went from a fantasy to a nightmare almost overnight.

II

One day while I was still living in Santa Rosa, she came down from Sacramento to see me. She was very distant and seemed upset. Naturally, I tried to find out what the problem was, only to have her shut me out for over an hour, being silent and not making eye contact. When my concern reached the point of near panic, I demanded she at least speak to me. I feared perhaps someone close to her had died or something else on that scale.

Instead, she began to talk of sensations that were welling up inside of her, feelings she couldn't seem to control or even articulate. After about three hours, she calmed down and seemed to settle but I had no way to know then, this was just the beginning.

As the next few months went on, the same behaviors grew more extreme, making her agitated and difficult. She began to recoil at my touch, to look at me as though she didn't know me, even as though I meant her harm! She would speak aggressively to me, become physically hostile sometimes, getting close to my face, saying weird stuff.

> *"I can see how pissed off you are! Why don't you hit me then?*
> *C'mon, do it, Hit me fucker. Hit me. I dare you!"*

It was as if she were hallucinating I was someone else. Maybe she was so out of her element in the relationship we were having, even though I respected her deeply and did my best to show it. She'd told me of abusive ex-partners she'd been with, some of the things she'd endured before. As you do when you're in love, I dismissed it as 'all in the past,' never stopping to suspect perhaps there was a reason why all of her past lovers had been abusive.

This is not to say she in any way deserved any of this, but instead she, like me, was choosing partners in adulthood who reflected the experiences of her childhood. And like me, hers was not good either. She never gave much in the way of specifics but alluded to a past full of physical abuse and neglect from her mom and an absentee dad who did not protect her as he should.

And so, when she became a woman, she immediately connected with men who were in possession of the same kinds of ugly traits – namely the desire to dominate and abuse the women in their lives. She suffered through man-after-man who berated her, belittled her and beat her physically. When I didn't do those things, she tried to goad me into action because it was what her conception of love was. So, she manufactured issues and in-fights, drama and discontent, creating conflict out of thin air, dragging me into the center.

This type of thing became a regular part of our relationship. She would calm down afterwards and we would make love, tender and succulent, feeding my deepest cravings. Grand apologies were offered. We would talk it over and discuss what we could do together about it. We fell into a macabre pattern of lurching between those ferocious episodes and the incredible tenderness that followed.

But here's the thing – the ferocious episodes were escalating in intensity.

She became irrational and aggressive, making ultimatums about needing to be placed ahead of my family (who I still held onto the illusion of normalcy with at this time) even my son. When I'd tell her the most anyone could hope for with me was to be considered on equal footing with those people, she would threaten to leave, or sometimes to hurt herself. I was so overwhelmed and so confused I slipped into a zombie-like state about the whole scenario. There would be times I'd sit in front of a mirror, look deeply my eyes and ask some questions

"Why are you still here? Why don't you simply leave?"

Try as I might, I could not find an answer – I just didn't have one.

I spent over five years trying to manage and normalize those behaviors I had blowing up in my face every day. She began demanding I keep our fights in our 'personal life' private from others, getting hugely angry when I'd tell her that I'd sought counsel from a friend or family member. She would cut off physical contact, scream at me, or accuse me of hating her. It was a mad house. It got to the point where she would stay in our room when Tobin was with us, or ignore him as much as she possibly could without raising my own ire.

One day, in a fit of desperation, I made an appointment with a psychiatrist who came highly recommended. I'd intended for both of us to go to couples counseling. Lila had agreed initially but when the time came, she flew into a blind rage at the idea, wrongly accusing me of trying to sabotage her and 'set her up.'

In an act of desperate anger, I shouted at her

"Fuck you then! Stay here and rot for all I fucking care! I'm going to see this lady and maybe, just maybe, find out why the fuck I'm still here with you!"

I stormed out of the house and got into my car. As I was starting the engine, Lila also came darting outside and literally jumped on the hood. I stopped. She got in, giving me a furious, dirty look. Then with the petulance of an eight-year-old who didn't get a pony for Christmas, she said to me

"If you're going, then I'm going! I'm not going to let you talk about me behind my back... Especially, to a goddamn shrink!"

We drove together in silence to the appointment. I had no idea why we were so incredibly angry at each other. I just knew something had to change. We arrived ten minutes early and waited in the car. Confronted with the imminent reality of being required to talk openly to another person about the drama happening between us, a grudgingly conciliatory air began to envelop us. We both calmed down a bit began to at least be civil again and set off to the appointment.

We walked up to the psychiatrist's door and opened it. We were greeted by a middle-aged, hippie-type lady.

She invited us in. We sat on her little couch and began talking. I couldn't have known it at the time, but this began the process that would complete the change in my life I'd been working on since the day I got sober, fifteen years earlier. This change I'd been struggling with all of my life. That moment, there in the psychiatrist's office was the beginning of the rest of my life.

III

It was that tiny little sanctuary I bought by the seventy-five minute stretch, where I would unravel some of the most perplexing issues of my existence. With her help, I would come to understand the dynamic between mom, my family and myself. I'd see why I was so dogged by recurring issues of money, love, friendship and the choices I made. I'd see, ultimately, why I had to leave Lila and why she had to leave me.

I'd love to be able to say it all happened quickly, or even over the space of a few months, but that was not the case. It was more a planting of seeds that would sprout into a clearer understanding of my own inner workings. And like seeds, it would take time for them to germinate, break the surface of the soil and reach for the sunshine. It did not, in fact, really come together fully until the day I found myself sat in the semi-circle at the family meeting (you read about at the beginning of this book.)

Our therapist, Marianne, was the epitome of someone who had found their calling in life. She was amazing. She never took notes, yet effortlessly recalled details from weeks earlier with ease and accuracy. She looked on from a perspective free from judgement and managed to validate both of us without alienating the other one – even when we were on opposite sides of an issue, which was most of the time.

I came to discover Lila was in fact, abused as a child, both physically and mentally. She was experiencing repressed memories, which were at least partly to blame for her sudden shifts from love to hate for me – shifts that could happen even though I'd done nothing intentional or unintentional to trigger them.

For my part, it took me a long time to realize I even had a problem. I kept focusing on everything Lila was doing. I learned that is called 'focusing on the diagnosed patient.' This is a fancy way of saying since her behavior was so big and hysterical, it was easy for me to avoid looking at my own inner issues. My issues were emotional withdrawal and subtle manipulations to get sex and attention. Though my behaviors were much less dramatic, they ran no less deep. In fact, they ran straight back to the beginning of my life.

It was also in the room with Marianne where I first began to wrap my head around why I had such erratic behaviors around the subject of money. All my life I struggled with being able to keep, manage and make sense of money. It had never occurred to me it might have something to do with the fact that I was raised in a commune environment where we all agreed that 'money was evil.'

Marianne was also the first to suggest I try on the term 'brainwashing' to explain my relationship with money and the term 'cult' to describe the commune I was raised in. At first, I resisted these new, sinister labels for those old familiar things but when Marianne asked me to look up the checklist for attributes of a cult, I was speechless. There the One World Family was listed, not only in name, but in description too. Point by point, it was all there. Unfailing devotion to a charismatic leader. Yep. Subversion of language. O.K. Group sex as dictated by said leader. Uh-huh. Surrendering of personal possessions to the organization. Err, yeah. Intentional isolation from the outside world. Mmm. And on down the line it went. Yes – I had clearly been raised in a cult.

Little-by-little, I began to see myself more clearly. It was easy for me to blame everything wrong in our relationship on Lila but if it were all her fault – why would I put up with the continual acrimony? What the hell was I doing there? Why was I staying? Clearly, she was not the only one in our relationship with issues. I had very soft, flimsy boundaries about women, stemming from the way mom was with me as a child. She was never there for me emotionally, unless it was to scold me. I can't remember ever – not once – getting held and nurtured by her as a child. Instead I was treated as little object, made to show off what I was good at in exchange for praise or attention.

By the time I became a young man, the patterns were set in stone within me. When a woman (or girl as the case was when I was young) gave me her attention, shone her light on me, I showed off, crowed, strutted and pranced. And when they took that light away, which they always seemed to do, I withdrew and became distant and insecure. I would mentally manipulate them into having sex with me, which was the most distilled form of approval I had found. I believe this dynamic was a big part of what hooked me so strongly with Lila. Our fights were cataclysmic, but our make-up sex was downright spiritual.

That was the surface level of our strong attraction but there was something else at work too. As I said earlier, humans are brought together to grow and to evolve and when it's our time to grow out of the deepest, most difficult, painful parts of ourselves, we require a very strong push. The intense levels of dopamine and serotonin hormones being released though my time with Lila were very compelling. They were all the more potent when added to a cocktail of powerful emotions. Grief, rage and confusion were jostling for position in my thoughts too. This heady concoction became far too strong to put down.

As it turned out, it was strong enough to make me walk down to rock bottom and into my own personal hell. It made make me confront the things I'd been unable to confront or even see, until then.

My time with Marianne was the real beginning of my new life I had been striving for. Sobriety got the ball rolling and gave me the tools to see there were clearly deep running issues with my family, money and the women that I habitually attracted. It just didn't help solve them.

Not only did she kick start a new phase of growth for me for me, Marianne, also gave me new ways to look at these long-standing issues. Together, we created me a sense of freedom and hope, where before, I only felt trapped and alone.

Time marched on, the way it always does. We were like detectives, uncovering deeper layers of our own truths, bit by bit, piecing together our own strategies that would allow each of us to become unstuck and to slowly rise above the dismal ways we had been living. I began to develop a sense life was finally pulling for me, not just dragging me from one tight spot to the next. At last, life was actually rooting for me.

Shortly before Lila and I met, I'd returned to one of my early passions, martial arts. I began studying Aikido. It's a discipline whose focus is blending with hostile energy, redirecting it, then diffusing it with the intent of protecting both you and your attacker. Unsurprisingly, I'd begun to view Julia as 'an attacker' and was using the Aikido philosophy in the way I approached our interactions. She would do something that felt like it was intended to make me upset or off-balance. I would not engage it, instead I'd let it go safely past me. After a while, when she decided she had nothing to fight against, she actually began to soften a bit towards me.

Julia was still making choices I didn't remotely agree with. However, with Aikido techniques, I was able to start acting less as an adversary to her and more as an advocate for Tobin, only speaking up when I thought he needed me to do so. I began to form a concept of physical conflict as a super-condensed, distilled example of all human interaction. A moment when each of our true selves comes to the forefront whether we like it or not. Through this discipline, I began to feel the tension slightly release between Julia and me.

Using the same idea, I began trying to interact differently with Lila, attempting to sidestep the temper outbursts and irrational flare-ups that were still very much a daily part of our life together. I learned to recognize the precursors to the big explosions and started practicing different ways of acting when I saw them coming. It worked to some extent but in the back of my mind, the fact that I was 'managing her' and using 'strategies' was always present. I didn't like it. I felt like my life had become like a balancing act at the circus. There I was, tiptoeing along the tightrope – one little slip either way and there would be dreadful consequences.

By the time we began seeing Marianne, everything I loved about my sex life with Lila together had virtually been taken off of the menu. All of the touching was now taboo. Kissing was non-existent. She wore shirts whenever she could during sex. Every position had become uncomfortable, or worse, it would often initiate one of her angry meltdowns. My solution was to dig my heels in and insist – at the very least – there was to be some kind of sex daily. Just once for 'maintenance' would be O.K.

Our sex life and the issue of sex became incredibly tense and awkward. I began to create elaborate rape fantasies in my head to justify to myself why she was in such a state of disgust when we were being intimate.

IV

What had started out as the most beautiful sex I'd ever had, had become nothing more than using a woman's body to masturbate. All of the feelings of connection were lost completely. Moreover, so was I. Yet again, unaware at the time, I was developing some issues around sex that would take me several years and lovers to overcome.

When I was not dealing with this, I was dealing with the Julia side of my personal balancing act, constantly dodging and sidestepping all manner of things that would come at me willy-nilly. Oddly, since I began the Aikido approach to co-parenting, she began to confide in me from time to time, when she wasn't trying to knock me off of my footing, that is. And so, as we do in the face of a protracted crisis, I settled into the life I was living. I found another level of coping. I was far from happy but I was dealing with everything and even being able to sometimes feel steady about it all.

But things don't work that way, at least not when you are in the midst of dealing with the issues most central to your existence. When you are in that process, life just keeps pushing you further and further, inching you toward your goal. Like it or not, you just keep plodding along.

And that is precisely what happened to me.

Just as I began to get some stability, a feeling of balance, Julia announced to me that Phillipe was coming home. He'd come to visit previously and they had apparently 'rekindled and reunited.' How this could have happened was beyond me – but it happened all the same. This was late 2007. It would be one year from then my work would dry up to nothing.

CHAPTER 21

THE TOP OF ROCK BOTTOM

I

In the short term, Phillipe provided a sense of stability for Julia and therefore for me, that part of my life eased up considerably. I still had my life with Lila to contend with, although we now had Marianne and the things we were learning with her, to make it more bearable. That was the most normal year I'd had in recent memory. Not 'peaceful' by any stretch of the imagination, but the 'highs and lows' were much less extreme than they had previously been. I should have known life was just marshaling its forces for the next big attack.

In the middle of 2008, as the global financial crisis started to bite, my work phone simply stopped ringing.

My friends who were contractors had been complaining for some time about how slow work had been. I'd been more fortunate. Up until the point when the calls stops, work for me had been going full-tilt. I was actually making so much money I treated myself a new car. And then, hey presto, all change, it just fucking stopped. It stopped and it didn't work again for eight months. I was about half way through that eight-month stretch when Phillipe called me one day to tell me he'd been given his new posting. It was in Maryland. He was moving across the country and Julia was going with him. She wanted to take Tobin.

By this time, the recession was biting hard. It was all over the news, there was no more trying to pretend things were going to bounce back any time soon. Every day the news was reporting more people being kicked out of their houses. The paint stores were actually laying people off, something I'd never heard of before. I didn't know what to do. For me this meant I had no way to provide for me and my son. Lila had a small inheritance but she and I had been burning through that little-by-little just to pay the rent.

Companies were closing left and right and the news was just getting worse. It was as if the whole country was a bigger of my life. I remember watching the news as AIG and Chrysler Motors were failing. Right there in front of my eyes, the pillars that held up the economic system I'd agreed to be part of were crumbling. There was nothing I could do about it. In my own life, things were getting more desperate by the day too.

I'd landed the biggest job of my career just before everything crashed down in flames. The foreman of the construction company I subcontracted to was grinding me on every tiny detail. Everywhere that he thought he could get an extra inch out of me, he was pushing for an extra foot. The atmosphere had become distinctly hostile between us. Terms like 'lawsuit' and 'breach of contract' had started being thrown around. I had selfish Julia wanting to take Tobin across the country for the foreseeable future. Unpredictable Lila was exploding in my face like old, unstable nitroglycerine. My entire family had left and gone to a city two hours from where I lived. Now, added to that already toxic mix was the imminent danger of being taken to court.

I had no place to go for respite from all this mess.

Everywhere I turned, there was crisis. Thanks to all the economic uncertainty, the whole country had seemingly adopted a 'look out for yourself' attitude and tightened its belt. I began losing sleep and weight as I dealt with all of the daily stressors confronting me. I could actually feel myself unravelling slowly. Living in such a state of stress and tension was affecting my judgement and making me into a walking disaster zone.

Julia, Phillipe and I had agreed to see mediator to decide how best to come to an agreement about Tobin. I remember walking into the mediation office, sitting down, beginning to talk and just splitting apart at the seams. I just stopped being able to keep my composure any longer, knowing full well I could not provide for my son in the immediate future. It killed me to admit it was actually in his best interest to let him go with them, at least then he would have a roof over his head and food in his belly. The idea of letting him go was the biggest failure I could possibly imagine. How could I do this terrible thing? I had to let my son go across the country, three thousand, two hundred and forty-three fucking miles from where I was.

Again, I was stuck. I could not move. I couldn't imagine the thought of him being so far from me, in the care of his mom and Phillipe. We were discussing the details and I broke. I fell backwards in my chair, flopped onto the floor, sobbing and wailing.

"I can't do this... I can't let him go... I can't."

My self-control was nowhere to be found.

"Please don't do this... Don't go... I can't let him go..." I wailed, to an impassive room.

Where I'd had such incredible fortune with mediators before, now I found no sympathy. I couldn't believe it! They just sat there and watched me fall to pieces. It took twenty minutes or more, to regain my composure – it took me twenty seconds to crumble again. I just couldn't face Tobin leaving and yet I needed to do this for him to keep him safe. I needed to give him over to the two people I least wanted him to be with.

With a heavy heart, I agreed.

II

The next day, Tobin set off by car to faraway Maryland. The agreement we struck upon was I'd have him summers and any significant breaks from school. Julia and Phillipe would pay his airfare to get him here, as it turned out, that wouldn't come up very often. I was devastated the day he left. It was the one time in our relationship where I can recall Lila being actually compassionate and nurturing. I cried in her arms for hours.

It was not long after Tobin moved that I decided to move as well. I felt that I should not be alone during a time like this and if truth be told, I didn't trust myself to be so untethered from everyone I held dear. In what would prove to be fate guiding my hand, Lila and I decided to move to Sacramento. This brought me to closer to my family, thinking that this might buy me some familial support. It also meant Lila would be back in familiar territory, supposedly to solve her problem of feeling as if she moved one hundred miles away for a man – a feeling she was very vocal about not liking.

I moved into what I think of as the 'endgame period' of my struggle to free myself from the binds of my upbringing. Of course, I have gone on learning and evolving since then but this was the final phase of the process of undoing the biggest obstacles inside myself, the ones keeping me in limbo. It was a period of spiritual growth that took the most faith. Throughout, I was wracked by the most awful self-doubt of the entire process.

When I finally made it through to the other side of this vortex, every single aspect of my life transformed. Nothing was left as it used to be. The phrase, 'it always gets darkest just before the dawn; was coming true. Lila and I had settled into a routine where we were literally trading sex for emotional connection. Our intimacy became transactional. She would give me her body and in return, I'd give her the non-sexual closeness she'd come to crave. I loathed the situation entirely. I felt cheapened and used, as I am sure she did and yet, neither of us would do what obviously needed to be done. Until one day, I picked up a book on Zen and the Mind of the Warrior.

In this book, the author laid out the true nature of what it means to be a warrior in the Zen tradition – to be utterly unafraid of loss. It means to accept all as it is and to ascribe no expectations whatsoever onto objective reality. 'Only this way,' the author wrote, 'can a warrior hope to be at their best and most effective. Only when the mind is free of the shackles of expectations and desires, can we give every ounce of ourselves to whatever task is set in front of us.'

The words hit me like an imaginary baseball bat to the head. The author continued. 'To fear no loss, even the loss of one's own life, is the way of the warrior. To be in a state of mushin [with an empty mind] and release all expectation of outcome is the only way that the mind can be free to activate at the highest level.'

When I read this, it hit me. I realized what I'd been doing wrong with Lila over those five long years. I'd been quietly, subtly, expecting her to change. I'd decided she had the problems, not me, not both of us – but her. In fact, I'd been holding on to huge expectations and desires about how things might be if I could only 'change her.' After all, she was smart, beautiful, talented, If only I could somehow coerce her into changing those things I didn't like, she would be perfect. That was the moment when I realized not only did I have to break up with her – but I could. After all this time, I was finally able to see my part in our relationship.

I could see how I was an equal contributor to our misery. Yes, her behavior was more dramatic than mine was and yes, it was easy for me to get sympathy from the rest of the world for all I was forced 'to endure' by being with her. I painted a picture for anyone who would listen, of what a victim I was. I only wanted to love her yet had been duped into committing myself to a person who was so broken that I ended up being emotionally blackmailed by her unreasonable demands.

But the truth is that just as she held my heart and emotions ransom, so did I hold ransom hers. For better or for worse, she was in love with me. She depended on me. I didn't have the maturity or awareness to leave when I knew the core of our relationship was dead. Instead I manipulated her and made demands of her so subtle that she could not explain them, though she could feel the effect of their presence just the same. I created an environment where the truth was implied, not stated All she had to do was become the kind of woman I wanted her to be and she could have all she'd come to want and desire from me.

The moment I realized what my role in this morbid charade had been, I called her and ended our relationship. I could not stand to think of myself as the type of person who would do those things to someone else. I separated from it immediately, knowing full well I was every bit as much to blame in our train wreck as she was. We were both abusers and victims in equal measure.

As I said before, Lila and I were each other's guides through the deepest, most fucked up parts of ourselves. Without her, I might still be stuck in that mire, that quicksand. I would be unable to free myself fully until the next teacher came along. I would pay a high price for that lesson.

A part of me still loves Lila, though not in the way once I did. I am grateful to have known her. I am humbled by our shared experience. She will live on, immortalized, in my memory.

Around then, Julia came back for the summer, chaperoning Tobin on his cross-country flight as agreed. When she came back, she brought Aiden with her and Annika, the newest child, who she had while they were in Maryland. (The speculation was that even though no one knew she was pregnant again, it had happened while she was still here.) I lost myself in work and spending my time with Tobin, seeing him whenever I could. He spent half of his summer with me in Sacramento and half with his mom in Santa Rosa. I'd frequently drive down and pick him up for weekend visits even when I was very busy.

The summer moved along and still Julia remained. Phillipe was not around nor was he ever mentioned. After about two months of Julia just not 'going back,' I called her up and quizzed her

> *"So, how are things with you and Phillipe? Anything you want to tell me?"*

When I asked her this, she let the flood gates open. I learned that she and Phillipe began to fall apart almost as soon as they arrived on the East Coast. She told a tale of fighting and alienation, of Phillipe not spending any time with the children and even starting to treat Tobin poorly. According to her, things culminated in a grand gesture from Phillipe. He rented a dumpster and threw all of her belongings into it as she was leaving with the kids to catch the plane back to the West Coast. Infidelity and email hacking were mentioned at different points in the discussion.

The upshot was that Julia was staying in California and she and Phillipe were getting a divorce. That also meant I was getting my son back.

Julia was pretty chewed up from her experience with Phillipe and seemed to want nothing more than to try to reestablish herself in California. For a time things were smooth and Tobin's life was actually becoming stable again. Then one day, a few months after they got back, Julia and I were talking on the phone and I asked her if she was seeing anyone new.

Her answer widened my eyes somewhat. She'd begun seeing a man from Israel who was here on a work visa. She told me that he was a 'good man' and, although they had only known each other a few months, he'd told her that he wanted to be with her and provide for her and her children. He also told her when he completed a training program he was in the midst of, he would need to move to wherever the best market for his new business was.

I asked what line of business he was in. She told me 'heating and air conditioning.' A very stable trade indeed. When I told her that the construction market was starting to rebound in California – me assuming they would naturally stay in California – she said 'Yes, he was looking into California, but that Michigan was also a very strong market right now and he had family near there.' She said this to me with the same perfectly even 'breakfast ordering' tone as last time, as though it were the most reasonable thing in the world.

I respond to this by saying I was glad for her and that while she could certainly do whatever she wanted with herself and her other children, I thought it was time for Tobin to come and live with me from now on.

That is how I got my son living with me full time.

Shortly after Tobin came to live with me, I was again talking to Julia. I asked her 'how she and her boyfriend were doing?' She told me 'he'd called her a few days earlier, from the airport, just about to board a plane back to Israel, with no plans to return.' Julia found herself alone with two children full time and one child who was primarily in my care.

Having secured Tobin's wellbeing, I was left to contend with the fact I was still in the midst of the greatest economic catastrophe of the last eighty years or so. I was getting work sometimes but most of it was still coming from my reputation in the Sonoma County area. Beggars can't be choosers so I had a 2-hour drive each way to contend with if I did get some Sonoma-based work. During this time, I thought I would to rely on my family to provide childcare for Tobin. Much to my utter surprise, this caused a great deal of tension between us.

Both mom and my sister were always very vocal about how much they wished that they could see Tobin more during the time when he was gone. Mom would often grumble about 'how she worried about his wellbeing and just wished that she could do something – anything – to help.' My sister mirrored this sentiment and added 'how nice it would be if only Tobin could grow up with his cousins.' But as is so often the case, fantasy and reality did not play out the same way.

When it came time for them to actually put their proverbial money where their mouths were, they were not as eager and willing to help as before. This isn't to say no help was offered, because it was. Instead of it being an opportunity for close family members to support each other, I was made to feel like a huge burden to them for needing help – even though I was busy doing the 'full time work' and 'single parent' thing. I began to internalize these feelings and to think I maybe was being a drain on my family. I felt as if my ideas about how families should behave were clearly idealistic and out of touch with reality.

During those days, I never felt at ease with my family but looking back, it's accurate to say I never ever felt at ease with it. Throughout my life, I was without doubt the 'odd man out,' the 'square peg in a round hole,' the classic 'black sheep.'

CHAPTER 22

BLOOD LETTING AND RELEASE

I

There is no easy explanation for why the 'black sheep phenomenon' occurs, but it is predictable within dysfunctional family units, so predictable in fact, they teach it in recovery books and classes.

I knew about it from the very beginning of my recovery, I just couldn't believe that I was being perceived that way. My family, the one I'd put on such a high pedestal for all of my life, were showing such base hues to be their true colors. It was so difficult for me to get to grips with. I spent months, even years, trying to see reality in a more flattering light. Alas, there were to be no flattering angles for my family.

I held tight to this comforting illusion of them, refusing to acknowledge the truth about my relationship with my family that I was stuck with. They were stuck viewing me through the same old lens. I hated that lens. There was me the lost child, me the lost sibling, me the one who just can't get his life together no matter how hard he tries. I was the one they really hope is going to make it all come together – but let's not get our hopes up too high. Never mind the fact that he's coming from so far behind the starting line that it's a miracle that he's gotten as far as he has. Never mind the fact that he's had so much shit dumped into his mind as a child it's a miracle that he's not in a fucking asylum. Never mind the fact that he's been through more than any of us have. Never mind the fact he's trying – and refuses to give up on – making something from the nothing. The less than nothing that he started with. Forget he's trying to give his child everything he never had, materially, emotionally, spiritually and in every other way. Let's miss the fact he's actually healing himself so that he doesn't screw his child up, going back painstakingly through all the individual little hells that made up his youth, so that he can stand toe to toe with every one of his motherfucking goddamn demons so that his child can deal with a better class of problems than he'd to deal with, or that what he's actually attempting is something that none of us have the courage, the discipline, the fortitude, the sheer balls swinging low and mighty to even attempt to accomplish. Never mind the fact that he fucking refuses, *refuses* to quit, to lay down, to be beat, no matter what we or life throws at him, refuses to think small as an excuse for not even bothering to discover his dreams, much less to actually go after them, to shrink his expectations until they fit where he is now. Never mind the fact that while we all sit here on the goddamn sidelines, criticizing every fucking move that he makes from our front row seats, judging instead of helping, taking bets on how and when he'll fail, that he just-keeps-on-going, pushing, pulling, fighting for something better than this absurd little life that we have all – each of us – silently agreed to be complicit in, where we give away our higher selves, little-by-fucking-little, bit-by-goddamn-bit, as we try to drag him down with our impossible to meet standard of what it will take for us to bequeath our fetid, acerbic, rancid, malignant approval upon him. Approval that he was never going to get in the first place and that we have never even bothered to examine, or to come up with any reasons whatsoever as to why it is like this, because to hell with going down THAT rabbit hole, easier to just sit here like tumors, As long as we all agree with each other then we must be right, RIGHT? Fuck any sort of objective self-examination or anything like that, it's easier to just huddle together and point the finger with our eyes turned inward, toward the center of our twisted little group...

I held tight to my illusion until the day of the so-called 'family meeting.' From that moment, the very instant that I told them to go fuck themselves I have not looked back.

II

I realized the futility of looking for any sort of real, meaningful approval or acceptance from my family. I took them down off of the pedestal I put them on, where they were quite happy to claim 'squatters rights.' I saw them for who and what they were – nothing more than broken, wounded, even wretched people, small, frail and inconsequential in this world.

I was freed.

Like sneaking backstage after witnessing the performance of a lifetime, only to catch the featured actors half out of their make-up, with their wigs off and their corsets loosed, no longer flattered by perfect lighting and looking sallow and bedraggled. Making guilty eye contact with you from the reflection in the dressing room mirror and all at once, the illusion gives way.

It was as though I'd finally uprooted a poisoned growth that I'd been yanking on for most of my life. It just let go all at once, roots and all and I was no longer in the struggle. When I told them to go fuck themselves, the lens had been changed, the paradigm had shifted. Afterwards, the good literally began to come into my life so fast, that I almost couldn't keep up with it.

CHAPTER 23

LEARNING TO FLY

I

There is a dream most of us know of. It is the one where you are falling and you'll die if you hit bottom before you wake up. One night, shortly, after I got sober, I was having that dream.

I'd been having an incredible array of dreams since my sobriety, dreams of wild and mysterious symbolism. But this one was something else – something special. As I was freefalling through a black and purple abyss, wind ripping through my hair and wakening the skin on my face, terror shooting electricity through my body, all my nerves screaming the chorus of someone who is about to die and they know it – a thought occurred to me.

What if I could stay asleep? What if I 'could fall' until I landed and see what happened? Hadn't I already had breakthroughs in my life that had come first from my dreams? The time I first flew, the first time I tapped into my power – that happened in a dream first, then years later in waking life.

Why not now?

There must be something to this dream if virtually everyone's had it. There must be something on the other side of it. I wanted to see if I could find out what it was. What's the worst that could happen?

In the dream, every fiber of my being was begging me not to do this thing. My mind was generating Technicolor scenarios of the moment of impact, slowing them down to last a lifetime. A familiar voice in my head begged

"Don't do this new thing. The pain will be beyond anything you can imagine. Your teeth will be pushed through the back of your head

and your lungs will explode. Just do what you always do, wake up, shake it off and go back to sleep. Stick to the plan, don't make waves."

But this time I also had another voice that was telling me to do it.

"Keep going! See what is on the other side of this stretching, dark unknown."

This place of fear could not possibly last, it reasoned, there must be more.

"You can't die from a dream." it said.

And I believed it.

I could tell that the ground was rushing up to meet me now. I was getting close. I began to tense for impact. Everything down to my fingernails and eyelashes was awake with adrenaline. My 'dream-body' hardened to the point where I couldn't move. I was paralyzed before the big hit even came.

And then, all at once, I decided to relax and trust I would somehow be OK. I began to breathe more slowly and deeply as my awake voice told me to have faith.

"Let it come. You're strong enough for this. You can do this, just surrender to what's real. It'll be O.K. It'll be O.K."

I could sense that the ground was right beneath me now, but I was soft, relaxed and calm. I'd found a place of total acceptance that somehow, in the most metaphysical way imaginable, seemed to straddle both the dream world and the waking one. This was big...

The moment of impact arrived and I smiled.

Then, instead of the smashing, splatting, heart-stopping, organ-rupturing sudden stop, there was an intense flash of warm, white light, too bright to see anything in and I felt my pace gently slow to a halt.

When I was able to see again, I was surrounded by little, grapefruit-sized orbs of different colored lights, like glass balls. They were warm and unbelievably nurturing. If I picked one up, warmth radiated out from it and down through the hand that was holding it and into my chest. I found that I was smiling and overcome by a deep sense of peace and wellbeing.

II

That so-called family meeting happened in late February 2011. As I said, the work didn't stop coming in from that afternoon on.

I was so energized that I must have been sending it out into the world, because the world was sending me back everything I needed. Job after job. Yes after yes. Everything just lined up in front of me. With the inevitability of having to move from my little condo, I called a friend of mine who had asked me on a couple of previous occasions if I knew anyone who was interested in renting one of his properties. In the past, I'd always said no, not having any one in mind, but now I called him on my own behalf to inquire whether he had a rental available.

With a full disclosure of my situation and my word I'd be an ideal tenant, I found myself with a new place to live. I went from a tiny condo at one thousand dollars a month, to a four-bedroom house in a quiet neighborhood for thirteen hundred dollars a month. A big step up for a guy who had just gotten evicted.

Having secured for myself a base of operations, I turned my focus to all the work I had coming in. I still had no vehicle of my own, so I began splitting jobs with other painting contractors I knew, provided they would do the driving. This went very well for a while but I knew a getting vehicle was a priority.

One day, while trying to find another contractor to split a very big job with, I called one of my old contacts, only to find out that he'd closed up his shop and moved to Utah. He told me that he was trying to sell what he had left of his operation, namely a work van full of top quality painting equipment and stacked high with ladders. He was throwing in a beautiful website that still generated a lot of traffic for him, even now when he was in another state.

I told him I'd be very interested in buying it but I didn't yet have enough money to buy it all outright. We hammered out a deal that allowed me to purchase a vehicle and everything I'd need to run three crews at the same time. I told him about my situation honestly and without any attempt at influence or manipulation. He sold the whole thing to me for eight hundred dollars down and monthly payments, choosing me over another potential buyer who was ready to purchase it all in one convenient lump sum.

Suddenly, I had a vehicle, equipment and a recognized business. Work kept getting better. By the middle of that summer, I had seven men working for me and we were averaging three paint jobs per week. Business was booming.

I began to date again, this time with some mental ground rules. I decided to operate from a place of abundance. I ditched my old habit of 'not being afraid of things not working out with any one girl.'

My new attitude was 'there were plenty of women in the world and anyone who could make it through all that I'd made it through must be a pretty good catch.'

When something seemed off between a new date and me I simply and honestly excused myself from the situation. This was the exact opposite of how I used to behave in those toxic relationships before.

I began to notice I was feeling more alive in the spiritual, physical and emotional senses, than I ever had in my life. Not only was everything going better for me, also I had a deep and persistent feeling of tremendous gratitude about it. I was experiencing a completely unprecedented amount of fulfillment in every area of my life – financial, spiritual and emotional. Even my physical realm was thriving, as it never had before. In fact, several chronic issues that I'd had with my back, knees and hips, all resolved themselves within a few months of my family 'catharsis.' I have literally never felt better.

Every day I'd wake up in happy disbelief at the monumental transformation that my life had undergone. It was so much more than a matter of degrees, it was a genuinely massive shift. It was the difference between sticking feathers up your butt and running down the street shouting 'Cock-a-doodle-doo,' and becoming a genuine, full-blown, magnificent rooster.

As my world changed, Tobin's did too. One of the most remarkable ways was in his relationship with his little brother. He went from being glad he never had to see his little brother, to wanting to spend time with him. We began to make it a point to have Aiden come up and visit us whenever possible. I could not believe how they just suddenly began to get along. When Aiden would visit, they would laugh and play together all day long, filling the house with the sound of happy children. I loved it when that happened. I made it a point to find as much time for his visits as possible.

On one such visit, as I was working in my office, Tobin and Aiden were in the other room together. They were having a great time by the sound of it. I found myself thinking how good it would be if Aiden could live with us too. I dismissed this immediately as ludicrous. After all, I had no legal claim to the boy whatsoever. He was in fact, the son of a man who had tried to sue me for custody of my own boy! This last thought made the whole notion seem even more ridiculous.

But just as I was pondering all of this, the two boys came into my room together. Tobin said to me (with his brother peering sheepishly out from behind his shoulder)

"Dad, I wish that Aiden could come and live with us."

I looked at both of them in disbelief.

"I was just thinking how cool that would be!" I said to them. "But I don't think it's possible guys, I'm sorry."

They both went from hopeful to dejected in the space of one breath. Tobin's shoulders slumped a little at my reply.

"Yeah, I know. It would be so cool though..."

"Yeah, buddy. That would really be great."

The boys went back to playing together. I went back to 'working' but I couldn't get the thought of Aiden moving in, out of my head. A couple days later after more cajoling from both boys on the subject, I decided to float the idea past Julia.

I told her it could work something like this. We could put Aiden into homeschooling like Tobin and he could stay here most of the time. I'd see to his education and all of his needs – at no cost to her. Since he and Tobin would both be in homeschool, they could both go to visit her often and frequently, bringing their schoolwork with them. It was clearly a great idea for the boys. We'd each need to make some sacrifices to accomplish it but it was achievable.

Initially she said 'no' – loudly. She couldn't stand the idea of another of her boys not being around her. On the other hand, she did acknowledge being able to see Tobin more often would be great for her.

I told her I understood. It was just so nice to see the boys getting along so well. I reminded her I was willing to do whatever I could to foster their relationship, knowing first-hand how much it hurts to have weak relationships with siblings. I valued those relationships for the boys very highly. I let the subject rest, knowing I never really had a much of a chance of selling something so farfetched in the first place.

Then, something unbelievable happened. Julia called me back.

It was a couple of weeks later when she did. She told me that she couldn't stop thinking about the suggestion. She told me – much to my surprise – that the positive effect I was having on Tobin was obvious and undeniable. She went on to point out Aiden was now the same age that Tobin had been when I took him full time. Much as it pained her to say so, she recognized he needed a male role model in his life now.

We talked about the effect on a little boy of having every man in his life go away, be it from death, in the case of his grandfather or simply abandonment, in the case of his dad.

We talked about how unhealthy the influences of her family were and about how she didn't want any of her kids exposed to it any more than absolutely necessary. After talking for a very long time, she said she'd come to agree it would be in Aiden's best interest if he lived with Tobin and I.

I couldn't believe my ears. Aiden would come and stay with us! I'd now have the opportunity to offer to two boys what I wished had been provided to me – guidance, love, shelter, parenting, a childhood.

When Julia decided to let Aiden come and stay with us, both of the boys were down at her house. She agreed to bring them back to my house the following weekend.

As the day approached, I began to prepare the house, setting up the extra room for our new arrival. As I cleaned and moved furniture around, turning an extra room into a bedroom, I was repeatedly struck by the way things had changed. I was about to begin looking after the son of the man who had attempted to gain custody of my son a decade earlier. The man who, when his attempts to wrest legal control of my child from me failed, simply walked away from his own.

The situation could not have been more poetic if it had been orchestrated and it was not lost on me.

Aiden coming to live us would fill our house with a joy and love that I didn't know was possible. He and Tobin would play and bicker together all day long, both of them wrangling a bit to figure out their places in the group but each clearly enriched by the presence of the other. I'd a newfound sense of purpose and mission with the two of them there. I prioritized my work and my days around the three of us spending as much time together as possible. I began to have a deeper understanding of what being a 'parent' meant to me.

In personality, Aiden was a joker to Tobin's thinker. Where Tobin was deeply cerebral and alarmingly sharp, even acerbic in his wit, Aiden, by contrast, was all witty one-liners and Tigger-like energy and enthusiasm. Both boys were both very intelligent, very different and somehow very similar. With the way Julia's life seemed to be going back then, there could not have been a better time for Aiden to have a strong, loving male role model enter his life, unless, of course it had been at the beginning.

My little family had grown.

Since then, I have met a wonderful woman, she herself a veteran of an obscene amount of trauma in her past, but a soldier, a warrior for change. She refuses to pass to her own daughter the dysfunction she was raised in.

Today all of us live under one roof, me, Jill, Tobin, Aiden, Gibbie, Pogo, Roofus, Peanut (the last three being our dogs.) Even when the hard days come – and they do – I face them with a ferocious sense of purpose and strength. The knowledge of my reason for being here bolsters me and gives me clarity. And today my house is a home and is filled – and I mean filled – to the rafters with love.

I feel like I am living my reward for the perseverance that got me through most of my life. Every day, in my house is full of children. I have a loving, solid woman by my side. Both of us feel a deep sense of privilege at the opportunity to break the chains of dysfunction that were put on us as children. Both of us feeling humbled by what we consider a sacred honor and duty – the duty of raising these incredible kids to be better than we are, to send them out into the world to connect with others and make great things happen.

All of them free from what we had to deal with.

Both of us aware that when we make better choices with our kids than our parents made with us, when we have the skills and the courage to act in spite of our conditioning, we not only free our kids but their kids and their kids' kids, on down through generations and in to posterity. We leave a legacy every day of love, respect, consideration and emotional health that will outlast us and them. It is the highest form of work we can engage in and we are grateful for the chance to do it.

I can look back on my own family now, through the lens of my life today and even find gratitude and forgiveness in my heart for them. I can look at my sister and see how she came to be who she is, the unique burdens she bears, just as I can see why mom is who she is and why she could never really understand or accept me. I know some of mom's upbringing and that of her mom too. I can see the strands stretch backward through time. The same strands I would have unknowingly carried with me into future generations but for the part of me that just knew something wasn't right – the Moral Man inside me – who wouldn't relent and wouldn't let me stop pushing for something better than what I was otherwise destined for.

If not for the fuel that my family provided me with, all of my frustrations and anger at being judged and misunderstood, I might not have been equal to the task. The task of uncovering my own, authentic self and being willing to accept it and me, where they never could. And so I am oddly grateful to them for their tremendous contribution in helping me to become me. Though I don't feel any kinship to them any longer, some things in life are bigger and more central to the human experience than even family.

In my case, when I found the strength and the courage to stay asleep and let myself die, to hit the bottom, where there is nothing left and to accept whatever was on the other side, openly, happily and without reservation, what I got was a new family.

I got a 'do over.' A chance to have things be the way I wished they could have been for me. I got to go back through everything and become the kind of man who I should have had raising me.

All of my life, at least the parts where I was paying attention, I heard from people that it is possible to turn your life around, to create, through hard work and sheer force of will, something different, something better for yourself.

I always wanted to believe this. I wanted it so bad I devoted the last twenty years of my life to seeking it. There were so many times when I wanted to quit. I had so many dark days and obstacles put in my path. I lost count of the number times when it would have been so easy to give up, to blame things on circumstances, or family, or anything else, just pack it in. But for some reason I kept going. And now I can tell you unflinchingly, with a calm confidence they were right.

When you change the way you think about the world, the people you let into your life, when you persist with the belief that you can be more, more than your inner voice tells you that you are, more than your family, or your boss, or whoever, tells you what you are, what you can do is revolutionary. You can have a totally new life. You've got to want it and it might not be easy. If you are like I was, then you know anything is better than settling for what other people tell you what you are.

Keep in Touch

You now know pretty much everything there is to know about me and the crazy life that led me to where I am today.

If you'd like to know more about what I do and how I do it, please visit my website:

- www.mannywolfe.com

Alternatively, you can connect with me on my Facebook page for the book:

- www.facebook.com/unbreakablefans

Also, you can follow my personal profile too:

- www.facebook.com/manny.wolfe1

Please do share your thoughts on the book with me. I'd love to hear from you.

- manny@mannywolfe.com

To your success,

Manny

P.S. Remember to grab a copy of my free audio download on charisma.

14909266R00176

Printed in Poland
by Amazon Fulfillment
Poland Sp. z o.o., Wrocław